"While many Christians are accustomed to hearing that there is good evidence for their faith, far less common are arguments that point out how other worldviews are far inferior in terms of both evidence and explanatory power. Ken Samples develops a cumulative case for Christianity, arguing well that no other thesis even comes close to accounting for what we know about reality. *7 Truths That Changed the World* is a very readable and recommended account that describes what Samples calls Christianity's seven dangerous ideas that best encapsulate the current state of the evidence."

—**Gary R. Habermas**, Distinguished Research Professor,
Liberty University

"Ken Samples has combined clear thinking with clear writing to give us a guided tour through basic Christian truths. He shows us what those truths are, why we should believe them, and how they make better sense of the world than the alternatives. This book serves all kinds of people: those wanting to know about Christian belief, those whose Christian belief is wobbling, and those who, like good athletes, want to renew their commitment to doing the fundamentals well. Thanks be to God for this helpful, encouraging, and challenging book!"

—**C. John Collins**, professor of Old Testament,
Covenant Theological Seminary

"Ken Samples has done it again. He has written about some of the most important issues in life, with seriousness and depth, and then made it accessible to everyone. I hope *7 Truths That Changed the World* is read in Bible studies and home groups around the globe. It has a transformative message and a style that can engage everyone."

—**Craig J. Hazen**, professor and director of Christian apologetics,
Biola University

"One of the most skilled and thoughtful apologists of our time, Ken Samples, has done it again. His *7 Truths That Changed the World* is a powerful reminder that Christianity is a truth claim which confronts the beliefs and values of our contemporary age at a number of critical points. But Samples is neither confrontational nor combative as he spells out seven aspects of the Christian truth-claim which stand in opposition to much of what our non-Christian neighbors hold dear. This is must reading."

—**Kim Riddlebarger**, senior pastor, Christ Reformed Church,
Anaheim, CA

Other books by Kenneth Richard Samples

A World of Difference: Putting Christian Truth-Claims to the Worldview Test

Without a Doubt: Answering the 20 Toughest Faith Questions

*Prophets of the Apocalypse: David Koresh and
Other American Messiahs* (with others)

*The Cult of the Virgin: Catholic Mariology and the
Apparitions of Mary* (with Elliot Miller)

*Lights in the Sky and Little Green Men: A Rational Christian Look
at UFOs and Extraterrestrials* (with Hugh Ross and Mark Clark)

7 TRUTHS THAT CHANGED THE WORLD

DISCOVERING CHRISTIANITY'S MOST DANGEROUS IDEAS

KENNETH RICHARD SAMPLES

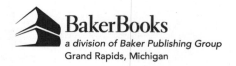

BakerBooks
a division of Baker Publishing Group
Grand Rapids, Michigan

Published by Baker Books
a division of Baker Publishing Group
P.O. Box 6287, Grand Rapids, MI 49516-6287
www.bakerbooks.com

Printed in the United States of America

Library of Congress Cataloging-in-Publication Data
Samples, Kenneth R.
    7 truths that changed the world : discovering Christianity's most dangerous ideas / Kenneth Richard Samples.
        p.   cm.
    Includes bibliographical references and indexes.
    ISBN 978-0-8010-7211-6 (pbk. : alk. paper)
    1. Christianity. 2. Apologetics. I. Title. II. Title: Seven truths that changed the world.
BR121.3.S259 2012
239—dc23   2011043952

Unless otherwise indicated, Scripture quotations are from the Holy Bible, New International Version®. NIV®. Copyright © 1973, 1978, 1984, 2011 by Biblica, Inc.™ Used by permission of Zondervan. All rights reserved worldwide. www.zondervan.com

Scripture quotations labeled NASB are from the New American Standard Bible®, copyright © 1960, 1962, 1963, 1968, 1971, 1972, 1973, 1975, 1977, 1995 by The Lockman Foundation. Used by permission.

Scripture quotations labeled NIV 1984 are from the Holy Bible, New International Version®. NIV®. Copyright © 1973, 1978, 1984 by Biblica, Inc.™ Used by permission of Zondervan. All rights reserved worldwide. www.zondervan.com

Scripture quotations labeled NLT are from the Holy Bible, New Living Translation, copyright © 1996, 2004, 2007 by Tyndale House Foundation. Used by permission of Tyndale House Publishers, Inc., Carol Stream, Illinois 60188. All rights reserved.

12   13   14   15   16   17   18   7   6   5   4   3   2   1

To Sarah
Your intelligence, beauty, strong work ethic, and committed faith
make your mother and me deeply proud.

Contents

Dangerous Idea #6: Humanity's Value and Dignity

Dangerous Idea #7: The Good in Suffering

Introduction

Historic Christianity's Dangerous Ideas

Who said anything about safe? 'Course he isn't safe. But he's
good. He's the King, I tell you.

C. S. Lewis, *The Lion, the Witch and the Wardrobe*

This line from my favorite book in C. S. Lewis's remarkable children's
series, *The Chronicles of Narnia*, makes it clear that Aslan, the Christ
figure in the story, is not a tame lion. But his being dangerous does not rule
out his profound benevolence.

Like Lewis's ferocious feline, ideas, including those of formal belief systems,
can also be dangerous. And if Christianity encompasses ideas that are not
safe, then is it not, therefore, a risky and even hazardous religion?

One of my longtime colleagues and friends, an atheist, agrees that historic
Christianity includes *dangerous ideas*. From his atheistic point of view, however, the Christian faith affirms irrational and superstitious ideas that are not
just unsafe but harmful. He believes these ideas are injurious both for those
who believe them as well as for those who are affected by them. In fact, the
emergence of the New Atheism movement was fueled by the conviction that
religion is not merely *false* but indeed *harmful*.

In philosophy, theology, and science, provocative ideas that challenge the
reigning paradigm reflect a radical shift in perspective. These ideas can have
major implications for how people view reality, truth, rationality, goodness,
value, and beauty, and they can sometimes contravene what many people
believe. Not only do such revolutionary ideas threaten accepted beliefs, but
they also contain explosive world- and life-view implications for all humanity.

Historic Christianity embodies numerous beliefs that are theologically and philosophically volatile (in the best sense of the term). The Christian faith contains powerful truth-claims that have transformed the church and turned the world upside down. Christianity's initial dangerous ideas started with twelve men (Jesus's apostles) and within three hundred years came to dominate the ancient Roman world. And for more than a thousand years after that, the historic faith dominated all aspects of Western civilization.

In the last couple of centuries, however, the world has been exposed to ideas that were dangerous in their own right. In the nineteenth century, Charles Darwin's theory of evolution and Friedrich Nietzsche's "God is dead" proclamation challenged everything Christian society held dear. These profound and unsettling naturalistic perspectives have propelled the secularization of today's educational institutions of the Western world. Accordingly, the public square in the West also increasingly reflects such beliefs and values.

The late twentieth century also saw the rise in the West of a new radical pluralistic and inclusivistic perspective. Postmodern thinking—in reaction to both traditional religion and secularism—reflects a mixture of relativism, subjectivism, and pluralism. Thus today's marketplace of ideas is a smorgasbord of skeptical, secular, and religious viewpoints.[1] But traditional religion now competes with religious inclusivism and pluralism.

The historic Christian truth-claims presented in this book can, then, be viewed as having a renewed sense of danger. The reason is that much of society today knows so little about the specific beliefs of classical Christianity. Therefore, many people are unaware of historic Christianity's unique perspective on God, Christ, the world, humankind, values, death, and suffering. The advance and entrenchment of secularism over the last couple hundred years make these Christian ideas fresh and explosive. Not safe, but good.

This book is divided into seven sections that address seven of historic Christianity's dangerous ideas. Each section is composed of two chapters that set forth why historic Christian truth-claims are both dangerous and good. The following summary gives you a brief foretaste of how these revolutionary ideas are framed, explained, and defended. This book is intended as an apologetic for the Christian faith's central beliefs and values.

Section 1 (chapters 1–2) starts with the secular perspective on the extreme brevity of human life and on our final end: death. In powerful contrast, arguably Christianity's *most dangerous idea*—Jesus's bodily resurrection—is presented in some detail and defended. Historic Christianity makes the startling claim that one man died a public death but did not remain dead.

Section 2 (chapters 3–4) begins with the controversy of religious pluralism: numerous and contradictory religions claim to speak for God. But historic Christianity's *most distinctive dangerous idea*—the incarnation (Jesus as God in human flesh)—is explained and shown to best account for the facts of Jesus's life. The Christian message is that God came to Earth to seek and save lost sinners.

Section 3 (chapters 5–6) shows how modern cosmology confirms an astonishing truth: the cosmos is fine-tuned and had a beginning. Amazingly, historic Christianity's *most far-reaching dangerous idea*—creation *ex nihilo*—comports with cutting-edge science. In fact, the dynamic enterprise of science itself was born and flourished within the context of the Christian worldview.

Section 4 (chapters 7–8) introduces the subject of atheism and shows how this philosophy seeks to explain reality without reference to God. Historic Christianity, on the other hand, affirms that the best arguments from virtually any aspect of life and the world clearly point to the existence of the God of Christian theism. God, then, as the best explanation for reality, constitutes the Christian faith's *most comprehensive dangerous idea*.

Section 5 (chapters 9–10) opens with the almost universal religious human belief: God will accept people based on their inherent goodness and their good works. In sharp contrast, historic Christianity's gospel message reveals the *most hopeful of dangerous ideas*: that salvation comes solely by grace through faith in Jesus Christ. Christianity stands alone as the universal religion of grace.

Section 6 (chapters 11–12) explains how, in rejecting God, secularism has also lost the value and dignity of human beings. In other words, if humans evolved by purely naturalistic means, they are not different in kind from the animals. But historic Christianity's *most humanitarian of dangerous ideas*— the *imago Dei* (humankind made in the image of God)—lays the foundation for the sanctity of human life. Christianity affirms humans as the distinctive crown of God's creation.

Section 7 (chapters 13–14) explores the problem of evil, pain, and suffering. In contrast to secularism, historic Christianity's *most comforting dangerous idea* is that God has a good reason for the evil and suffering that he allows. Furthermore, God has defeated evil in and through the life, death, and resurrection of Jesus Christ and will eliminate suffering in his future eternal kingdom. Thus the Christian faith has the best and most hopeful explanation concerning evil and suffering.

If as a Christian you find that these dangerous ideas don't rock your worldview, then maybe your faith has become far too safe. And if you're not a Christian, then welcome to Christianity's dangerous, but good, ideas. For those who are courageous enough to seek deeper understanding, the historic Christian faith has many more incredibly explosive truths to reveal.

Soli Deo Gloria,
Kenneth Richard Samples
Advent 2011

NOT ALL DEAD MEN STAY DEAD

1

Easter Hope

> For the religious believer [theist], the last word lies not with
> death but with God.
>
> John Polkinghorne, "God and Physics"

Most people feel uncomfortable talking about their own mortality. Research in the field of thanatology (the study of death and dying) indicates that some individuals even believe if they don't think about death, it may not happen to them.[1] But, as Walter Martin, original host of *The Bible Answer Man*, often said, "The real death rate is one per person."[2]

A dangerous thinking in its own right, this denial of one's mortality constitutes a serious departure from reality. Given that for the last couple of centuries secularism has gained influence within the Western world (especially in the universities), let's explore how that worldview conceptualizes death.

Welcome to the Worldview of Naturalism: Life's One-Way Ticket

Assume the reductionistic worldview of naturalism for a moment. This is the secular view that the material, physical cosmos is the sole reality. Therefore, the infinite, eternal, tripersonal, spiritual God of Christian theism does not exist. In fact, there simply are no spiritual realities such as gods, angels, or immaterial human souls. And no supernatural realm such as heaven exists.

Life—a fortunate accident—emerged on Earth somehow through the purely natural forces of physics and chemistry.[3] Humankind evolved from the lower primates and now stands atop the amazing evolutionary ladder. Now the one referred to as the *naked ape* or *Homo sapiens sapiens* recognizes his chance origin and must contemplate his personal destiny. From a naturalistic perspective, human beings, unlike the impersonal cosmos itself, possess an evolved consciousness and are able to ask the *why* questions. (Strangely enough, the impersonal and nonrational forces of naturalistic evolution have produced a creature that is both *personal* and *rational* and thus capable of reflection.)[4]

As they reflect, humans realize both the fragility and brevity of life—the unequivocal existential dilemma. The grave is the final end of each person's collective life, existence, and consciousness. After death a person will never think again. Never experience again. Never love again. Only oblivion awaits. And nothing more.

The Naturalist's Existential Predicament

The naturalist faces a fourfold existential predicament:

1. I will die.
2. I will die soon.
3. I will die alone.
4. I will remain dead forever.

Some might characterize the human condition as being stalked by death. Death is a constant companion. It's not a matter of *if* but only *when*. Each new day is fortuitous but also ominous. It's one day closer to that which is even more certain than taxes: the *final end*.

Humans may be called *cosmic orphans*. They are doomed to die, yet they have the inherent capacity to ask the big, existential questions. This melancholy naturalistic scenario leads some to angst and despair. Others feel a sense of urgency to live every moment to the hilt before relinquishing the precious life force within them. Yet even if convinced of a secular view toward life, most people seem unable or unwilling to seriously consider this bleak eventuality. Fear, or in some cases inner terror, keeps people from seriously contemplating death and all that it entails.

Some people succumb to the irrational state wherein they subconsciously entertain the idea that they can successfully avoid death. Philosopher Stephen T. Davis notes, "Human beings are the only animals who know that they must die, and thus the only animals who try to hide from themselves the fact that they must die."[5]

Death: Knocking at My Back Door

Given such a stark naturalistic fate, the temptation to deny the reality of death runs strong. Yet without faith in God, this amounts to little more than irrational escapism. But it's not only the naturalist who dodges even the mention of the word *death*. What is it about death that frightens people so much? Davis offers six reasons for humankind's fear of death:

1. Death is inevitable.
2. Death is mysterious.
3. Death must be faced alone.
4. Death separates us from our loved ones.
5. Death puts an end to our hopes and aims.
6. Death ends in oblivion.[6]

Everyone has some natural fear of the unknown, including death. But Davis's six reasons are amplified when one adopts a naturalistic worldview. Why? Because from a naturalistic perspective this life is everything! And this unexpected and accidental life is inevitably slipping away; it can't be held on to. And it will never return again.

It gets worse. The big picture reveals a devastating outcome for all life and the energy and configuration of the cosmos itself. The inevitable outcomes according to the naturalistic worldview include the following:

- The individual dies.
- Humanity collectively goes extinct.
- All life on Earth goes extinct.
- Earth, its solar system, and the Milky Way galaxy literally come apart as humankind's once-hospitable location in the universe disperses.
- Finally, the entire grand cosmos itself inevitably grows lifeless and cold due to a universal heat death. The physics law of entropy will have the last say on the matter.

Thus the fate of each individual, humanity as a whole, and the universe will inevitably be the same regardless of what any person thinks, says, or does. The outcome of the naturalistic view is utter hopelessness. Ironically, many naturalists have failed to reflect sufficiently on their worldview perspective and blind themselves to this desperate predicament.

Danger Ahead

Yet it is at this very point of naturalism's projection of ultimate gloom and doom for humanity that historic Christianity's most dangerous idea comes to bear. Its *dangerous proclamation* is that, though Jesus Christ was condemned by Pontius Pilate and publicly executed through crucifixion, he nevertheless rose bodily from the dead three days later on the first Easter morning.

The absolutely astounding claim of primitive Christianity is that one man in history died but didn't stay dead! In light of human experience and uniform human testimony, this declaration of a literal bodily resurrection from the dead is an utterly incredible claim. If true, there is no more important message for humankind to hear and heed. The resurrection of Jesus Christ would be the ultimate of all dangerous ideas!

Historic Christianity's Most Dangerous Idea: The Resurrection of Jesus Christ

From a historic Christian perspective, both the nature and truth of Christianity uniquely rest on Jesus Christ's bodily resurrection from the dead.[7] The claim that Jesus Christ was raised to life three days after he was executed resides at the heart of the Christian gospel (doctrine) and is Christianity's central supporting fact (apologetics). According to the apostle Paul, historic Christianity's greatest advocate, the truth of Christianity stands or falls on Christ's resurrection. In his own words, "If Christ has not been raised, our preaching is useless and so is your faith. . . . If Christ has not been raised, your faith is futile; you are still in your sins" (1 Cor. 15:14, 17).

Because the truth-claims of Christianity hinge so closely on the resurrection, the New Testament accounts of Christ's resurrection warrant careful analysis and reflection. Not only do the New Testament writers report the resurrection as a factual event, but they also place it within a theological context and explain its overall significance in God's historical redemptive plan.

Let's first summarize the Christian story of Jesus's resurrection; then we'll examine the evidence that supports it and respond to naturalistic alternatives and objections. Later we will return to the amazing implications that the resurrection of Jesus Christ holds for humanity in light of our deadly dilemma.

The New Testament Resurrection Scenario

The four New Testament Gospels and various New Testament Epistles reveal the following historic Christian narrative concerning Jesus Christ's death and resurrection[8] (see Matt. 26:47–28:20; Mark 14:43–16:8; Luke 22:47–24:53; John 18:1–21:25; Acts 9:1–19; 1 Cor. 15:1–58).

Jesus of Nazareth was arrested and tried for blasphemy by the Jewish religious leaders (chief priests and elders). He was subsequently found guilty before the Sanhedrin and taken to the Roman governor of Judea, Pontius Pilate, for execution. At the instigation of some of the Jewish religious leaders, Pilate condemned Jesus to death as an insurrectionist. He was beaten and crucified at the hands of Roman soldiers.

Jesus's lifeless body was taken down from the cross, covered with a burial cloth, and placed in the newly cut tomb of Joseph of Arimathea (a wealthy and prominent member of the Sanhedrin). A large boulder was placed at the entrance of the tomb, and guards were stationed there to ensure that Jesus's body was not stolen.

At dawn three days later (Sunday morning, the first day of the week) there was a violent earthquake at the tomb. An angel of the Lord appeared and rolled away the stone. The guards were terrified to the point of paralysis at the sight of the angel. Some women followers of Jesus subsequently arrived at the tomb and discovered it empty. The women encountered the angel who informed them that Jesus was not in the tomb because he had risen from the dead. Having heard about the women's encounter at the burial site, some of Jesus's disciples went to the tomb later that morning and also found it empty.

Following the empty tomb event, the risen Christ appeared to specific individuals and groups, starting on that original Easter and extending over a forty-day period. According to the New Testament Gospels and Epistles, the resurrected Jesus appeared to individuals, small groups, large assemblies, friends and enemies, believers and nonbelievers, women and men, in public and in private, and at different times and locations.

Jesus's Resurrection Appearances

The New Testament specifically mentions twelve different resurrection appearances:

1. to Mary Magdalene (John 20:10–18)
2. to Mary and the other women (Matt. 28:1–10)
3. to Peter (Luke 24:33–34; 1 Cor. 15:4–5)
4. to two disciples on the way to Emmaus (Luke 24:13–35)
5. to ten apostles (Luke 24:36–49)
6. to eleven apostles (John 20:24–31)
7. to seven apostles (John 21)
8. to all of the apostles (Matt. 28:16–20)
9. to five hundred disciples (1 Cor. 15:6)
10. to James (1 Cor. 15:7)
11. to all the apostles again (Acts 1:4–8)
12. to Paul, somewhat later (Acts 9:1–9; 1 Cor. 15:8)

The distinct characteristics of Jesus's resurrection body can also be cataloged:

- His resurrection body still bore the marks of the cross in his hands, feet, and side (John 20:19–20).
- His body could be seen, touched, and handled (Matt. 28:9).
- It was a body of flesh and bone, and he invited people to handle and examine it (Luke 24:37–40; John 20:20, 27).
- Jesus even ate and drank with his disciples after his resurrection (Luke 24:41–43; Acts 10:41).

Jesus's resurrection body was certainly material and physical in nature (being the same body that had been crucified), yet it had been transformed into a glorious, immortal, and imperishable body. It was clearly capable of things that ordinary mortal bodies are not; for example, it could appear and disappear in a closed room; it could ascend heavenward; and it was free from the constraint of gravity. Therefore, there was both continuity and discontinuity between Jesus's pre- and post-resurrection body.

What Specific Evidence Supports the Resurrection of Jesus Christ?

The basic reason people reject the idea of resurrection is that they intuitively know dead people stay dead. Therefore, given the extraordinary statements made in the New Testament concerning Jesus's unique bodily resurrection, powerful evidence must be marshaled to defend this claim. Christian apologists through the centuries have appealed to seven credible strands of historical evidence as support for the factuality of the resurrection of Jesus.[9]

1. Jesus's Empty Tomb

One of the best-supported facts surrounding Jesus's resurrection is that after his death he was buried in a tomb that three days later was discovered empty. Most New Testament scholars, even most critical scholars (those who doubt the truth of Jesus's resurrection), agree that solid historical facts stand behind the claim in the Gospels that Jesus's tomb was empty on that original Easter morning.[10]

Several sound reasons exist for believing that the story in the Gospels of Jesus's burial is historical in nature and not a legendary invention:

1. *The burial accounts originated early on.* They became part of a primitive creedal statement that formed long before any of the New Testament books were written (more on this creedal statement later).
2. *The accounts of Jesus's burial also come from multiple independent sources.* They also remain clear and straightforward, without signs of embellishment, exaggeration, or excessive theological or apologetic adornment.

3. *Historians have no good reason to doubt the existence of any of the key people mentioned in the burial scenario.* Prominent among these is Joseph of Arimathea. If a pious fiction had been hatched, it would hardly depict a member of the controversial Jewish Sanhedrin (the responsible agents in Jesus's arrest and trial) as serving the cause. Moreover, since these burial reports surfaced early, they could have been discredited for factual inaccuracy. Yet no alternative burial tradition about Jesus emerged.

4. *The Gospel accounts indicate that Jesus's women followers were actual witnesses of the crucifixion, burial, and empty tomb.* If the story were false, it is highly unlikely that such an important role would have been granted to women. In the first century, the testimony of women was considered far less reliable than that of men.

In summary, the details of the empty tomb story conform well to what is known historically. For example, far from myth or legend, the report of the empty tomb carries a very early date, even using the primitive expression "on the first day of the week" instead of the later theologically developed "on the third day." The vacated burial site also fits well with what is known of the times archaeologically (i.e., concerning burial customs, construction of tombs, timing of ceremonial events). And the empty tomb was never challenged, let alone refuted, by the contemporary enemies and critics of Christianity.

Just how important is the evidence for the empty tomb? Well, if the Jews or Romans had produced the body of Jesus, Christianity would have been immediately falsified. They could have exhumed the body and put it on public display. Even a partially decomposed body of Jesus would have been enough to severely damage the apostolic message and the movement it launched. Furthermore, if Jesus's body had remained in the tomb, the Jewish and Roman authorities had the motive, means, and opportunity to publicly produce it. But this was never done, though there were plenty of people who desired to quash the primitive faith.

The disciples would not have proclaimed a bodily resurrection unless Jesus's tomb was indeed barren. For in ancient Judaism, the concept of resurrection was considered only bodily in nature, not a spiritual resurrection. Yet the apostles proclaimed Jesus's bodily resurrection just fifty days after his crucifixion in the very locale in which he had been executed and buried.

It should also be noted that the first alternative naturalistic explanation for the resurrection presupposed the truth of the vacated tomb. The Jewish authorities insisted that the tomb was empty because Jesus's disciples had come in the night and stolen the body (Matt. 28:13). There was no mention of the body of Jesus being in a different tomb, buried in a common grave, or eliminated in any other manner (such as devoured by dogs, which is the view set forth by controversial cofounder of the Jesus Seminar, John Dominic Crossan).[11]

The preeminent evangelical Christian specialist on the resurrection, William Lane Craig, notes, "There is simply no plausible naturalistic explanation available today that accounts for the empty tomb of Jesus."[12] For two thousand years Christians have argued that when the facts of the empty tomb are combined with Jesus's postcrucifixion appearances, the only genuinely consistent explanation for this data is found in early Christianity's proclamation that Jesus Christ rose bodily from the dead.

2. Jesus's Postmortem Appearances

According to the New Testament, numerous people (as many as five hundred) had intimate, empirical encounters with Jesus Christ after his death (postmortem). These appearances were attested by a variety of people, at different times and places, and under various circumstances. The witnesses of the resurrection claimed to have seen, heard, and touched the glorified Christ. The same person whom they had seen executed three days earlier was now alive and in their midst. He even manifested the physical marks of crucifixion. These in-time-and-space physical appearances, which were reported soon after the encounters, cannot reasonably be dismissed as mythical or purely psychological in nature.

The resurrection appearances that the disciples claimed to witness are not like religious visions or hallucinatory phenomena. The encounters with the risen Christ involved the observers' five senses—much different from strictly religious visions. And the resurrection appearances were part of the observers' long-term memory, unlike hallucinations that are experienced and then fade from memory. Resurrection expert Gary Habermas says about this eyewitness testimony of Jesus's resurrection, "Probably a majority of contemporary critical scholars are impressed by the evidence that first century Christians genuinely believed they had seen Jesus after his crucifixion."[13]

In summary, specific characteristics of the postmortem appearances of Jesus include:

- He appeared to women and men.
- He appeared to friends and enemies.
- He appeared to individuals, small groups, and large groups.
- He was observed indoors and outdoors.
- He was encountered in the morning and evening.
- He was seen, heard, and touched.
- He ate and drank with the disciples.
- His appearances were physical and bodily.
- He appeared to some people a single time and to others multiple times.
- His encounters demonstrated natural and supernatural qualities.

3. *Short Time Frame between Actual Events and Eyewitness Claims*

Powerful evidence for the historical authenticity of Jesus's resurrection from the dead comes from eyewitness testimonies that were reported soon after the events transpired. The apostle Paul claims both that he saw the resurrected Christ (Acts 9:1–19; 22:6–16; 26:12–23) and that prior to his experience he received the firsthand testimony from others who were eyewitnesses to the resurrection (1 Cor. 15:3).

In Paul's first Epistle to the Corinthians, he employs a creedal statement about the resurrection that dates to the most primitive period of Christianity. This creedal statement is believed even by critical scholars to be part of the original Christian kerygma (the earliest preaching and teaching message of Christianity). This early statement of faith that Paul relays mentions by name two of Jesus's disciples who said they had seen the resurrected Christ. These two disciples are Peter (one of the original twelve apostles and principal spokesperson of early Christianity) and James (the brother of Jesus).

> For what I received I passed on to you as of first importance: that Christ died for our sins according to the Scriptures, that he was buried, that he was raised on the third day according to the Scriptures, and that he appeared to Cephas [Peter], and then to the Twelve. After that, he appeared to more than five hundred of the brothers and sisters at the same time, most of whom are still living, though some have fallen asleep. Then he appeared to James, then to all the apostles. (1 Cor. 15:3–7)

Paul's statement gives us a fourfold formula of the primitive Christian kerygma:

1. Christ died.
2. He was buried.
3. He was raised.
4. He appeared.

Three independent sources confirm this formula:

> With a loud cry, Jesus breathed his last. . . . Joseph [of Arimathea] bought some linen cloth, took down the body, wrapped it in the linen, and placed it in a tomb cut out of rock. . . .
> [The women] saw a young man dressed in a white robe sitting on the right side, and they were alarmed.
> "Don't be alarmed," he said. "You are looking for Jesus the Nazarene, who was crucified. He has risen! . . . Go, tell his disciples and Peter, 'He is going ahead of you into Galilee. There you will see him, just as he told you.'" (Mark, told to him by Peter, in Mark 15:37, 46; 16:5–7; see 15:37–16:7)

> Though they found no proper ground for a death sentence, they asked Pilate to have him executed. When they had carried out all that was written about him,

they took him down from the cross and laid him in a tomb. But God raised him from the dead, and for many days he was seen by those who had traveled with him from Galilee to Jerusalem. They are now his witnesses to our people. (Luke, in Acts 13:28–31)

For what I received I passed on to you as of first importance: that Christ died for our sins according to the Scriptures, that he was buried, that he was raised on the third day according to the Scriptures, and that he appeared to Cephas [Peter], and then to the Twelve. (Paul, in 1 Cor. 15:3–5)

Paul also mentions that within a couple of years of his own conversion (brought about by seeing the resurrected Christ), he journeyed to Jerusalem to meet with Peter and James. Most scholars agree it was during the meeting with these two early Christian leaders that he received this early creedal message and then later relayed it in his first Epistle to the Corinthians. Habermas explains the close time frame of these events:

The majority of critical scholars who address the issue think that Paul received his traditional material on the death and resurrection of Jesus from Peter and James the brother of Jesus while he was in Jerusalem approximately a half dozen years after the crucifixion of Jesus.[14]

Given the short interval of time between the early eyewitness testimonies about Jesus's resurrection and the event itself, these accounts must be considered historically reliable. Furthermore, this time frame also places the original proclamation by the first apostles about Jesus's resurrection near to the time of Jesus's death and resurrection. This development has led even critical New Testament scholars to be amazed at the early and reliable testimony evident in Paul's writings. In fact, distinguished New Testament scholar James D. G. Dunn states, "This tradition [of Jesus's resurrection and appearances], we can be entirely confident, was *formulated as tradition within months of Jesus's death*."[15]

Six prominent witnesses to Jesus's resurrection are named in 1 Corinthians 15:3–8:

1. Peter
2. the Twelve
3. more than five hundred brothers and sisters
4. James
5. all the apostles
6. Paul

The testimony of the eyewitnesses also provides an estimated timeline for the resurrection and the events that followed:

AD 30: Jesus's crucifixion

AD 30–31: early creedal proclamation or report of Jesus's resurrection circulates

AD 31–33: Paul's conversion

AD 34–36: Paul's first visit with Peter and James in Jerusalem (where and when Paul receives the creedal report)

AD 48: Paul's second visit with Peter, James, and John in Jerusalem

AD 50: Paul visits the church in Corinth

AD 54–55: Paul writes his first Epistle to the Corinthians (which includes the creedal report found in 1 Cor. 15:3–8)

4. Extraordinary Transformation of the Apostles

The book of Acts describes a dramatic and enduring transformation of eleven men. These terrified, defeated cowards after Jesus's crucifixion (as revealed in the Gospels) soon became courageous preachers and, in some cases, martyrs. They grew bold enough to stand against hostile Jews and Romans even in the face of torture and death. Such radical and extensive change deserves an adequate explanation, for human character and conduct does not transform easily or often. Considering that the apostles fled and denied knowing Jesus after he was arrested, their courage in the face of persecution seems even more astounding. The apostles attributed the strength of their newfound character to their direct, personal encounter with the resurrected Christ. In Christ's resurrection, the apostles found their unshakable reason to live—and die.

According to the earliest testimony concerning the resurrection of Jesus, three of the people Jesus appeared to were either initially skeptical of the truth of the resurrection or were outright opposed to Jesus and his messianic claims. Those three were Thomas, James, and Paul, all of whom were predisposed to reject the truth of the resurrection. Since Paul's conversion will be addressed later, let's consider the extraordinary impact Jesus's resurrection had on Thomas and James.

DOUBTING THOMAS BECOMES BELIEVING THOMAS

While Thomas was one of the original twelve disciples, he was not among the first of Jesus's followers to see the risen Christ. Upon hearing the testimony from his fellow disciples concerning Jesus's bodily resurrection, he doubted its truth. The Gospel of John conveys Thomas's skepticism: "Unless I see the nail marks in his hands and put my finger where the nails were, and put my hand into his side, I will not believe" (John 20:25).

Though a follower of Jesus, Thomas was highly skeptical and needed direct, empirical evidence of Jesus's actual bodily resurrection before he would believe the claim of his compatriots. Thomas demanded evidence of a concrete nature. He demonstrated tough-mindedness when it came to claims of the miraculous even when the testimony came from his close friends and associates. Yet according to John's Gospel, Thomas soon had an encounter with the resurrected Jesus that more than satisfied his skepticism:

> A week later his disciples were in the house again, and Thomas was with them. Though the doors were locked, Jesus came and stood among them and said, "Peace be with you!" Then he said to Thomas, "Put your finger here; see my hands. Reach out your hand and put it into my side. Stop doubting and believe."
>   Thomas said to him, "My Lord and my God!" (John 20:26–28)

Thomas went on to serve as an ardent disciple of Jesus Christ throughout his life. The transformation of Thomas from doubter to worshiper and servant is strong evidence in support of the truth of Jesus Christ's bodily resurrection from the dead.

While some critical scholars have attempted to dismiss John's report of Thomas's encounter with the resurrected Jesus as a mere invention, most readers hear in John's testimony the ring of historical truth. If a mythical story had been invented to support the resurrection, it is highly unlikely that it would claim that one of the original twelve disciples doubted Jesus's resurrection.

JAMES THE FAMILY SKEPTIC

The Gospels report that prior to the resurrection Jesus's brothers were highly critical of Jesus's messianic claims (see Mark 6:3–4; John 7:5). In fact, Jesus's family viewed him as suffering from mental delusion (Mark 3:21, 31–35). Yet the early creed that Paul had been given by the apostles (which included James) reported that Jesus had appeared to his brother James (1 Cor. 15:7). James then became one of the most important leaders of the early Christian church, even holding unique authority at the Jerusalem Council (Acts 15:12–21). Sources in church history report that James was later martyred for his belief in Jesus Christ.

What accounts for James's amazing transformation from (undoubtedly) being embarrassed by his brother's claims to becoming a distinguished leader in the early church and finally to suffering martyrdom? The resurrection seems to best account for this radical change in James's understanding and perspective. James saw his brother alive after his public execution, and that event changed everything. It was a *dangerous* idea, but a real one.

5. *The Greatest Conversion in History*

Saul of Tarsus was a distinguished, first-century Hebrew scholar of the Torah (the Law), a member of the Jewish party of the Pharisees, and a Roman citizen (Acts 21:37–22:3). Zealous in his devotion to God and in his desire to protect ancient Judaism from what he perceived as false and heretical teaching, he became the principal antagonist of the primitive Christian church. Saul expressed his intense hatred toward Christians by having them arrested and instigating physical persecution and execution of believers, including Stephen (Acts 7:54–8:3; Gal. 1:13–14). Traveling on the road to Damascus to further persecute the church (ca. AD 31–33), Saul underwent a life-changing experience. According to his claim, Saul encountered (saw and spoke with) the resurrected Jesus of Nazareth (Acts 9:1–30; 22:5–13). Following his dramatic conversion to the movement he once loathed, he used the Gentile name "Paul" and became the greatest protagonist of the newfound Christian faith.

Besides Jesus Christ himself, the apostle Paul is clearly the second most important figure in the history of Christianity. Paul went on to become Christianity's greatest missionary, theologian, and apologist as well as the inspired author of thirteen books of the New Testament.

What caused Paul's conversion—arguably the greatest religious conversion in history? To understand the true magnitude of this conversion, let's consider what may be the modern equivalent of Paul's first-century conversion to Christianity.[16] Imagine the British prime minister and statesman Winston Churchill becoming a Nazi. Or American president Ronald Reagan becoming a communist. Or Führer Adolf Hitler becoming a convert to Judaism. Whatever equivalent one chooses, Paul's conversion to Christianity was such an absolutely astounding event.

According to Paul himself, the incredible transformation of one of Western civilization's most influential religious leaders and thinkers was due to the appearance of the resurrected Christ. The conversion of the apostle Paul, not to mention his life and accomplishments, seems truly inexplicable apart from the fact of the resurrection.

Yet there are still many skeptics. Scottish philosopher David Hume (1711–76) is considered one of the foremost critics of claims of miracles. Christian philosopher Stephen T. Davis summarizes one of Hume's major objections to claims of the miraculous: "Hume's main complaint is that no purported miracle that he knows about has been supported by the testimony of a sufficient number of people of unquestioned good sense, education, learning, and integrity."[17]

Would the claims of the primitive Christian church expressed in Paul's creedal statement in 1 Corinthians 15 about Jesus's resurrection meet Hume's standard? Consider these three points:

1. *The early church claimed that Jesus had appeared alive to more than five hundred people and to Paul.* Many of these people were alive and available to testify at the time Paul penned the first Epistle to the Corinthians. That seems a sufficient number of witnesses to validate a miraculous event.

2. *The skeptical converts to Christianity—namely Thomas, James, and Paul—seem to possess very strong intellectual, educational, and moral qualities that qualify them as credible witnesses.* All three men came to believe in the resurrection after initially doubting or rejecting it.
3. *A number of the major, early Christian leaders died as martyrs for their affirmation of Jesus Christ's bodily resurrection from the dead.* As A. J. Hoover explains,

> When a man undergoes persecution, contempt, beatings, prison, and death for a message, he has a good motive for reviewing carefully the grounds of his convictions. It is extremely unlikely that the original disciples of Jesus would have persisted in affirming the truths they affirmed if Jesus hadn't actually risen.[18]

It was this reasoning that motivated the Christian thinker Blaise Pascal (1623–62) to state, "I only believe histories whose witnesses are ready to be put to death."[19]

6. *Emergence of the Historic Christian Church*

What started this movement that within three hundred years dominated the entire Roman Empire and over the course of two millennia dominated Western civilization? Christianity in a very short time developed a distinct cultural and theological identity apart from that of traditional Judaism. According to the New Testament, this unique Christian faith came into being directly because of the resurrection of Jesus Christ.

The extraordinary, historical emergence of the Christian church needs an adequate explanation. According to the New Testament, the apostles turned the world upside down with the truth of the resurrection, and the historic church emerged. This is why many have called the historic Christian church *the community of the resurrection.*

7. *Emergence of Sunday as a Day of Worship*

The Jews worshiped on the Sabbath, which is the seventh day of the week (sundown Friday to sundown Saturday). The early Christian church, however, gradually changed the day of their worship from the seventh to the first day of the week (see Acts 20:7; 1 Cor. 16:2; "the Lord's day," Rev. 1:10). For the early Christian church, Sunday commemorated Jesus's resurrection from the dead.

Reflection on Christ's resurrection to immortal life transformed Christian worship, uniquely influencing the formulation of the sacraments of the early church (baptism and communion), and thus it distinguished the Christian faith in its theology and practice from traditional Judaism. Apart from the resurrection, no reason existed for early Christians (as a sect of Judaism) to view Sunday (the first day of the week) as having any enduring theological or ceremonial significance. The resurrection of Jesus therefore set historic Christianity apart from the Judaism of its day. That same truth sets the faith apart from all other religions through the centuries.

Such a dangerous idea has been subjected to all manner of skeptical scrutiny. What are the counterexplanations and how do they fare? Do they pose a danger? We'll review them in the next chapter.

2

Objections Examined

If Christ is risen, nothing else matters. And if Christ is not—
nothing else matters.

Jaroslav Pelikan (1923–2006),
Yale Department of History Newsletter

No one ever argued when *Star Trek*'s McCoy uttered his famous catch-phrase, "He's dead, Jim." He was, after all, a doctor. Yet when it comes to the dangerous idea of Christ's resurrection, questions and alternative theories abound. These alternative theories ask whether Christ's death on the cross was genuine or if there is a natural explanation that can rule out the resurrection claim.

Can the Events Surrounding Jesus's Resurrection Be Explained Naturally?

A good explanatory theory includes logical consistency, explanatory power and scope, fidelity to known facts, avoidance of unwarranted assumptions, and assertion of claims that can be tested and proven true or false. Using these objective standards, let's examine eight naturalistic theories that have gained some popularity over the years.

1. Legend Theory: The Resurrection of Jesus—Legend or Myth?

Most critical scholars acknowledge that the first reports of Jesus's resurrection can be traced to early creedal pronouncements dating back to within the first couple of years (if not earlier) after Jesus's death and proclaimed resurrection. Such creedal statements—or traditions, as they were called—existed long before any of the books of the New Testament were written. These creeds tended to summarize the essence of the Christian truth-claims as seen in the references to 1 Corinthians 15:3–6 in the previous chapter.

For the most part, New Testament scholars acknowledge that the reports of the resurrection date back to the earliest part of the Apostolic Era to the original disciples themselves, who claimed to be eyewitnesses of the resurrection. On that basis, the resurrection cannot be adequately explained as either accruing myth or embellished legend. Therefore, the interval of time between the events of Jesus's life, death, and resurrection and the subsequent writings of the New Testament are appropriate to show that reports of the resurrection are not the product of myth or legend. One can assume that the closer the New Testament documents are to the events that they report, the more historically reliable they may be considered.

Many of the New Testament books (the Gospels and various Epistles) were written soon enough after the events they report that there wasn't sufficient time for legends and myths to enter into the biblical accounts. Consider the following two arguments.

First, while Jesus's death probably took place in AD 30, there are good reasons to believe that the Synoptic Gospels (Matthew, Mark, and Luke) existed by the early 60s (possibly the late 50s for Mark), which was within a generation of the events surrounding the life, death, and resurrection of Jesus Christ. Neither the Gospels nor the book of Acts mentions three significant events that transpired between AD 60 and 70: (1) the persecution of Christians by Roman Emperor Nero (ca. mid-60s); (2) the martyrdom of the apostles Peter and Paul (ca. 64–66); and (3) the fall of Jerusalem under the Roman military leader Titus (ca. 70).[1] These significant events would have undoubtedly been of great interest to Christians, so the fact that none of them are mentioned in the Gospels causes some New Testament scholars to conclude that the Synoptic Gospels were already in existence by the early 60s.

Second, since the book of Acts follows the Gospel of Luke as a companion work, and since Acts does not mention the events listed above, this seems to place the dates of the Synoptic Gospels even earlier—especially if one assumes Markan priority (the dominant theory in modern New Testament scholarship that Mark was the first Gospel written).

Not only were the Gospels written too early to have incorporated legends, but other written and oral sources (such as the creedal statements mentioned previously) also bridge the gap between the time of Jesus's death and the time when the Gospels were actually written. Some of the apostle Paul's Epistles

(Galatians; 1 and 2 Thessalonians) were probably written as early as the late 40s or early 50s. Source criticism (the study of sources that stand behind the written text) indicates there were oral and possibly written sources to support the Greek Gospels, which again fills the timeline between the events of Jesus's life and the written records. New Testament scholar Craig Blomberg sees ample reasons to believe that Matthew, Mark, and Luke used such sources. "Source criticism cannot demonstrate that the first accounts of the various portions of Jesus's life were entirely trustworthy, but it can suggest that those accounts arose in a time and place in which many who had personally known Jesus still lived."[2]

The mythologizing theory (the idea that myth has encrusted the facts of Jesus's life) seems possible only if one postulates several generations over which the mythology grew up around Christ.[3] In fact, A. N. Sherwin-White, Oxford scholar of ancient Greek and Roman history, argues that the span of two full generations is not sufficient time for myth and legend to accrue and distort historical fact.[4] Legend expert Julius Müller states that legend cannot replace fact as long as the eyewitnesses remain alive.[5]

A further reason for rejecting the myth and legend theory is that the apostles of Jesus recognized the difference between myth and factual, eyewitness testimony, and they solemnly asserted that they were eyewitnesses of actual historical events (see Luke 1:1–4; John 19:35; 1 Cor. 15:3–8; Gal. 1:11–12; 2 Peter 1:16; 1 John 1:1–2). Rather than creating myth, the apostles tried to squelch rumors and untruths before they could spread (John 21:22–25). The Gospel writers also paid attention to historical details: the Gospels contain particular points about the historical time period of Jesus—including names, dates, events, customs, and so on. Historically speaking, the central criterion for including the Gospels in the New Testament Canon was that they emerged from within apostolic circles (eyewitnesses or associates of eyewitnesses).

The Gospel accounts also seem incongruous in style or in content with other known mythical writings.[6] Biblical miracles are neither bizarre nor frivolous like other mythological literature (i.e., Greek mythology). Jesus's miracles are always performed within the context of his ministry, specifically to the glory of God and in response to legitimate human need. The historical stand side by side with the miraculous in the Gospels in a way that is not found in mythological literature.

Some have attempted to tie the resurrection of Jesus to the alleged resurrection of fertility gods in ancient pagan religions (e.g., Osiris, Adonis, Attis, Mithras).[7] In reality, these comparisons are superficial, inexact, and often based on late sources. There are no clear parallels in other religions to Jesus's resurrection. Thus, they have no historical connection with or influence on Christianity. None of these pagan religious stories have the factual historical foundation that surrounds the resurrection of Jesus Christ.

Advocates of *demythologizing* (exposing the myth of) the Gospel accounts also typically reason in a fallacious manner. They tend to set forth circular arguments for rejecting the Gospels as history. Consider the following:

- They reject the divinity of Christ because they reject the Gospel texts.
- They reject the Gospel texts because they think they are myth.
- They think they are myth because of the miraculous events that speak of God becoming man (i.e., the divinity of Christ).[8]

This reasoning clearly begs the question—that is, the premises illegitimately depend on the assumed conclusion—and it exposes an antisupernatural bias. This reasoning reveals a problem of having a basis on presuppositions rather than actual history.

Because good evidence supports the conclusion that the Gospels reflect early sources about the life and death of Jesus, one can assume that if the Gospel writers had departed from the historical facts (either by exaggeration or out-right invention), hostile witnesses conversant with the events of Jesus's life could have and would have exposed the untruths. As textual scholar F. F. Bruce writes, it could not have been easy "to invent words and deeds of Jesus in those early years, when so many of His disciples were about, who could remember what had and had not happened."[9] The apostles, confident in their testimony, appealed to the firsthand knowledge of unbelievers who were conversant with the facts of Jesus's life (see Acts 2:22; 26:25–27).

Viewing the resurrection of Jesus Christ as a legend or myth ignores the solid historical support (oral and written) behind the event, seems rooted in unsupported antisupernatural presuppositions, and fails to recognize the short interval of time between the emergence of the Gospel writings and the events they describe. Accordingly, this must be considered a highly implausible and inadequate explanatory theory.

2. Fraud Theory: Someone Stole the Body

According to the Gospel records, after hearing about the empty tomb some of the Jewish religious leaders bribed the guards to say that they had fallen asleep on their watch and that Jesus's apostles had come in the night and stolen the body (Matt. 28:11–15). Regardless of how this story started, it became (in effect) the first alternative explanation of the resurrection scenario. On that basis it deserves analysis.

This theory disregards the fact that the apostles themselves at first did not believe that Jesus had risen. It also fails to account for the dramatic conversion of James, who was opposed to Jesus's ministry and was turned around only through *seeing* the risen Jesus (see Mark 6:1–5; 1 Cor. 15:7; Gal. 2:9). The same is also true of Paul, who earlier had persecuted the early believers and was converted only through a direct encounter with the resurrected Christ. These factors also contradict the claim that someone other than the disciples stole Jesus's body.

Now let's examine further the idea that the disciples stole the body and pulled off a fraud. One must ask whether the apostles were even capable of stealing the body. In order to steal it, they would have had to bypass the guards and move the large, sealed stone (weighing possibly between one and a half and two tons) in front of the tomb. This makes a theft highly unlikely, especially since the apostles acted cowardly after Jesus's initial arrest. Moreover, if the guards were asleep, then how did they know the identity of whoever stole the body?

What possible motivation would the apostles have for stealing the body anyway? They had nothing to gain and virtually everything to lose. Creating a resurrection hoax would only bring them meaningless hardship, persecution, martyrdom, and possible damnation for blasphemy. If the apostles had, in fact, stolen the body and then created a hoax for the resurrection appearances, would they then be willing to die as martyrs for what they *knew* was false? Such a scenario seems totally unrealistic and ridiculous.

If the apostles were actually involved in creating a resurrection hoax, the conspiracy would have undoubtedly come apart under pressure, both external and internal. Plenty of adversaries were more than willing to expose the apostles' fraud. After all, religious and political leaders hated, scorned, excommunicated, imprisoned, and tortured them. And if the apostles were deceivers, then their dishonest behavior went against everything they had been taught by Jesus about truth and integrity. Yet in the Gospels the apostles come across not as charlatans or mythmakers, but rather as simple, honest men.

If the apostles or others did invent the story of the resurrection, they deserve Academy Awards. Apologists Peter Kreeft and Ronald K. Tacelli note, "If they made up the story, they were the most creative, clever, intelligent fantasists in history, far surpassing Shakespeare, or Dante or Tolkien. Fishermen's 'fish stories' are never that elaborate, that convincing, that life-changing, and that enduring."[10]

Overall, this hoax theory seems extremely implausible. It doesn't fit the facts, and it lacks true explanatory power and scope. Understandably, even most critical scholars now reject this explanation.

3. Wrong Tomb Theory: The Women Were Mistaken

It seems plausible that in their grief and confusion following Jesus's crucifixion, the women followers of Jesus might have mistakenly gone to the wrong tomb. But if they had, their error would have been quickly corrected. Wouldn't Joseph of Arimathea have known the correct location of his own property? Wouldn't the apostles have responded by correcting this mistake?

Are we to assume, as well, that the soldiers commissioned to guard Jesus's tomb also guarded the wrong one?

Because it served the best interest of both the Jewish and Roman officials to crush Christianity, if Jesus's body actually lay in another tomb, the Jews and Romans had both the motive and the manpower to locate it, produce the body as evidence, and thus put an end to Christianity before it really began.

Furthermore, the wrong tomb hypothesis offers no explanation for the resurrection appearances, the apostles' transformation, or the Christian church's formation and growth. This hypothesis plays fast and loose with the facts and lacks genuine explanatory power and scope.

4. Relocated Second Burial Theory: Jesus's Body Was Moved

A twist on the wrong tomb theory suggests that Jesus's body was relocated to another grave site after his initial burial in Joseph of Arimathea's tomb.[11] According to this naturalistic explanation, Joseph of Arimathea hurriedly buried Jesus in his own tomb because the Sabbath was fast approaching. Then after the Sabbath day was over, Joseph moved Jesus's body to a graveyard for criminals. Therefore, Jesus's initial tomb was found empty on the first Easter morning because the body simply had been moved.[12]

Though interesting, this theory suffers severe problems.

First, while reburial was common in ancient Israel, it wasn't characterized by relocating bodies to a different grave site (not even in the case of criminals). Rather, the body was left in the original tomb for one year until only the bones remained. At that time, family members removed the bones, placed them in an ossuary (a stone bone box), and then placed the ossuary in a family cemetery. Thus the theory that Jesus's body was relocated to a second burial site fails to correspond with the common reburial practice.

Second, no evidence exists anywhere in the biblical reports or elsewhere that Jesus's body was relocated. Nor has any tradition emerged pointing to an alternative burial site. Mark's Gospel indicates that Joseph of Arimathea's tomb was Jesus's exclusive burial site (Mark 15:42–47; 16:6).

This reburial theory—even if successful—offers limited explanatory scope. It fails to account for the postmortem resurrection appearances of Jesus, the extraordinary transformation of the apostles, or the emergence of the Christian church. Thus this alternative theory simply doesn't fit the facts.

5. Apparent Death Theory: Jesus Wasn't Really Dead

This theory claims that Jesus only appeared to be dead when he was taken down from the cross. Subsequently Jesus revived in the tomb and appeared to his disciples as the "risen Lord."

This theory fails to recognize that the Roman executioners were very good at their task. Crucifixions were their specialty. Furthermore, they operated under the constant threat of the death penalty if they allowed a convict to escape. According to the Gospel accounts, the Roman soldiers thrust a spear into Jesus's side to confirm that he was in fact dead on the cross. The wound produced blood and water from his pierced heart. In light of Jesus's confirmed death, they found no need to break his legs, which would have hastened his suffocation (John 19:34–37).

Could Jesus have survived after suffering severe torture, crucifixion, and exposure in a cold tomb with no medical attention? Could the guards have been overcome by a nearly dead man? Could Jesus have convinced his disciples that he had gloriously and triumphantly risen from the dead when his medical condition was, at best, *critical*? And if this incredible story was somehow true, where did Jesus go?

This *swoon* theory makes Jesus of Nazareth out to be a fraud, an intentional deceiver. But there is nothing known about the historic Jesus that leads one to believe he was a charlatan. It also fails to account for Paul's subsequent conversion resulting from a glorious appearance of the risen Jesus. This theory seems totally implausible and lacks real explanatory power.

6. Hallucination Theory: Jesus's Followers Suffered from Hallucinations

Hallucinations are commonly understood to be private, subjective, and individual mental experiences (or mental projections) that do not correspond to objective reality. They are usually brief (lasting seconds or minutes, then fading away) and are often induced by drugs or by extreme deprivation of food, drink, and sleep.[13] They also typically occur among people described as extremely nervous or high strung.

The resurrection appearances, however, were experienced by various people, at various times, in various places, and under various circumstances over a period of forty days. The hallucination hypothesis simply cannot reasonably account for this array of data. Grieving Mary in the garden may have been a candidate for a hallucination, but what about those who were not favorably disposed to the cause of Jesus, such as his brother James or the openly hostile Saul of Tarsus? It seems impossible that the more than five hundred brethren Paul says witnessed the resurrected Christ (1 Cor. 15:6) all shared the same hallucination.

The disciples described intimate encounters with the risen Jesus in which they saw, heard, touched, conversed, and ate with him. These personal encounters fit with and corresponded to their relationship with Christ before the resurrection. These kinds of experiences don't correspond to what is known of hallucinatory states.

Furthermore, the apostles, as orthodox Jews, did not believe in individual resurrection. Their concept of resurrection was limited to the general resurrection of humankind in the future divine judgment. Because hallucinations are mere projections of what is already in the mind, and since the apostles had no resurrection expectations, they would have had no basis for a resurrection hallucination.

The hallucination theory fails to account for the empty tomb and, like most of the other naturalistic alternatives, it fails to account for all the facts. Thus it lacks any authentic explanatory power.

7. Twin Brother Theory: Jesus Had an Identical Twin

This theory claims that Jesus and his identical twin were separated at birth. Then after the crucifixion, this twin returned to impersonate his brother as the resurrected Christ.

Imagine the improbable state of affairs if this twin theory were true.[14] This Jesus look-alike had to somehow discover his amazing resemblance to Jesus of Nazareth, then study the public ministry of Jesus, lurk in the shadows awaiting Jesus's death, only then to present himself—for a brief period only—as the resurrected Christ. To get rid of Jesus's body he would have to bypass the guards and move the large sealed stone in front of the tomb to steal the body of Jesus. Would conspirators have helped him? Would the marks of crucifixion on his hands, feet, and side be perfectly imitated? How would he pull off appearing and disappearing within closed rooms? After forty days of fame, this man would then disappear completely. How? What happened to him? And what would motivate a person to do such bizarre things?

This relatively new and creative naturalistic hypothesis has no clear basis in either the Gospel accounts or any other document. It clearly contradicts what Luke reveals about the personal details of Jesus's birth (i.e., a single child born to Mary and Joseph in Bethlehem, Luke 2:1–20). Like some of the other theories examined above, it is, in effect, nothing more than an ad hoc hypothesis emerging from antisupernatural presuppositions. Some people presuppose that miracles don't happen, and they therefore reason that there must be some natural explanation—no matter how unusual and implausible.

8. Disembodied Visions Theory: Jesus Appeared to the Apostles in a Nonphysical Way

The idea that the apostles had visionary experiences of Jesus after his death is popular today among critical scholars. Because the *subjective* visions (hallucination) theory is so highly inadequate and untenable, many scholars propose that Jesus really did appear to the apostles, but in a nonphysical manner. It is important to note that this viewpoint is a departure from the purely naturalistic alternatives previously discussed. In this view, the appearances of Jesus involve a phenomenon that moves beyond the natural realm.[15]

Yet visions of a disembodied Jesus after his death go against the Jewish belief that resurrection will be bodily and physical in nature in addition to not being individual. Moreover, the various appearances of Jesus involved activities associated with a physical body. His appearance to more than five hundred people at the same time would be difficult to conceive of in noncorporeal terms. And how did Jesus eat and drink with his disciples without a real body? Similarly, the resurrection accounts describe Jesus as being touched, which indicates the presence of a physical body.

Thus, while the disembodied visions theory is quite distinct from the other purely naturalistic theories, it still defies logic and appears unable to adequately explain the data revealed in the resurrection accounts.

Superior Explanatory Theory: Jesus Christ Did Rise Bodily from the Dead

After almost two millennia, the most reasonable explanatory theory for the events surrounding Jesus's death remains that the apostles told the truth: Jesus was raised bodily from the dead. The resurrection corresponds to Christ's specific predictions and his followers' claims to be historical eyewitnesses of that resurrection (see Acts 2:32; 3:15; 5:32; 10:39). Jesus anticipated his own resurrection numerous times (see Matt. 16:21; Mark 9:10; Luke 9:22–27; John 2:19–22). The event gains plausibility in light of Jesus's matchless personal character, fulfillment of Old Testament messianic prophecy, and many miraculous works, culminating in his personal conquest of death.

The proper way to evaluate such a miraculous claim is to scrutinize the evidence and follow it wherever it leads. It is logically illegitimate to reject the resurrection a priori based on a preconceived commitment to naturalism (a case of begging the question). As amazing as the resurrection may be, it has the ring of truth on many different levels. The proclamation of the resurrection of Christ by the apostles makes more sense than all naturalistic alternatives. It manifests genuine explanatory power and scope. Christian apologist William Lane Craig comments,

> One of the greatest weaknesses of alternative explanations to the resurrection is their incompleteness: they fail to provide a comprehensive explanation of all the data. By contrast the resurrection furnishes one, simple, comprehensive explanation of all the facts without distorting them. Therefore, it is the better explanation.[16]

Death and Resurrection

The question of the resurrection—Christianity's most dangerous idea—plays out in very practical and existential terms. As each person contemplates the inevitability and imminence of death, these thoughts can quickly lead to existential angst, desperation, and despair. Only the promise of the one whose resurrection is a historical fact can deliver anyone from this dreaded human predicament.

The idea that Jesus truly did rise from the dead is indeed the most dangerous idea on Earth, for it tells us that *not all dead men stay dead*. Given the inevitability of death, this truth is the greatest news that mortal human beings could ever hope to hear.

Unfortunately, Christ's followers today sometimes fail to appreciate the truly dangerous nature of ignoring this distinctly historic Christian doctrine. Believers often take this astounding truth for granted. As Stephen T. Davis says, "Christians today do not seem to be astonished at the idea of resurrection (after nearly two thousand Easters, we seem to have gotten used to the idea), but we ought to be."[17]

The fact of the resurrection tells us God loves us and wants to rescue us from the desperate plight brought upon all humanity by original sin. God himself through the person of Jesus Christ entered history to bring about redemption through his life, death, and resurrection. Jesus Christ conquered sin on the cross, and at the empty tomb he proved his power to banish death forever. The resurrection teaches profound lessons about God's love, power, and sovereign plan for humankind.

Until the Lord returns at his glorious second coming, believers will continue to face death. But Christians know that just as the Lord was raised, so too will their mortal bodies be raised and transformed into bodies fit to live and reign in God's kingdom forever. Saint Augustine expresses the historic Christian view regarding life and death in his work *Confessions*: "I was born into this life which leads to death or should I say—this death which leads to life?"[18]

A Dangerous Idea That Changed the World

The history of Western civilization is inconceivable without Jesus Christ. And it was the resurrection that produced the Christian community. Starting with only twelve followers, Jesus altered the course of history. Within a few hundred years his followers, his *church*, came to dominate the Roman Empire. In the next millennium, Christianity was the driving force in the spread of truth, culture, and worldview. The historic Christian church has been the most powerful force for good in the history of the world. Its very existence is an enduring evidence of Christ's bodily resurrection from the grave.

There is no adequate explanation for the existence of this believing community apart from the resurrection. The historic Christian faith did not emerge from Jewish or pagan influences. As theologian Merrill Tenney notes, "Faith in the resurrection of Christ is the secret of the church's origin. United by a common conviction that Jesus was not dead but living, the disciples proceeded to proclaim His victory and to win others to their cause."[19]

A. J. Hoover asks,

How in the world, without the Resurrection, could the frightened followers of a crucified "Messianic Pretender" have become the nucleus of a militant church, a community which has now endured for nineteen centuries? You may be prejudiced enough to reject everything found in the New Testament but you can't possibly pass off the church as legend.[20]

A Personal Reflection on Dying Well

Christians talk a lot about what it means to live well, but seldom do they discuss what it means to die well. So what is a *good death*? The word *euthanasia* comes from the Greek language and literally means "good or happy death" (*eu*—"good" or "happy"; *thanatos*—"death"). In the context of hospice, a good death involves the easing of a dying person's suffering. But in the broader scope of life, what constitutes a good death?

Since childhood I have found death both intriguing and puzzling. I was always more fascinated by funerals than by weddings. Just how and why a person could be alive one moment and dead the next struck me as one of life's greatest enigmas. Of course I came to understand that biological systems break down, but still death remained mysterious.

I had a number of candid discussions about the subject with my father, a World War II veteran. As a frontline combat soldier in the bloodiest war in human history, he had seen more death than anyone else I knew (historians estimate that sixty to seventy million people died in World War II). While he found it difficult to talk about deeply personal issues, he shared his anticipation—borne of his historic Christian belief—of an afterlife in the presence of his risen Lord and Savior Jesus Christ.

Two of my close childhood friends, Paul Goff and Scott Claud, both died tragically in automobile accidents when they were young adults. Though it has been many years since their deaths, I still think of them and remember the pain of the losses to their families and to me. It is especially difficult to see friends die when they are only of high school or college age. These friends were literally here one day and gone the next.

When I was just out of high school, my older brother Frank took his own life after a long battle with drugs, alcohol, and mental health challenges. At the time, I was not a Christian and was embarrassed by my brother's reckless lifestyle and horrified by his final desperate act. Upon reflection, however, I realized that like my brother I was also searching for meaning, purpose, and hope in life. To paraphrase the great Christian philosopher Søren Kierkegaard (1813–55), I was looking for "a reason to live and a reason to die." My brother's premature death forced me to come to grips with death and all of its scary implications. By God's grace, I discovered the person of Jesus Christ and his extraordinary life, death, *and* resurrection. I came to believe that because he rose, I will also rise from the dead on the last day.

For many people, dying well is greatly complicated by the fact that the aging process takes a heavy toll on a person's body and mind. Because the Bible presents human beings as a union of body and soul (the material and the immaterial, see Gen. 2:7; Matt. 10:28; 2 Cor. 7:1), the decline of the body severely limits the expression of mental and spiritual faculties. Weakness, along with physical and emotional suffering, makes the dying process difficult and challenging.

Yet in spite of the difficulties, many Christians have exhibited a *good death*. It has been said of many Christian martyrs in church history that they "died well." They faced death with faith, hope, courage, and resolve because of their solid confidence in Jesus Christ's bodily resurrection from the grave. They were convinced that Jesus's bodily resurrection had defeated death and the fear that it wields (1 Cor. 15:54–55).

The good news for those who don't seem to have martyrlike faith is that God always provides exactly what we need to face trying times (2 Cor. 12:9). In this case he grants what many have called *dying grace*. Christians are able to face death with the deep assurance in the death-defying idea of Jesus Christ's historic, bodily resurrection from the grave.

Further Suggested Reading

Bauckham, Richard. *Jesus and the Eyewitnesses*. Grand Rapids: Eerdmans, 2006.

Craig, William Lane. *Knowing the Truth about the Resurrection*. Revised edition. Ann Arbor, MI: Servant, 1988.

Habermas, Gary R. *The Risen Jesus and Future Hope*. Lanham, MD: Rowman and Littlefield, 2003.

———, and Antony G. N. Flew. *Did Jesus Rise from the Dead? The Resurrection Debate*. Edited by Terry L. Miethe. San Francisco: Harper and Row, 1987.

———, and Michael R. Licona. *The Case for the Resurrection of Jesus*. Grand Rapids: Kregel, 2004.

Swinburne, Richard. *The Resurrection of God Incarnate*. Oxford: Oxford University Press, 2003.

Tenney, Merrill C. *The Reality of the Resurrection*. New York: Harper and Row, 1963.

Wright, N. T. *The Resurrection of the Son of God*. Minneapolis: Fortress, 2003.

Discussion Questions

1. What is the naturalistic worldview's perspective on death?

2. Why is the resurrection of Jesus Christ described as historic Christianity's most dangerous idea?

3. What is the strongest single strand of evidence for the resurrection of Jesus Christ? Why?

4. What is the basic problem with the alternative naturalistic explanations of Jesus's resurrection?

5. How does the resurrection meet the greatest existential need of human beings?

GOD WALKED THE EARTH

3

Religious Pluralism and God in the Flesh

> In an age when so many reject the idea that any one viewpoint
> is superior to another, that Jesus is regarded as uniquely God
> incarnate is the epitome of intolerance.
>
> Robert M. Bowman Jr. and J. Ed Komoszewski,
> *Putting Jesus in His Place*

I was twenty years old and a new Christian when I first encountered a Jehovah's Witness (a member of the American-based Watchtower religious sect that denies the deity of Jesus Christ). We met playing basketball together at a local park near my home in Southern California. After the game, we got into a lengthy theological discussion. At the time I was not well grounded in my understanding of essential Christian doctrines and the biblical basis for their support. While I believed in God's triune nature and in Jesus Christ's full deity, I had a very frustrating time trying to communicate my faith to this experienced Witness. This fellow twisted me into a doctrinal pretzel with ease.

After this humiliating encounter, I told the Lord in prayer that I would study to be prepared in future encounters. Not long after that I discovered the apologetics (counter-cult) ministry of Walter Martin. Within a few years I joined Martin's staff at the Christian Research Institute. Working in this apologetics context helped me discover that getting Jesus Christ's true identity (the God-man) correct is absolutely critical if one is to embrace authentic

Christianity. Every non-Christian sect denies the true deity of Jesus Christ, and a defective Christology infects all other areas of doctrine.

Today as a teacher in my church, I strive to help all members appreciate the critical nature of sound Christian theology. I constantly bring my students back to the true identity of Jesus Christ as revealed in the historic Christian doctrine of the incarnation.

Historic Christianity's Second Dangerous Idea: The Incarnation of Jesus Christ

It's a mind-boggling idea for sure—God becoming a human. And first a baby. How can that be? This fascinating yet dangerously supernatural notion has empowered millions of people to change societies for the better. We'll explore it and discuss its implications, and in the next chapter we will take on challenges.

Three Truth Problems with the World's Religions

Humanity's ever-present religious quest has led to the designation *Homo religiosus* ("religious man"). While the major religions of the world (Buddhism, Hinduism, Islam, Judaism) meet some important human needs, a fundamental issue remains unanswered: What is ultimate truth? Or, which religion is God's true religion? Finding the true and living God in and among the world's religions can be a challenge. Here's why.

1. World Religions Are Divided

The religions of the world do share some common beliefs and moral values, but fundamental and irreconcilable differences divide them on many crucial issues, including the nature of God (or ultimate reality), the source and focus of revelation, the human predicament, the nature of salvation, and the destiny of humankind.[1]

A plethora of views exist just on the issue of God's nature, personhood, and relationship to the cosmos. For example, some religions affirm monotheism (one God); others, polytheism (many gods); still others, pantheism (all is God); and some even atheism (no God).[2] In Judaism and Islam, God is personal and singular; in Christianity, God is more than personal and singular (superpersonal and triune); while in strands of Hinduism and Buddhism, God is less than personal and singular (apersonal and diffuse).[3] Clearly, *no universal agreement exists among the world's religions as to who or what God really is.*

To give a perspective on the various views of God among the world's religions, let's consider their beliefs concerning what and who God is.

What Is God?

One:	Judaism, Christianity, Islam
Many:	Popular Hinduism (330 million gods)
All:	Philosophical Hinduism
None:	Theravada Buddhism

Who Is God?

A Personal Being:	Judaism, Islam
A Superpersonal Being:	Christianity (triune)
An Impersonal Entity:	Hinduism, Buddhism

These distinct, metaphysical visions of what is ultimately real and true about God cannot all be correct. The central question remains: Exactly which religious point of view speaks for God?

2. World Religions Are Irreducible

Some people argue that no particular religion speaks for God. They suggest instead that when the world's religions are reduced to their lowest common denominator, a consensus emerges that reflects God's voice. This reductionistic approach to religion, however, is fraught with problems. The world's religions are so diverse in belief and in worldview orientation that they defy attempts to synthesize them to a single common theme or essence. In fact, in light of this complex array of religious perspectives, religious reductionism appears to be an altogether dubious venture.

Furthermore, reducing religions to their simplest common denominator usually succeeds only in distorting them. Homogenizing religions in hope of solving the problems of religious diversity comes at great cost. In the end it forces the sacrifice of the very features that make the religions unique and appealing in the first place.

3. World Religions Are Contradictory

The religions of the world teach different things about ultimate issues (namely God), and those specific theological conclusions can't be reduced to a convenient pluralistic consensus. But the difficulty is greatly magnified by the fact that the essential beliefs held by the various religions contradict one another.

Even the religions that hold the most theological ground in common—such as the monotheistic faiths (Judaism, Christianity, Islam)—take positions that logically clash with one another. The world's largest religion, Christianity, affirms that Jesus Christ is God incarnate (God in human flesh). But the world's second largest religion, Islam, asserts that Jesus was merely a human being. Traditional Judaism also denies the deity of Jesus of Nazareth.

But Jesus Christ cannot be both God incarnate (Christianity) and *not* God incarnate (Judaism, Islam) at the same time and in the same respect (the Law of Noncontradiction; see table 1). Contradictory religious claims have opposite truth value, meaning that they negate or deny each other. Therefore, exactly one can be true and the other false. Accordingly, Jesus Christ must either be God incarnate or not be God incarnate; there is no middle position possible (the Law of Excluded Middle; see table 1).

Table 1. Applying Logic to the Incarnation

1. Jesus *is* God incarnate (Historic Christianity). 2. Jesus *is not* God incarnate (Judaism, Islam).	
The Law of Noncontradiction: (A cannot equal A and equal non-A) Necessitates that the above statements cannot both be true.	The Law of Excluded Middle: (A is either A or non-A) Necessitates that either one or the other of the statements is true.

For a seeker of truth, it seems that an all-inclusive religion offers no hope. But it is at this low point of the world's religions' contradictory claims about God that historic Christianity's second dangerous idea comes to bear. That dangerous proclamation is: God has indeed revealed his own objectively true identity by taking on human flesh and walking the earth as the God-man.

Is there evidence to back the claim?

The Christian Theistic View of God and the Incarnation

The doctrine of the incarnation should be understood within the broader theological framework of the Christian theistic view of God. The God disclosed in Scripture and later enunciated in the historic creeds and confessions of Christendom is the one sovereign and majestic Lord. Historic Christianity thus affirms belief in one infinitely perfect, eternal, and yet tripersonal God, the transcendent Creator and sovereign Sustainer of the universe. This one God is triune, existing eternally and simultaneously as three distinct and distinguishable but not separate persons: Father, Son, and Holy Spirit. All three persons in the Godhead, or divine being, share equally and completely the one divine nature and are therefore the same God, coequal in attributes, nature, and glory. The doctrine of the incarnation properly emerges from this explicit trinitarian teaching.[4]

The term *incarnation* is of Latin origin and literally means "becoming in flesh" (Latin, *in carne*). While the term does not appear in our English translations, the original Greek uses its equivalent in 1 John 4:2, "Jesus Christ has come in the flesh [*en sarki*]." The doctrine of the incarnation is at the heart of the biblical message, for it reveals the person and nature of the Lord and Savior Jesus Christ. The incarnation teaches that the eternal *Logos* (Word), the second person of the Trinity, took to himself a fully human nature without diminishing his deity. Specifically, this doctrine holds that a full and undiminished divine nature and a full and perfect human nature (untainted by Adam's sin) were inseparably united in the one historical and divine person of Jesus of Nazareth. According to Holy Scripture, Jesus Christ is God the Son in human flesh (Greek, *theanthrōpos*, the God-man).

The Hypostatic Union

As the incarnate Son of God, Jesus Christ is one person with two natures. In accord with the definition in the Creed of Chalcedon (discussed later in this chapter), these two natures (divinity and humanity) remain "distinct, whole, and unchanged, without mixture or confusion so that the one person, Jesus Christ, is truly God and truly man."[5] Christ is one in substance (*homoousios*) with the Father in regard to his divine nature and one in substance with humanity in regard to his human nature. The two natures are perfectly united forever in the one person (*hypostasis*) of Jesus Christ. The hypostatic union refers, therefore, to the union of the two distinct natures in the one person of Jesus Christ (neither dividing the person nor confounding the natures). Philosophically speaking, as the God-man, Jesus Christ is two *what*s: a divine *what* (or nature) and a human *what* (or nature) and one *who* (i.e., a single *person* or *self*).

Kenosis

The concept of kenosis[6] (from Greek, *ekenosen*; Phil. 2:7, "made himself nothing" NIV, or "emptied Himself" NASB) is an attempt to explain how the two natures of Christ related to each other in God becoming a human. While there have been many so-called kenotic theories in the modern era, two models warrant consideration here.

The first contemporary model states that in order for Jesus to have been truly human he must have divested himself of such divine attributes as omnipotence, omniscience, and omnipresence. This kenotic theory interprets "emptied himself" as meaning that Christ laid aside divine attributes. Thus the incarnate Christ is something less than God and therefore not fully equal to God.

Historic Christian orthodoxy, however, considers this position as heresy (a significant departure from Christian truth), for if God the Son is deprived of any divine attribute, then he is obviously not deity. Christian theologian Bruce Milne identifies the equation for this kenotic theory as "incarnation = God minus."[7] It runs contrary to the creeds and to Scripture and is therefore rejected by theologically orthodox Christians.

The second model suggests that instead of Christ divesting himself of divine attributes in the incarnation, he retained all divine attributes through his divine nature, but in union with his human nature, he may have voluntarily chosen to refrain from exercising certain attributes in his earthly sojourn as a human. According to this position, Jesus's deity is undiminished. This view understands Philippians 2:7 as not a literal emptying of attributes but rather as a sign of Christ's humility in voluntarily giving up the status and privileges that were his in heaven. According to this position, he surrendered divine glory rather than divine attributes. Milne identifies the equation for this approach as "incarnation = God plus,"[8] because Christ retains his deity and yet takes on himself a truly human nature. This second model benefits from biblical and creedal support and thus is embraced by orthodox Christians.

Incarnation Verified in Scripture and Creeds

Scripture explicitly teaches the doctrine of the incarnation. Following are six examples (see also 1 Tim. 3:16; Heb. 2:14; 5:7; 1 John 1:1–3):

The Word became flesh and made his dwelling among us. (John 1:14)

Regarding his Son, who as to his earthly life was a descendant of David, and who through the Spirit of holiness was appointed the Son of God in power by his resurrection from the dead: Jesus Christ our Lord. (Rom. 1:3–4)

Theirs are the patriarchs, and from them is traced the human ancestry of the Messiah, who is God over all, forever praised! Amen. (Rom. 9:5)

Have this attitude in yourselves which was also in Christ Jesus, who, though He existed in the form of God, did not regard equality with God a thing to be grasped, but emptied Himself, taking the form of a bond-servant, and being made in the likeness of men. (Phil. 2:5–7 NASB)

For in Christ all the fullness of the Deity lives in bodily form. (Col. 2:9)

This is how you can recognize the Spirit of God: Every spirit that acknowledges that Jesus Christ has come in the flesh is from God. (1 John 4:2)

The most important creedal statement concerning the incarnation is the Creed of Chalcedon. It was the Council of Chalcedon (the fourth ecumenical council) in AD 451 that laid down the basic boundaries of the orthodox view of Christ's person and nature. According to this council, Jesus Christ is one divine person in two natures (divinity and humanity). Thus the Chalcedon Creed became, and continues to be, the normative standard for the orthodox doctrine of Christ. All of Christendom (Roman Catholic, Eastern Orthodox, and Protestant) affirms the Chalcedonian affirmation that Jesus Christ is both God and man. This creed enunciates the orthodox doctrine of the incarnation—specifically Christ's two natures:

We all with one voice confess our Lord Jesus Christ to be one and the same Son, perfect in divinity and humanity, truly God and truly human, consisting of a rational soul and a body, being of one substance with the Father in relation to his divinity, and being of one substance with us in relation to his humanity, and is like us in all things apart from sin. He was begotten of the Father before time in relation to his divinity, and in these recent days was born from the Virgin Mary, the *Theotokos* [God-bearer], for us and for our salvation. In relation to the humanity he is one and the same Christ, the Son, the Lord, the Only-begotten, who is to be acknowledged in two natures, without confusion, without change, without division, and without separation. This distinction of natures is in no way abolished on account of this union, but rather the characteristic property of each nature is preserved, and concurring into one Person and one subsistence, not as if Christ were parted or divided into two persons, but remains one and the same Son and only-begotten God, Word, Lord, Jesus Christ; even as the Prophets from the beginning spoke concerning him, and our Lord Jesus Christ instructed us, and the Creed of the Fathers was handed down to us.[9]

Although the Chalcedonian formulation does not explain just *how* the two natures are united in one person, it does set the crucial theological parameters for orthodox biblical Christology (doctrine of the person and nature of Christ). In other words, this statement generally tells us *what* the doctrine of the incarnation means and doesn't mean, but is silent about *how* it is that Christ is actually God and man.[10]

Biblical Support for the True Deity of Jesus Christ

The Bible attests in numerous ways to the full and undiminished deity of Jesus Christ. The following material provides examples of the affirmation of Christ's deity found in Scripture.[11]

Divine Titles Proclaimed by or Attributed to Jesus Christ

God:	John 1:1, 18; 20:28; Romans 9:5; Titus 2:13; Hebrews 1:8; 2 Peter 1:1
Lord:	Mark 12:35–37; John 20:28; Romans 10:9–13; 1 Corinthians 8:5–6; 12:3; Philippians 2:11
Messiah:	Matthew 16:16; Mark 14:61–62; John 20:31
Son of God:	Matthew 11:27; Mark 15:39; John 1:18; Romans 1:4; Galatians 4:4; Hebrews 1:2
Son of Man (in light of Dan. 7:13–14, this title indicates someone who possesses the prerogatives of deity):	Daniel 7:13–14; Matthew 16:28; 24:30; Mark 8:38; 14:62–64; Acts 7:56

Prerogatives or Actions of Yahweh (God) in the Old Testament Proclaimed by or Attributed to Jesus Christ

Worship of Yahweh:	Isaiah 45:23; Philippians 2:10–11
Salvation of Yahweh:	Joel 2:32; Romans 10:13
Judgment of Yahweh:	Isaiah 6:10; John 12:39–41
Nature of Yahweh:	Exodus 3:14; John 8:58
Triumph of Yahweh:	Psalm 68:18; Ephesians 4:8

Divine Roles Proclaimed by or Attributed to Jesus Christ

Creator:	John 1:3; Colossians 1:16; Hebrews 1:2, 10–12
Sustainer:	1 Corinthians 8:6; Colossians 1:17; Hebrews 1:3
Universal ruler:	Matthew 28:18; Romans 14:9; Revelation 1:5
Forgiver of sins:	Mark 2:5–7; Luke 24:47; Acts 5:31; Colossians 3:13
Raiser of the dead:	Luke 7:11–17; John 5:21; 6:40
Object of prayer:	John 14:14; Acts 1:24; 7:59–60; 1 Corinthians 1:2; 2 Corinthians 12:8–9
Object of worship:	Matthew 28:16–17; John 5:23; 20:28; Philippians 2:10–11; Hebrews 1:6
Object of saving faith:	John 14:1; Acts 10:43; 16:31; Romans 10:8–13
Image and representation of God:	Colossians 1:15; Hebrews 1:3

Divine Qualities Proclaimed by or Attributed to Jesus Christ

Eternal existence:	John 1:1; 8:58; 17:5; 1 Corinthians 8:6; Colossians 1:17; Hebrews 13:8
Self-Existence:	John 1:3; 5:26; Colossians 1:16; Hebrews 1:2
Immutability:	Hebrews 1:10–12; 13:8
Omnipresence:	Matthew 18:20; 28:20; Ephesians 1:22–23; 4:10; Colossians 3:11
Omniscience:	Mark 2:8; Luke 9:47; John 2:25; 4:17–19; 16:30; Colossians 2:2–3
Omnipotence:	John 1:3; 2:19; Colossians 1:16–17; Hebrews 1:2
Sovereignty:	Philippians 2:9–11; 1 Peter 3:22; Revelation 19:16
Authority:	Matthew 28:18; Ephesians 1:22
Life in himself:	John 1:4; 5:26; Acts 3:15

Biblical Support for the True Humanity of Jesus Christ

The Bible attests in numerous ways to the full and essential humanity of Jesus Christ. Consider the following references:[12]

Jesus Christ Calls Himself or Others Speak of Him as a Man

Jesus Christ was conceived super-naturally but born naturally:	Matthew 1:25; Luke 2:7; Galatians 4:4
Jesus Christ had an ancestral lineage:	Matthew 1; Luke 3
Jesus Christ experienced normal growth and development:	Luke 2:40–52; Hebrews 5:8
During his earthly ministry:	John 8:40; Acts 2:22; 1 Corinthians 15:21; Philippians 2:7–8
After his resurrection:	Acts 17:31; 1 Corinthians 15:47; 1 Timothy 2:5; Hebrews 2:14

Jesus Christ Was Subject to Real Physical Limitations

Weariness:	John 4:6
Hunger:	Matthew 21:18
Need for sleep:	Matthew 8:24
Thirst:	John 19:28
Sweat:	Luke 22:44
Temptation:	Matthew 4:1–11
Lack of knowledge:	Mark 5:30–32; 13:32

Jesus Christ Experienced Pain

Physical pain:	Mark 14:33–36; Luke 17:25; 22:63
Physical death:	Luke 23:33; John 19:30

Jesus Christ Manifested the Full Range of Human Emotions

Joy:	Luke 10:21; John 17:13
Sorrow:	Matthew 26:37
Friendship love:	John 11:5
Compassion:	Mark 1:40–41 (NASB)
Weeping:	John 11:35
Astonishment:	Luke 7:9
Anger:	Mark 3:5; 10:14
Loneliness:	Mark 14:32–42; 15:34

Jesus Christ Possessed All the Essential Physical Qualities of a Human Being

Body:	Matthew 26:12
Bones and Flesh:	Luke 24:39
Blood and Soul:	Matthew 26:28
Will:	John 5:30
Spirit:	John 11:33

Who Was Jesus Christ?

Several times in the Gospel accounts Jesus directed his disciples and others (including his enemies) to consider his true identity (Matt. 22:41–46; John 8:24–28, 53–58). Here's one provocative example:

> When Jesus came to the region of Caesarea Philippi, he asked his disciples, "Who do people say the Son of Man is?"
>
> They replied, "Some say John the Baptist; others say Elijah; and still others, Jeremiah or one of the prophets."
>
> "But what about you?" he asked. "Who do you say I am?"
>
> Simon Peter answered, "You are the Messiah, the Son of the living God."
>
> Jesus replied, "Blessed are you, Simon son of Jonah, for this was not revealed to you by flesh and blood, but by my Father in heaven." (Matt. 16:13–17)

Historic Christianity is all about Jesus Christ—his identity, message, and mission. As the divine Messiah (God incarnate), Jesus preached and taught about the kingdom of God, and he presented his life, death, and resurrection as God's means for forgiving the sins of repentant sinners. In fact, at the core of Christianity is the assertion that Jesus Christ provided redemption on the cross for human beings specifically because he was God incarnate. If this belief can stand the test of reason and history, then Christianity's central truth-claim can be powerfully supported as an intellectually credible assertion.

Did Jesus View Himself as God?

While for centuries various individuals and groups have denied that the New Testament presents Jesus as both fully God and fully human, a fair assessment of the scriptural data leaves little doubt that the New Testament witness presents Jesus as the divine Messiah (the preceding lists bear witness to this claim). Viewing Jesus Christ as the God-man is the historic and orthodox consensus of Christendom (Catholic, Orthodox, and Protestant). But this question must be addressed: Did Jesus view himself as divine? Some critics assert that Jesus never claimed to be God and that the Christian church has erroneously drawn that conclusion.[13] What follows is a summary of the biblical data that shows Jesus did see himself as the divine Messiah.

While it is true that Jesus never actually said the words, "I am God," an examination of the Gospels reveals, nevertheless, that Jesus did view himself as divine. The following four points illustrate that Jesus was conscious of his own deity and that he deliberately made that fact known to others.

1. Jesus Equated Himself with the Father (Yahweh)

In his public ministry, Jesus so closely associated himself with the Father that one is compelled by logic to conclude that relating to Jesus is relating to

God himself. His insistence on this unique relationship with the Father was largely the reason some of the Jewish religious leaders charged him with blasphemy. Jesus associated himself with God in at least ten identifiable ways.[14]

1. To *know* Jesus is to know God: "If you really know me, you will know my Father as well" (John 14:7).
2. To *see* Jesus is to see God: "Anyone who has seen me has seen the Father" (John 14:9).
3. To *encounter* Jesus is to encounter God: "Believe me when I say that I am in the Father and the Father is in me" (John 14:11).
4. To *trust* in Jesus is to trust in God: "Trust in God, and trust also in me" (John 14:1 NLT).
5. To *welcome* Jesus is to welcome God: "Whoever welcomes me does not welcome me but the one who sent me" (Mark 9:37).
6. To *honor* Jesus is to honor God: "That all may honor the Son just as they honor the Father" (John 5:23).
7. To *hate* Jesus is to hate God: "Whoever hates me hates my Father as well" (John 15:23).
8. To *come* to Jesus is to come to God: "No one comes to the Father except through me" (John 14:6).
9. To *love* Jesus is to love God: "The one who loves me will be loved by my Father" (John 14:21).
10. To *obey* Jesus is to obey God: "Anyone who loves me will obey my teaching. My Father will love them, and we will come to them and make our home with them" (John 14:23).

2. Religious Leaders Considered Jesus's Claims Blasphemous

Being strict monotheists, many of Jesus's Jewish contemporaries were outraged at his claims to divine authority. Their reaction illustrates that they understood him to be claiming deity for himself. Consider four such instances:

Jesus said to them, "My Father is always at his work to this very day, and I too am working." For this reason they [the Jews] tried all the more to kill him; not only was he breaking the Sabbath, but he was even calling God his own Father, making himself equal with God. (John 5:17–18)

As discussed earlier, Jesus's constant insistence that he had an intimate and special relationship with God the Father infuriated many Jews. Notice that Jesus didn't speak of God as "*our* Father," but as "*my* Father."

"Very truly I tell you," Jesus answered, "before Abraham was born, I am!" At this, they picked up stones to stone him. (John 8:58–59)

Jesus's use of "I am" (Greek, *egō eimi*) was tantamount to saying, "I am God," for he was applying to himself from the Old Testament "one of the most sacred of divine expressions."[15] In the Old Testament, Yahweh specifically references himself as "I am" or "I am he" (Isa. 41:4; 43:10, 13, 25; 46:4; 48:12). Jesus may also have been appealing to Exodus 3:14 where Yahweh refers to himself as the great "I AM." In a Jewish context, this is how someone would assert deity for himself. Again, the fact that the Jews reacted by wanting to stone Jesus (the prescribed penalty for blasphemy, Lev. 24:16) contextually supports the deity claim.

> "I and the Father are one." Again the Jews picked up stones to stone him, but Jesus said to them, "I have shown you many great miracles from the Father. For which of these do you stone me?"
>
> "We are not stoning you for any of these," replied the Jews, "but for blasphemy, because you, a mere man, claim to be God." (John 10:30–33 NIV 1984)

The Greek word for "one" (*hen*) in this verse is in the neuter form; thus it does not say Jesus and the Father are the same person. It could be translated: "I and the Father, *we* are one." The oneness between Jesus and the Father is more than a unity of purpose or action; it clearly has metaphysical overtones (deity).[16] The Jews understood Jesus's statement as a reference to his deity, for again they sought to stone him.

> Again the high priest asked him, "Are you the Messiah, the Son of the Blessed One?"
>
> "I am," said Jesus. "And you will see the Son of Man sitting at the right hand of the Mighty One and coming on the clouds of heaven."
>
> The high priest tore his clothes. "Why do we need any more witnesses?" he asked. "You have heard the blasphemy. What do you think?"
>
> They all condemned him as worthy of death. (Mark 14:61–64)

Jesus was arrested, tried, and sentenced to die by the Jewish religious leaders for the crime of blasphemy because his statements before the high priest were understood to be claims of deity. Notice four things in Jesus's brief exchange with Israel's high priest:

1. He affirmatively identifies himself as Israel's Messiah.
2. He uses the title "Son of Man," which in certain contexts was viewed as a divine title (see Dan. 7:13–14).
3. Sitting at the "right hand" of God implies that Jesus possesses the authority of God.
4. "Coming on the clouds" identifies himself as the future judge of humanity.

3. Jesus Invoked Divine Prerogatives

During Jesus's ministry, he engaged in functions that were reserved for God alone.[17] In a context of strict Jewish monotheism, the following four activities were considered blasphemous for anyone other than God.

1. Jesus expressed his *authority to forgive sins*, even sins not committed against him personally—a prerogative reserved for God alone:

   > When Jesus saw their faith, he said to the paralyzed man, "Son, your sins are forgiven."
   >
   > Now some teachers of the law were sitting there, thinking to themselves, "Why does this fellow talk like that? He's blaspheming! Who can forgive sins but God alone?" (Mark 2:5–7)

2. Jesus accepted *worship* from other human beings—a prerogative reserved for God alone:

   > Then the eleven disciples went to Galilee, to the mountain where Jesus had told them to go. When they saw him, they worshiped him. (Matt. 28:16–17)

3. Jesus exercised the *power and authority to raise the dead*—a prerogative reserved for God alone:

   > For just as the Father raises the dead and gives them life, even so the Son gives life to whom he is pleased to give it. (John 5:21)

4. Jesus claimed to possess the *authority to judge humanity*—a prerogative reserved for God alone:

   > Moreover, the Father judges no one, but has entrusted all judgment to the Son. . . . And he has given him authority to judge because he is the Son of Man. (John 5:22, 27)

4. Jesus Invoked Various Divine Titles

Jesus referred to himself by various Old Testament titles that, in certain contexts, carry the implication of deity. A good example is that in his trial before the Sanhedrin, Jesus used the titles "Son of God" and "Son of Man" as designations for himself. Jesus's use of these titles (among other things) led the high priest of Israel to condemn Jesus as a blasphemer worthy of death (Matt. 26:62–66). Jesus's consistent reference to Old Testament divine titles infuriated the Jews.

More could be said about Jesus's provocative identification with deity,[18] but the four points discussed provide sufficient evidence that Jesus of Nazareth claimed to be God. In addition, support for the truth of Jesus's claim of deity is found in such particulars as his matchless (and unchallenged claim of) moral perfection, his specific fulfillment of biblical prophecy, and his many miraculous works—culminating in his own bodily resurrection from the dead.

The skeptic may still ask if there's a way to explain the life and person of Jesus without concluding that he was really God incarnate. Is this idea too dangerous—perhaps too fanciful—to be true? The focus of the next chapter will turn to an evaluation of various alternative explanatory theories concerning Jesus of Nazareth.

4

Explanations for Christ's Life

> The Son of God became a man to enable men to become
> sons of God.
>
> C. S. Lewis, *Mere Christianity*

Of all the world's religions, only Christianity proclaims that God has become embodied as a human being. Of all the founders of the world's great religious traditions, only Jesus Christ claims to be God. Only the historic Christian faith proclaims that to encounter Jesus Christ is to directly and personally encounter God himself.

Indeed at the very heart of historic Christianity is a truly astounding—one may say *dangerous*—truth-claim. This central article of the Christian faith is the incarnation: *God became man in Jesus of Nazareth*. This truth is a distinctive feature of the Christian faith, for it is unique to Christianity to discover a God who not only takes the initiative in becoming flesh but also does so in order to redeem sinful human beings.

Alternative Explanations for Jesus's Identity

Obviously, not everybody accepts the traditional Christian interpretation of the New Testament documents as accurate historical records. Various groups and individuals have proposed a number of alternative explanations for the

New Testament account of Jesus of Nazareth. The six most widely proffered explanations warrant a response.

Each view will be scrutinized to see which one ultimately has the most genuine explanatory power. By a logical process of elimination, the one that can stand up to sustained critical analysis will emerge as the best explanation. Before considering these specific views, however, it is important to explore how one goes about arriving at a good—as in reasonable and reliable—explanation.

Most people recognize two basic ways of reasoning or arguing in logic: deductive and inductive. But logicians sometimes speak of a lesser-known way of thinking called *abductive reasoning*.[1] This third form of reasoning attempts to arrive at the best explanation for an event or a given series of facts. Unlike deduction, abductive reasoning provides something less than total certainty in its conclusion. Similar to induction, it yields only probable truth, and yet it doesn't attempt to predict specific future, probable occurrences. Rather, it seeks to provide the most plausible broad, explanatory hypothesis. Abductive reasoning can be helpful in efforts to determine which argument for a given event is best. For example, one may use an abductive approach to decide which explanation best settles the controversy surrounding the assassination of President John F. Kennedy (lone gunman theory versus conspiracy theory).

While no hard and fast testing rules have been formally set forth by logicians, they generally accept the best explanatory hypothesis meets the following six criteria:

1. Offers a balance between complexity and simplicity
2. Is coherent
3. Corresponds to the facts
4. Avoids unwarranted presumptions and ad hoc explanations
5. Can be tested
6. Successfully adjusts for possible counterevidence[2]

The hypothesis that scores highest on these criteria can be said to have genuine explanatory power and scope.

Beware of the False Alternatives Fallacy

Examining the various alternative theories about how to interpret the New Testament data involves a logical process of elimination. While in that process, however, one must be careful to avoid committing the false alternatives fallacy. Logician T. Edward Damer defines this fallacy as "an oversimplification of a problem situation by a failure to entertain or at least recognize all its plausible alternative solutions."[3] One commits the false alternatives fallacy when proposing too few alternatives and then assuming one of those limited alternatives must be correct or true.

Some evangelical apologists have been accused of committing the false alternatives fallacy when presenting the options for Jesus's identity in a too narrow way. For example, the argument is sometimes formulated in terms of a "trilemma."[4] Because Jesus claimed to be God, he must be either a lunatic, a liar, or the Lord (God). Critics of this argument, however, suggest that it ignores other plausible alternatives (for instance, maybe the claims about Jesus in the New Testament are mythical in nature).

The way to avoid the false alternatives fallacy is to give careful consideration to what may constitute a plausible explanation. One should attempt to include all *possibly reasonable* explanations, although there is a limit to the number of reasonable explanations that can be given for any set of data, including data about the identity of Jesus. It is also fallacious to reserve judgment of a reasonable hypothesis because one hasn't exhausted all possible or conceivable alternatives.

Avoid the Ad Futurus Fallacy

Sometimes skeptics commit the *ad futurus* (appeal to the future) fallacy by insisting that the future will undoubtedly reveal a natural or nontheistic explanation for the life of Jesus. This appeal exhibits a presumptuously optimistic confidence in the unknown, and it ignores that one must live and reason in the present.

Alternative Hypotheses for the Identity of Jesus

It makes sense to try to reason to the best explanatory hypothesis among known alternatives. Then if a new, reasonable alternative is discovered, critically analyze it as well.

Let's apply this schema in evaluating the various explanations for the identity of Jesus. We will consider six alternative hypotheses.

1. Legend Hypothesis

This hypothesis is that Jesus never claimed to be the divine Messiah. His claims of divinity are mere legend brought on by his followers. The following facts shed significant light.

First, even most critical scholars today affirm that the claims about Jesus's life and ministry date to the earliest stage of Christianity—back to the apostles themselves. Even two decades before the books of the New Testament were written, and only a few years after Christ's crucifixion, there were already creedal statements and traditions that support the facts later presented in those books. Moreover, many of these same scholars also recognize that a high Christology (calling Jesus "Lord," which means *divine*) can be traced to the earliest period of Christianity.[5]

Second, as stated earlier, since the Gospels (which present a divine Jesus) were written within a generation after the events they describe, there simply wasn't sufficient time for legends and myths to have entered into the New Testament accounts. And this is especially true given the fact that oral and written apostolic sources bridged the gap between the events of Jesus's life and the written Gospels themselves. A mythical Jesus seems possible only if a long period of time separated the actual, historic Jesus from the eyewitness apostolic proclamation of who he was (the Lord God) and what he did (accomplished redemption). Given that the Gospels reflect primitive eyewitness testimony, myth had insufficient time to overtake fact. The narrow time frame between when Jesus lived and when the written sources about him emerged argues against the legendary hypothesis.

Third, the Gospel writers knew the difference between legend on one hand and truthful eyewitness testimony on the other. They testified that they were eyewitnesses of Jesus's claims and actions (see Luke 1:1–4; John 19:35; Acts 2:22–38; 17:30–31; 1 Cor. 15:3–8; Gal. 1:11–12; 2 Peter 1:16; 1 John 1:1–2). In addition, cogent arguments can be marshaled to show that the authors of the Gospels were either original apostles of Jesus (and thus eyewitnesses) or close associates of the apostles.[6]

Fourth, if the Gospel writers had departed from the historical facts, hostile forces who were still alive and conversant with the events of Jesus's life would have exposed them as frauds.

Fifth, the followers of Jesus had no good reason to deify a mere human, especially one who had seriously disappointed them. As first-century, monotheistic Jews, their theological orientation did not allow them to exalt a mere human being to the level of the divine. And they certainly knew that an attempt to deify Jesus would lead to persecution, prosecution, and even the damnation of their souls. No one in the early church ever confessed to making it up—even when faced with torture and martyrdom. The Gospel writers had no reasonable motive to concoct a story, especially in light of the punishment that awaited them. Thus, inventing a divine Jesus makes no sense.

Sixth, if the followers of Jesus were going to invent a Messiah, it seems reasonable that they would have created one who corresponded more to the Jewish messianic expectations of the time (such as a purely human Messiah who would function as a political-religious leader and break Rome's dominance over Israel). Yet the Jesus presented in the Gospels is in many ways counter to what first-century Jews thought the Messiah would accomplish on their behalf.[7]

Finally, first- and early second-century secular and Jewish sources (historians, government officials, and religious writers) report general information about the life and ministry of Jesus that corresponds well to what is conveyed in the Gospels. The existence and content of these early, extrabiblical and non-Christian sources make it extremely difficult to support a mythical theory concerning the life of Jesus.[8]

Dismissing Jesus's claims to deity as mere myth ignores the early historical sources (oral and written) that stand behind those claims. Moreover, this hypothesis also seems deeply indebted to unsupported, antisupernatural presuppositions and doesn't recognize the short period of time between the emergence of the Gospel writings themselves and the events they record. Therefore, this view must be considered implausible and an inadequate explanatory hypothesis.

2. Learned Man Hypothesis

This hypothesis claims that Jesus was nothing more than a great man or a great sage. Many people gravitate toward this position because it seems respectful while preserving their preference for the natural over the supernatural. But once a person grants that the New Testament portrait of Jesus is based on sound, historical sources, then viewing Jesus as a great man becomes intellectually untenable. In light of the reliable New Testament witness, Jesus couldn't be a great man for two basic reasons:

1. *A person could not be a great man and say the kinds of things that Jesus said.* If Jesus were only a man, he would be considered one of the world's greatest megalomaniacs. Why? Because Jesus frequently talked about himself in what would be deemed incredibly grandiose ways, even for a great man.[9] Consider a few of his "I am" statements from the Gospel of John:

> I am the resurrection and the life. The one who believes in me will live, even though they die; and whoever lives by believing in me will never die. Do you believe this? (John 11:25–26)

> I am the way and the truth and the life. No one comes to the Father except through me. (John 14:6)

> I am the light of the world. Whoever follows me will never walk in darkness, but will have the light of life. (John 8:12)

> I am the bread of life. Whoever comes to me will never go hungry, and whoever believes in me will never be thirsty. (John 6:35)

A great man who was *only* a man would not say the things that Jesus said. His boasts, if he were only a man, would certainly disqualify him from being regarded as great.

2. *Not even the greatest of men and women can do the kinds of things Jesus did.* He claimed to forgive other people's sin (including offenses not

committed against himself). He allowed other human beings to worship him. He claimed he could raise the dead and that a person's eternal destiny rested on what they thought of him personally. A great man who was only a man would not do or say these sorts of things.

How could Jesus be a great man if he claimed to be God and was not? Viewing Jesus as a great moral teacher when he said and did the kinds of things he did seems a logically preposterous conclusion. Bear in mind the analysis of Christian thinker and former atheist C. S. Lewis:

> You can shut Him up for a fool, you can spit at Him and kill Him as a demon; or you can fall at His feet and call Him Lord and God. But let us not come with any patronising nonsense about His being a great human teacher. He has not left that open to us. He did not intend to.[10]

If Jesus professed to be God (as the well-attested historical documents convey) but was not, then he was either a morally bad man or a mentally deranged man. But he certainly was not a great man or a great sage.

3. Liar Hypothesis

This hypothesis claims that Jesus intentionally lied about being the divine Messiah. For Jesus to say and do the things he did—all the while knowing that he was a mere human being—would make him a bad man. Intentional spiritual deception is perhaps the worst kind of deceit. Yet in light of everything known about Jesus, to consider him a diabolical liar creates a deep dissonance. The Jesus presented in the Gospels reflects an extraordinary personal and moral integrity, one who transcends the frail and imperfect human moral condition.

During his three-year ministry, Jesus consistently endured challenging moral dilemmas, personal pressures, and trying circumstances, including physical torture and death. Yet he never exhibited even a trace of moral weakness or the various vices so common to humankind. When the pressure is on, deceivers—usually among their inner circle of associates—almost always leave clues about their true motivation. Yet Jesus's closest friends, and even some of his enemies, insisted that he faced every event and circumstance with courage, honesty, and resounding moral virtue (Acts 3:14; 1 Peter 2:22–23; 1 John 3:4–5). In sharp contrast to known deceivers, Jesus showed no sign of being motivated by wealth, fame, power, or pleasure. Rather, the motivating factors of his extraordinary life were love, truth, mercy, and justice. Viewing Jesus as a charlatan runs contrary to both his unparalleled character and his uniquely insightful ethical teachings.

While it is true that certain cult leaders have made claims to divinity, evidence shows that many, if not all, were intentional frauds. Father Divine, Jim Jones, and David Koresh all gave clear signs of being motivated by a combination of greed, power, and sexual lust.[11] And none of these cult leaders can be even reasonably compared to Jesus when it comes to intellectual and moral virtue, let alone Jesus's divine credentials (miracles, fulfilled prophecy, resurrection).

Jesus's moral example and teachings laid the foundation for much of the ethical theory adopted throughout Western civilization. He is widely considered even by non-Christians as the ideal pattern of moral virtue. Is it reasonable to conclude that the person who has had arguably the greatest impact on human history in terms of moral virtue was in reality a colossal liar about his real identity? History, reason, and common sense say a resounding No.[12]

Frankly, for those who have examined the life of Jesus carefully, accepting him as the divine Messiah is much easier than concluding that he was a moral and spiritual fraud. Jesus's life and character in no way match the typical profile of a deceitful liar. This hypothesis is both weak and exceedingly improbable. One must look elsewhere for a satisfactory explanation of the life and character of Jesus of Nazareth.

4. Lunatic Hypothesis

According to this hypothesis, Jesus was a lunatic with the delusion of being the divine Messiah. Today, people who claim to be God generally end up in a mental health institution. Such delusions of grandeur result from severe mental disorders that leave patients out of touch with reality. The *divinity complex* carries with it the severe symptoms of egocentrism and narcissism. Jesus of Nazareth showed no signs of being mentally deranged or out of touch with reality. He showed no signs of emotional instability as would someone who is mentally ill.

Of all humans, Jesus seems to have had a fundamental grip on reality and constantly exhibited a profound mental and emotional stability. In every crisis Jesus confronted, whether being interrogated by his enemies or undergoing the horrific punishment of crucifixion, his mind reflected an amazing clarity, sobriety, and underlying emotional balance. As arguably the world's greatest teacher, he was always clearheaded, lucid in thought and in argument, and eloquent in speech. Jesus rose to every occasion with grace, poise, and strength. Even his enemies were amazed at his teaching and his unprecedented authority. Those who knew and observed him did not give the slightest impression that he was psychologically imbalanced.

> When Jesus had finished saying these things, the crowds were amazed at his teaching, because he taught as one who had authority, and not as their teachers of the law. (Matt. 7:28–29)

> Coming to his hometown, he began teaching the people in their synagogue, and they were amazed. "Where did this man get this wisdom and these miraculous powers?" they asked. (Matt. 13:54)

> "No one ever spoke the way this man does," the guards replied. (John 7:46)

Perhaps this *lunacy* viewpoint has some explanatory power if Jesus was not insane but merely wrong about his being God. This argument says that mental illness is not an all-or-nothing proposition. Rather, mental instability is measured in degrees. After all, other religious figures have made divine claims (Father Divine, Jim Jones, David Koresh) without appearing to be outright insane. So couldn't Jesus have been simply mistaken about his identity without being a certifiable lunatic? Like other geniuses, maybe he was only eccentric—just a *little* crazy.

Christian philosopher Ronald Nash responds to this argument with these words: "There are little mistakes and then there are big—*really big*—mistakes."[13] For a first-century Jewish rabbi raised on the strict, monotheistic teachings of the Torah to identify himself as God definitely would have been a *big* mistake. In fact, an error of this magnitude would have been perceived within Judaism as the biggest mistake imaginable—one he himself would have abhorred (Lev. 24:13–16). If Jesus made a mistaken claim of being the divine Messiah of Israel, it would have constituted a serious departure from reality. As Christian apologist John Warwick Montgomery asks, "What greater retreat from reality is there than a belief in one's divinity, if one is not in fact God?"[14]

How does Jesus compare, then, with seemingly noble religious leaders who have made extraordinary religious claims? For example, the Dalai Lama, leader of the Tibetan monks, claims to be a *bodhisattva* and the fourteenth successive incarnation of a Buddha-like figure.[15] Yet in spite of this exalted claim, he received the 1989 Nobel Prize for peace. Doesn't he prove that extraordinary religious assertions don't necessarily equate with insanity?

Jesus's situation, however, is quite different from that of the Dalai Lama in three important respects:

1. *The Dalai Lama doesn't claim to be God in human flesh.* As exalted as his title is, he doesn't say he is the transcendent Creator of the universe and Redeemer of the world.[16] The Dalai Lama claims only to have an enlightened or awakened consciousness within a solely human nature. Jesus's title as the divine Messiah carries far greater magnitude.

2. *Jesus knew he would face fierce opposition.* Because his claims to deity were in direct contrast to the orthodox religious views of his time, Jesus was fully aware he would be confronted with severe opposition—which was well-deserved if his claims were false. While the Tibetan Buddhists have suffered real persecution in their part of the world, it is not because of the Dalai Lama's personal religious declarations. His claims are not out of step with mainstream Buddhist tradition. Jesus's deity claims therefore carried greater personal risk.

3. *The Dalai Lama makes no claim of moral perfection.* Although he may indeed be a morally decent man (a contrast to various cult leaders), his excellent character still pales in comparison with Jesus's sterling moral example. In

addition, he obviously lacks Jesus's divine credentials—notably Jesus's power to raise people from the dead.

Even if mental illness is measured in degrees, Jesus doesn't show the slightest sign of mental instability or eccentricity. In fact, the opposite is true. Those informed of the life and teachings of Jesus would likely concur with the insightful conclusion drawn by psychiatrist J. T. Fisher:

> If you were to take the sum total of all authoritative articles ever written by the most qualified of psychologists and psychiatrists on the subject of mental hygiene—if you were to combine them, and refine them, and cleave out the excess verbiage—if you were to take the whole of the meat and none of the parsley, and if you were to have these unadulterated bits of pure scientific knowledge concisely expressed by the most capable of living poets, you would have an awkward and incomplete summation of the Sermon on the Mount. And it would suffer immeasurably through comparison.[17]

Could this blueprint for optimum mental health have been laid down by a lunatic or even by someone just slightly unstable? Reason and informed psychological analysis say otherwise. Jesus transcended all categories of human mental health, emotional stability, and moral virtue. He exhibited the character traits of supreme wisdom and goodness—the very virtues that lunatics and liars lack. A powerful reason for concluding that Jesus was indeed God incarnate is that he was so fundamentally different from every other human being who has ever lived. Even Socrates, the Buddha, Confucius, and Moses fall short in comparison to him. In fact, human goodness is measured according to Jesus's life and character.

5. Lama Hypothesis

Some hypothesize that Jesus was a mystical guru. His claims of divinity were meant in the Eastern mystical sense that all human beings are divine.

With the influx of Eastern religions into the West over the past several decades, along with the rise of so-called New Age religions,[18] some suggest Jesus was really a mystical guru. New Age advocates insist that during Jesus's so-called lost years (between the ages of twelve and thirty, prior to his public ministry) he traveled east to India, Tibet, Persia, and the Near East to learn from various spiritual masters.[19] Jesus therefore developed his "Christ consciousness" and his miracle-working ability during his trek through Eastern mysticism. How credible is this view of Jesus as a mystic?

Let's consider three points:

1. *There is almost no evidence for this position.* As Christian theologian and New Age specialist Ron Rhodes notes, "The historical, hard evidence for the

Jesus-goes-East accounts is virtually nonexistent."[20] Further, the various stories that speak of Jesus's alleged journey to the East are contradictory in nature and filled with historical inaccuracies.[21] These stories also stand in contrast to the well-established historical Gospels that imply Jesus spent his early life in Nazareth, in submission to his parents, studying the Hebrew Scriptures (Luke 2:51–52), and keeping the Mosaic law. These texts also indicate that during Jesus's public ministry, people recognized him and his family as local citizens and acknowledged that he was the son of Joseph, the local carpenter (Matt. 13:55–56).

2. *The core of Jesus's beliefs as an orthodox Jew, which he strongly affirmed, are at odds with many of the essential beliefs of Eastern religions.*[22] For example, the Torah explicitly condemns such beliefs as polytheism and pantheism (Exod. 20:3, 23; 34:14–15; Deut. 32:17), instead teaching a strict monotheism (Deut. 4:35, 39; 6:4; 32:39). The Hebrew Scriptures also recognize a sharp distinction between the Creator and the creature (Gen. 1:26–27); thus, in direct opposition to Eastern thought, human beings are not gods. And the heart of the Old Testament revelation centers on the issue of divine redemption (Ps. 19:14; Isa. 44:6), not mystical enlightenment. Moreover, some Eastern religions view the time-space-matter world as illusory, whereas Judaism views the cosmos as real and good.

3. *New Age advocates consistently misinterpret Scripture.* They read into the text Eastern concepts and meanings that have no objective basis in the Judeo-Christian revelation. This is especially evident when New Agers invoke their esoteric system of interpreting the Bible (finding hidden or inner mystical meanings).[23] In this method, mysticism overrides rationality, and the attempt to discover the historical, grammatical, and contextual (exoteric, public) meaning of the text of Scripture is lost. Viewing Jesus as a mystical guru or spiritual master has no objective scriptural basis whatsoever.

This hypothesis is incoherent, fails to fit the facts, and is based entirely on unwarranted assumptions. Therefore, it should not be taken seriously as an explanation for the life and identity of Jesus of Nazareth.

6. *Lunar Alien Hypothesis*

This hypothesis claims that Jesus was not the biblical God but rather an extraterrestrial. Some readers may be surprised that anyone considers Jesus an extraterrestrial, but various UFO-based religions have held this viewpoint for several decades.[24] Given the growing popularity of UFO-related speculations, the extraterrestrial position warrants a response. I must note at the outset that this hypothesis seems to require *otherworld* reasoning, including claims concerning Jesus that are directly at odds with the basic teaching of Scripture.

According to alleged UFO-based revelations, Jesus is not a man but rather a visitor from outer space. But both Scripture and other historical documents depict Jesus as a real man (though not merely a man, but rather the God-man). Although Jesus was conceived supernaturally, he was born naturally. He had ancestors and experienced normal growth and development as a human being. Jesus lived and died as a real man; he made no mention of other worlds in space.

Ironically, UFO religions are centered on occult beliefs and practices that are directly contrary to Jesus's specific views and are explicitly condemned in the Jewish Torah. These UFO-related beliefs and practices include mediumistic *channeling* of so-called alien beings, automatic writing, telepathy, teleportation, dematerialization, levitation, and psychokinesis.[25] All of this is expressly condemned in the Scriptures upon which Jesus based his life and ministry (Exod. 22:18; Lev. 19:31; Deut. 18:10–12). Further, the theological messages promulgated by various UFO cults match more closely with New Age mysticism than with the teaching of the Bible.[26]

In fact, UFO cults read into the biblical text subjective and esoteric interpretations that have no objective basis. In effect, they interpret the Bible in light of UFO phenomena rather than according to sound historical and exegetical principles.

Finally, many UFO-based groups embrace the *extraterrestrial hypothesis*: the notion that UFOs are an objective, physical reality, and that literal metallic spacecrafts are piloted by interplanetary visitors. This viewpoint suffers from insurmountable scientific, philosophical, and evidential problems.[27]

Viewing Jesus as an extraterrestrial cannot be accepted as an intellectually credible theory. It doesn't fit the facts, it involves incredible presumptions, and it lacks logical coherence.

The Superior Explanatory Theory: Jesus Christ Is God Incarnate

Was Jesus actually the unique, divine Messiah (God in human flesh)? Given that the previous six hypotheses represent the best alternatives to the true identity of Jesus of Nazareth, then by the logical process of elimination, the historic Christian claim that Jesus is God incarnate stands firm. While other challenges to the traditional Christian position may be presented, reasonable responses can be made. If one refrains from arbitrarily presuming a naturalistic worldview (which constitutes begging the question), then of the various hypotheses analyzed here, the most reasonable explanation of Jesus's identity is the historic Christian one. If other seemingly reasonable alternatives arise in the future, then they should be similarly evaluated. Nevertheless, viewing Jesus of Nazareth as the God-man is an explanatory hypothesis that corresponds to history, psychology, logic, human intuition, and common sense.

Jesus's credentials as the divine Messiah are formidable. They include:

- matchless personal character
- incalculable influence on history
- fulfillment of prophecy
- miracle-working power
- extraordinary teaching
- bodily resurrection

Alternative views that deny Jesus's true divinity offer no adequate explanation for his incomparable wisdom or his capacity to heal incurable diseases, raise the dead, or command other forces of nature (such as calming the storm).

In light of his legacy, it is reasonable for one to ask the same penetrating question that he asked of his disciples: "But what about you?" he asked. "Who do you say I am?" (Mark 8:29). Historic Christianity's christological argument is this:

1. Jesus has been variously identified as the Lord or as a legend, mere learned man, liar, lunatic, lama, or lunar visitor.
2. The claims that he was a legend, mere learned man, liar, lunatic, lama, or lunar visitor have been shown to be unreasonable and implausible.
3. Therefore, the most reasonable and plausible conclusion is that *Jesus is Lord* (in accord with historic Christianity's primitive creed).

Christianity's Most Distinctive Dangerous Idea and Humankind's Search for God

The *enfleshing* (incarnation) of God is historic Christianity's most distinctive truth-claim.[28] To become a historic Christian begins with the affirmation, "Jesus is Lord" (Jesus is *Yahweh* [God], Rom. 10:9). And Jesus's unique lordship by definition excludes all others who make the claim (Caesar, Krishna, Allah, etc.). Thus, to affirm that Jesus is God in human flesh is to identify oneself with what can variously be described as apostolic, biblical, orthodox, or creedal Christianity.

Competing religions of the world reflect humankind's search for God, but they are hopelessly divided over who and what God really is. Outside of Jesus, none of the great religious leaders possess the qualities and prerogatives of divinity. They may reflect extraordinary human lives, but they remain solely human. Their death testifies to the truth of their mere humanness. And because these religious leaders are not divine, they cannot speak unequivocally for God.

Historic Christianity's distinctive and shocking truth-claim is that God himself took the initiative to come to humanity. He accepted the constraints of physical life on Earth to reveal himself to humanity in an up close and personal way. In light of the incarnation, J. B. Phillips describes Earth as the "visited planet."[29] Unlike all other religions, the Christian faith presents a God who has appeared in the world—the physical cosmos of time and space. As amazing as it was for American astronauts to first walk on the moon in 1969, Christianity's unprecedented claim is that God walked on Earth.

The implications of the incarnation are utterly astounding. God is not merely a reasonable inference in a logical argument but rather a person who appeared in history. Therefore, to see and hear Jesus Christ through the historic Gospel testimony is to see and hear God himself. Those who claim they would believe in God if he showed himself need only consider the historic person of Jesus Christ.

To read of Jesus's unique life, death, and resurrection is to encounter God taking on human form and acting in the world to reconcile fallen, sinful humans back to their holy Creator. The truth of the incarnation both reveals God and confirms the dignity and value of human beings: Jesus became the God-man to reconcile humans with God. Moreover, in the incarnation God enters into the human condition and suffers with and for humanity, thus dignifying human suffering and giving life objective meaning and purpose.

How Historic Christianity's Most Distinctive Dangerous Idea Changed the World

Western civilization became inextricably linked to historic Christianity and thus to the person of Jesus Christ. It began with Jesus's disciples as their direct encounter with the life, death, and resurrection of Jesus convinced them that he was the Lord God Almighty in human flesh. Those disciples then turned the Roman world upside down by presenting Jesus as the risen Lord and Savior: the divine Messiah come to Earth. In turn, the growing Christian community transformed Western culture and civilization through its Christo-centric gospel message.

Though not a political or revolutionary figure per se, Jesus Christ has had an incalculable influence, especially on the Western world. Yet all this influence is tied to Christ's unique identity. Because he is the God-man, he can reconcile God and man (Savior). Because he is God in human flesh, he is the universal King (Lord). And the Christian church has sought to spread Christ's legitimate lordship to all areas of life. Thus the reach of the historic Christian world- and life-view extends to all human endeavors, including the arts, charity, economics, education, government, justice, medicine, morality, science, vocation and labor, warfare, and so on. Dutch theologian and politician Abraham Kuyper (1837–1920) proclaimed, "There is not a square inch in the whole domain of our human existence over which Christ, who is Sovereign over *all*, does not cry: 'Mine!'"[30]

This great Sovereign, once so humbled in his incarnate birth, is mine, yours, and ours as we embrace the dangerous idea of the God-man.

Further Suggested Reading

Bowman, Robert M., Jr., and J. Ed Komoszewski. *Putting Jesus in His Place*. Grand Rapids: Kregel, 2007.

Bray, Gerald. *The Doctrine of God*. Downers Grove, IL: InterVarsity, 1993.

Evans, C. Stephen. *Why Believe? Reason and Mystery as Pointers to God*. Grand Rapids: Eerdmans, 1996.

Harris, Murray J. *Jesus as God*. Grand Rapids: Baker, 1992.

Kreeft, Peter. *Between Heaven and Hell*. Downers Grove, IL: InterVarsity, 1982.

Morris, Thomas V. *The Logic of God Incarnate*. Ithaca, NY: Cornell University Press, 1986.

Reymond, Robert L. *Jesus, Divine Messiah*. Phillipsburg, NJ: Presbyterian and Reformed, 1990.

Warfield, Benjamin B. *The Person and Work of Christ*. Philadelphia: Presbyterian and Reformed, 1950.

Discussion Questions

1. In what ways did Jesus claim to be God incarnate?

2. How can abductive reasoning help in examining the various views concerning Jesus?

3. Which alternative concerning Jesus's identity is most popular today? Why might that be?

4. Can you think of any other reasonable alternatives concerning the possible identity of Jesus?

5. Should one use Jesus's question: "Who do you say that I am?" as an effective evangelistic and apologetic method with today's nonbelievers?

A FINE-TUNED COSMOS WITH A BEGINNING

5

Cosmology and Creation Out of Nothing

> It would be very difficult to explain why the universe should
> have begun in just this way, except as the act of a God who
> intended to create beings like us.
>
> Stephen Hawking, *A Brief History of Time*

The last one hundred years have witnessed a revolutionary change in how scientists view the origin of the universe. Scientific cosmology has jettisoned belief in an eternal universe in favor of a cosmos with a distinct beginning. Consider the words of esteemed cosmologists Stephen Hawking and Roger Penrose: "Almost everyone now believes that the universe, and time itself, had a beginning at the Big Bang."[1]

A Fine-Tuned Earth and Solar System

Astrophysicists understand that our solar system exhibits an amazing degree of fine-tuning that allows for the existence of complex and intelligent life. Specifically, the relationship of the earth, sun, and moon provides a rare habitable zone for life to thrive on planet Earth. Though scientists are only beginning to discover and study planets outside our solar system, these *just-right* conditions of the bodies of our solar system seem unmatched from what scientists yet know about other systems. In fact, the number and exquisite combination of factors that require fine-tuning to allow for life are so exceedingly improbable through natural means as to provide probative evidence for cosmic design.

Though admittedly skeptical of the claims of traditional theistic religion, eminent physicist and cosmologist Paul Davies says, "The impression of design is overwhelming."[2] This exquisite fine-tuning seems to comport well with a theistic worldview, but it appears out of place and unexpected from an atheistic, naturalistic perspective.

Historic Christianity's Third Dangerous Idea: Creation *ex Nihilo*

One of the things that makes historic Christianity's teaching about creation so dangerous is the fact that it resonates with the findings of modern cosmology. Consider this idea for a moment: *The basic cosmology revealed in an ancient religious book matches quite well with modern science.* How often has that happened?

Let's explore what historic Christianity teaches about the doctrine of creation *ex nihilo* (out of nothing). This unique perspective on creation differs from that of other philosophical and religious teachings. In fact, this dangerous idea of creation has literally changed the world.

Two Interconnected Theological Truths

God's sovereign actions and providential ordering in creation[3] represent two foundational tenets of the historic Christian perspective. These two critical doctrines—of creation *ex nihilo* and God's providence (his unique act of sustaining and guiding his creation)—reveal his character and care and provide an anchor of truth for the overall Christian worldview. (See the following chapter for further discussion of God guiding his creation.) Examining the various aspects of creation and providence shows how historic Christianity stands in contrast to alternative positions and competing religious belief systems.

FOUNDATIONAL IMPORTANCE OF CREATION

Throughout Christian history, the concept of biblical creation has been critically important for three basic reasons:

1. *Creation is foundational to addressing the big questions of life.* Where did I come from? Who am I? Where did the universe come from? Why is the world an orderly cosmos rather than disorderly chaos?

All adequate worldview systems must answer these crucial questions in order to provide meaning and purpose for humanity. Creation addresses questions about ultimate truth and reality—issues foundational to each person's world- and life-view.

2. *The doctrine of biblical creation affects other areas of biblical thinking.* For example, God's action as Redeemer presupposes his action as Creator (Isa. 44:24). A God who made the world and exercises complete, sovereign authority over it can also guarantee his people's salvation and destiny. The God of the Bible is therefore known as the Creator-Redeemer (Acts 17:24–31).

The biblical concept of creation also greatly impacts regard for human life. The distinguishing characteristic of humans—being made in the image and likeness of God (Gen. 1:26–27)—gives humankind special value and dignity (see chapters 11–12).

This pattern shows how biblical creation powerfully impacts virtually all other areas of Christian thought. It demonstrates that the historic Christian *big picture* of reality is unified and possesses explanatory power.

3. *The doctrine of creation helps set Christianity and the historic Christian worldview apart from other religions and worldviews.* As demonstrated later in this chapter, God's unique relationship to the universe highlights his astonishing attributes. For example, God has no limitations or boundaries with regard to the categories of time, space, and knowledge.

Throughout history, some of the very best arguments for God's existence and for the truth of Christianity have appealed to various aspects of the doctrine of biblical creation. The Apostles' Creed begins with this most far-reaching of historic Christianity's dangerous ideas: "I believe in God, the Father Almighty, creator of heaven and earth."

From First to Last

The very first verse in Genesis declares God's creation of the totality of all things.[4] Many references to God's involvement occur in that book's early chapters. But this important biblical truth also appears in every major section or genre of Scripture. In the Old Testament, creation is addressed in the Pentateuch, in the Major Prophets, and in the wisdom literature. Some of the most significant discussions of this doctrine can be found in the individual books of Job, Psalms, and Isaiah.[5]

The concept of creation receives prominence in the New Testament as well. The first verse of John's Gospel takes readers back to the moment before the cosmos began (Greek, *en archē*, in the beginning). This text introduces the preexistent "Word" (Greek, *logos*), Jesus Christ. Before his incarnation as the God-man, Jesus was with God the Father in the beginning before anything else existed. Jesus shared the same divine essence with his Father (John 1:1) and was directly involved in the formation of all things (John 1:3).

Creation is mentioned throughout the New Testament, including the Gospels (John 1:1–3), Acts (14:15–17), the Epistles (Rom. 2:14; 4:17; 5:12, 18–19; 1 Cor. 11:7–9; Heb. 11:3), and even the book of Revelation (4:11; 10:6). Several of the most important references can be found in the Pauline Epistles of

Romans (1:18–23), 1 Corinthians (8:6), and Colossians (1:15–17), as well as in the book of Hebrews (1:2–3).

Creation: From, Through, and By the Triune God

According to Scripture, each person within the divine Godhead was involved in the work of creation. While God the Father initiated the act (1 Cor. 8:6; Eph. 4:6), nevertheless God the Son (John 1:3; Col. 1:15–17; Heb. 1:2, 10–12) and God the Holy Spirit (Gen. 1:2; Ps. 104:30) served as his divine coagents. Thus, the Triune God created all things.

According to Christian theology, when one member of the Godhead is involved in a work, then in some way all three members participate.[6] But clear examples demonstrate that sometimes one member of the Trinity is recognized as the primary agent in performing a given task. For instance, the Father is the compelling force behind creation, whereas the Son plays this role in salvation, and the Holy Spirit performs this function in human beings who experience regeneration (spiritual rebirth).

Evangelical theologian Millard J. Erickson explains further:

> It appears from Scripture that it was the Father who brought the created universe into existence. But it was the Spirit and the Son who fashioned it, who carried out the details of the design. While the creation is *from* the Father, it is *through* the Son and *by* the Holy Spirit.[7]

The Whats and Whys of Creation ex Nihilo

Historical theologian Richard Muller defines the Latin term *ex nihilo* as a reference to "the divine creation of the world *not* of preexistent, and therefore eternal, materials, but out of nothing."[8] This doctrine teaches that there was originally nothing except God (an infinite, eternal, and tripersonal spirit). By means of his incalculable wisdom and infinite power, God alone brought the universe (all matter, energy, time, and space) into existence from nothing (not from any preexistent physical reality such as matter and its connected realities).

To elucidate further, creation *ex nihilo* means that God created out of or from nothing, therefore *nothing* should not be understood as being an actual *something*. In other words, *nothing* is not itself an entity; it is literally *no thing*. Creation out of nothing means that God spoke or called all things (material and spiritual) into existence out of nonexistence. The implication is that all of creation had a singular beginning and is completely dependent on God for its coming into being and for its continued existence.

This doctrine is implicitly drawn from several passages of Scripture. Illustrating its prominence, the very first verse of the Bible begins with creation *ex nihilo*: "In the beginning God created the heavens and the earth" (Gen. 1:1). This verse implies a singular beginning or origination to creation; the universe has not always existed. The expression "the heavens and the earth" reveals that God created everything in its *totality* or that God created the *sum total of reality*.[9]

A passage from the wisdom literature of the Old Testament follows suit, informing readers that merely "by wisdom the LORD laid the earth's foundations, by understanding he set the heavens in place" (Prov. 3:19). There's no mention of any preexisting materials used in God's creative actions.

The psalmist pronounces, "Before the mountains were born or you brought forth the whole world, from everlasting to everlasting you are God" (Ps. 90:2). Therefore, only God is eternal, everlasting, and without beginning or end. The created order is not eternal, for it had a distinct beginning from nonexistence.

AND GOD SAID, "LET IT BE"

The psalms proclaim that God spoke, or commanded, and the created order sprang forth: "By the word of the LORD the heavens were made, their starry host by the breath of his mouth" (Ps. 33:6). "Let them praise the name of the LORD, for at his command they were created" (Ps. 148:5).

Further backing for creation *ex nihilo* emerges from the New Testament, where the apostle John states that through the preincarnate Son, Jesus Christ, "all things were made; without him nothing was made that has been made" (John 1:3). Jesus Christ, who shares the one divine nature with the Father and the Holy Spirit (trinitarian monotheism), is identified as taking part in the work of creation. John also identifies Jesus as the "Word" (Greek, *logos*) who brings about the created order.

The author of the book of Hebrews also recognizes Jesus Christ as the Creator by proclaiming that he is the one "through whom also he [God the Father] made the universe" (Heb. 1:2). And the apostle Paul adds explicit support for the doctrine of creation out of nothing by asserting that it is God who "calls things that are not as though they were" (Rom. 4:17 NIV 1984). This passage signifies God's unique capacity to create in an *ex nihilo* fashion. Paul, in consensus with the other New Testament authors, also identifies Jesus Christ as the Creator, noting that he made "all things," which includes "things in heaven and on earth" as well as things that are "visible and invisible" (Col. 1:16).

The writer of Hebrews even provides what some Christian theologians believe to be an even more *explicit* statement about creation *ex nihilo*.[10] He says, "By faith we understand that the universe was formed at God's command, so that what is seen was not made out of what was visible" (Heb. 11:3). This verse conveys the central thrust of the doctrine of creation out of nothing. And there is no reason to think the author of Hebrews had an invisible preexistent reality or entity in mind when he used the words "what was visible."

Christian philosophers Paul Copan and William Lane Craig note, "The author of Hebrews is not making a metaphysical point about different types of matter (visible versus invisible) or that God created out of invisible matter rather than visible."[11] The clearly preferable understanding of this verse in context is that it speaks of God creating out of nonexistence, or creation *ex nihilo*.

In numerous places the New Testament refers specifically to the universe as having a beginning, using such expressions as "the beginning of the world" (Matt. 24:21) or "the creation of the world" (Rom. 1:20).[12] In light of these verses, Copan and Craig state, "The biblical data are not ambiguous, as some contend; indeed, creation *ex nihilo* is the most reasonable inference to make in light of biblical texts."[13]

Weighty Theological Implications

While the Bible does not claim God created the universe out of preexisting materials (such as matter and its constituent realities), neither does it claim he made the world out of his own being. Scripture asserts that God alone is infinite, eternal, transcendent, and independent; while all of creation is finite, temporal, and contingent—matter, energy, space, and time are not eternal but result from the amazing word of God's power.

Creation *ex nihilo* teaches not only that the cosmos had a singular beginning but also that the created order is continually dependent on God's sustaining power. Since creating the cosmos, the sovereign God continues to uphold, preserve, and direct his creation (Acts 4:17–28; Col. 1:17; Heb. 1:3). This action is addressed in more detail later under the doctrine of providence (see chapter 6).

The Bible therefore reveals God as the transcendent Creator and immanent Sustainer of all things. This wondrous intervention into his creation through divine providence rules out the deistic view of God, which sees the divine as wholly transcendent (creating alone, but not intervening or providentially upholding the universe).

A profound, practical implication of the doctrine of creation *ex nihilo* is that only the sovereign Creator (who is also our benevolent Redeemer) deserves worship, adoration, and devotion. A denial of creation *ex nihilo* implies that matter is self-existent and constitutes a challenge to God's independence and sovereignty. Scripture explicitly warns people not to fall prey to idolatry by engaging in the false worship of the world or of particular things in the world (Exod. 20:3–6; Rom. 1:18–23).

While not a proper object of worship—because God created it—the universe possesses objective meaning, purpose, and significance. And these characteristics are all the more true of human beings made in the expressed image and likeness of God (Gen. 1:26–27) and who will live even after the present creation ceases to exist (2 Peter 3:7, 10, 13; Rev. 21:1). Talk about a truly dangerous, even shocking idea! The implications of the historic Christian doctrine of creation are indeed far-reaching.

An important qualification to God's creation out of *nothing* is this: the concept applies only to God's *initial* creation of the universe. For example,

God's subsequent creation of the animals (Gen. 2:19) and of humankind (Gen. 2:7) involved the use of preexisting elements ("the dust of the ground").

It is critically important to know what the doctrine of creation *ex nihilo* means. The following points serve to clarify:

1. The cosmos had an absolute origination (coming into being).
2. The cosmos had an absolute beginning (start in time).
3. God solely initiated and caused the created order.
4. At the point of creation, the cosmos became a distinct, temporal entity.
5. While the cosmos is an independent reality from God, it nonetheless continually depends on God's intervening and sustaining power for its continued existence.
6. Nothing other than God manifests an eternal, independent, ontological existence.

It is also equally important to know what the doctrine of creation *ex nihilo* does *not* mean. The following points serve to explain:

1. The cosmos was created either in God or out of God's being (i.e., as part of God or emanating from God).
2. The cosmos was made of preexisting materials, such as matter.
3. God created the cosmos out of a *nothing* that was an actual *something*.
4. God *wound up* the cosmos so it could then run on its own power.

WHAT CREATION *EX NIHILO* REVEALS ABOUT GOD

God did not *need* to create the universe, for he was in no way desperate or incomplete in personhood or being. Within the Godhead three eternally distinct (but not separate) persons live in loving community with each other. Theologian Cornelius Plantinga explains:

> The persons within God exalt each other, commune with each other, defer to one another. Each person, so to speak, makes room for the other two. . . . From eternity God has had a communal life and didn't need to create a world to get one. Nothing internal or external to God compelled him to create.[14]

This eternal community of fellowship among the three members of the Trinity solves philosophical problems for which unitarian concepts of God have no answer. For example, arguably the greatest of the church fathers, Saint Augustine (AD 354–430), explained in his monumental work *De Trinitate* (*On the Trinity*) that only a God who has plurality within unity can adequately account for love and for thought. If God were a solitary person (such as in Islam or Unitarianism), then before creation he had no one to love. Also, he could not distinguish between the knower and the known (a requisite of self-knowledge).

In this way, the Trinity becomes quite practical. Because human beings are created in the image of the fully relational Triune God, concepts such as love, family, and community take on a new dimension. Redemption in Christ is adoption into the family of God.[15] These ideas, then, are uniquely tied to Christianity's affirmation of God's triune nature (yet another dangerous idea).

Creation was a totally free act of God, an expression of the divine will (which stands in contrast to pantheism's view of divine emanation). The universe is not eternal, but neither was it an accident. Copan and Craig state, "Creation out of nothing expresses, among other things, the unhindered freedom, sovereignty, and graciousness of God."[16] It is obvious from Scripture that God took enormous care and delight in his creation of all things.

In addition, God's creation of the universe out of nothing is consistent with God's *aseity*,[17] or the concept that he is a self-existent and necessary being (a being who must exist). Because God created all existing entities, and he himself is an eternal and everlasting being who is completely self-sufficient, God is therefore an absolute being who cannot *not* exist. As the transcendent Creator and immanent Sustainer of the universe, the God of the Bible is the sovereign Lord over all. And he has exhibited his infinite power and wisdom by creating all things out of nothing.

Three Big-Picture Perspectives on the Origin of the Cosmos

Three basic philosophical positions compete to explain the origin of the cosmos. Those three viewpoints are: (1) creation *ex materia*, (2) creation *ex Deo*, and the previously discussed (3) creation *ex nihilo*.[18] Let's briefly explore the first two positions and contrast them with the historic Christian viewpoint of creation *ex nihilo*.

1. Creation ex Materia

This view asserts that matter (and its constituent parts, including energy) is eternal in some form. Thus the cosmos has in some way always existed. Accordingly, to the extent that the universe was created (or better yet *formed*) then it came *out of preexisting materials*.

The position of creation *ex materia* has been adopted both by those who affirm God's existence and by those who deny a divine reality. As an example of the former, the ancient Greek, dualistic philosopher Plato (427–347 BC) proposed that a divine craftsman (the Demiurge) shaped an orderly cosmos into existence out of disorderly matter. This divine builder formed matter but did not originate it because matter is eternal. Thus the divine craftsman gave shape to the eternal stuff of the universe. Interestingly, Plato, whom some view as a proto-theist, saw value in the design argument for God's existence (called the *teleological argument*).

From ancient times to the present, the creation *ex materia* has been adopted by secular materialists (naturalists) who deny a divine reality. Atomists (fifth century BC), Marxists, and other contemporary advocates of naturalism (the view that the physical cosmos is the exclusive reality) all view the universe in materialistic and physicalistic terms. Today's advocates of creation *ex materia* believe that the material cosmos consists of a closed physical system that is somehow self-generating and self-sustaining. These naturalists believe either that matter is eternal in some form or that it emerged from nothing without a cause.

Contemporary advocates of this position affirm the following philosophical tenets:

1. Matter is eternal in some form.
2. No supernatural creator exists.
3. Human beings are solely physical entities and thus mortal.
4. Humans have evolved naturalistically from animals; thus, humans differ only in degree (instead of kind) from the animals.

2. *Creation* ex Deo

This metaphysical perspective reflects the worldview position of pantheistic monism (all reality is one, and that single reality is God). Pantheistic monism takes two forms in attempting to explain the cosmos in relationship to the ultimate reality of God.

The first form of pantheistic monism is called *absolute pantheism*. It affirms that only mind or spirit exists and matter is an illusion (maya). Hindu philosopher Shankara (ca. AD 788–821) proclaimed that ultimate reality is God, and therefore, the physical cosmos is an illusion. One may analogously think of the illusory universe coming forth from God as a dream comes forth from a mind.

The second stripe of this Eastern, mystical philosophy is *nonabsolute pantheism*. It may be thought of as taking a more flexible approach to ultimate reality. While believing all is one in God, this perspective accepts a form of multiplicity within the unity. Accordingly, this position views the cosmos as springing from the essence of God.

Pantheistic monism asserts that the cosmos is either an illusory entity or an emanation from the being of God. In both cases, all is God and God is all.

Advocates of this mystical viewpoint affirm the following philosophical tenets:

1. All reality is one, and that single reality is God.
2. No absolute distinction can be made between creator and creation; thus, creator and creation are one.

3. The cosmos is either an illusion from God or an emanation of God's being.

4. The true human *self* (atman) is God (Brahman).

3. *Creation* ex Nihilo

As discussed previously, historic Christianity's position affirms that God brought the cosmos into being from nothing. Since God is an eternal and necessary being, he brought all things into existence through his wisdom and power alone. Before examining the critical worldview implications of creation *ex nihilo*, let's note why the biblical God cannot have created either *ex materia* or *ex Deo*.

First, God cannot have created the cosmos *ex materia* because if matter were eternal, it would compete with God's sovereign ontological status. In other words, God would have an eternal competitor.

Second, the God of Christianity cannot have created *ex Deo* because he is a simple being (without division or parts). He cannot take a part of himself and make the universe.

It should also be noted that the historic Christian perspective of creation *ex nihilo* views God as a necessary reality (a being who cannot *not* exist), whereas the creation is a contingent reality (a reality that could conceivably be nonexistent).

Worldview Implications of Creation *ex Nihilo*

Profound theological and philosophical implications of the biblical doctrine of *creation of something from nothing* set historic Christianity apart from alternative worldview perspectives. The twenty points that follow explain these implications and their significance.

1. *The universe is not an extension or emanation of God's essence or being.* Thus pantheism (the Eastern mystical view that all is God and God is all) and panentheism (the view that God is in the world but is more than the world) must be false.[19] The Christian theistic view of God's simplicity rules out the idea of the universe as a *part* of God's being (contra creation *ex Deo*).

Three Competing Views on the Origin of the Cosmos

1. Materialism's *ex materia* (out of preexisting materials)
2. Pantheism's *ex Deo* (out of God)
3. Theism's *ex nihilo* (out of nothing)

2. *God created a universe with a distinct existence of its own (though always dependent on God's power for its continuance)*. Therefore, metaphysical views that assert monism, the belief that all reality is one or that reality is a seamless garment, must be false. These include various forms of: (1) Eastern mysticism, which affirms that everything is divine; (2) idealism, the belief that everything is mind or idea; and (3) metaphysical naturalism or physicalism, the belief that everything is physical or material.[20] A necessary feature of Christian theism is the affirmation of the Creator-creature distinction (see table 2).

Table 2. Christian Theism's Creator-Creature Distinction

Creator (Maker)	Creation (Made)
Uncreated	Created
Infinite	Finite
Eternal	Temporal
Necessary	Contingent
Immutable	Mutable
Sovereign	Subject

3. *The world is a distinct reality that cannot be denied*. As a result, religions and worldviews that view the physical universe as illusory or as apparently real (such as the pantheistic-oriented religions of Vedanta Hinduism, Buddhism, Sikhism, Gnosticism, Christian Science, and other mind-science religions) must be false.[21] Christian theism affirms a *realism* to the cosmos that serves to anchor the scientific enterprise.

4. *The world is a finite and contingent creation of God and therefore not a proper object of worship*. Thus, religious systems that engage in this type of devotion and deification (such as animism, popular polytheism, and folk religion) must be wrong.[22] Jewish and Christian teachings explicitly forbid the worship of nature.

5. *Matter was created by God and is therefore neither eternal nor the sole reality*. Therefore, philosophies that affirm the eternity of matter, whether dualistic (considering matter and God as eternal) or materialistic (believing that everything is reducible to or explainable in terms of matter) must be false.[23] Only God has an eternal, independent ontological status (contra creation *ex materia*).

6. *The universe is neither self-sufficient, self-explanatory, nor self-sustaining*. Whereas the universe is not self-caused and did not pop into existence as the result of a quantum accident, a worldview that asserts such things (such as metaphysical naturalism—nature is the sole reality) must be regarded as false.[24] Christian theism views the created order as finite, temporal, and contingent.

7. *Everything has value and meaning as implied by the doctrine of creation ex nihilo*. Therefore, philosophies that discount significance and worth (such

as nihilism) must be false.[25] In a biblical context, the cosmos derives its value and meaning from the Creator.

8. *The natural, material, and physical universe was created by a super-natural, personal divine agent.* As a result, methodological naturalism (which accepts only natural, scientific explanations for things) must be false.[26] The scientific enterprise will naturally reflect theistic implications.

9. *God's creation of the world from nothing demonstrates his complete power and control over all things (his sovereign lordship).* Thus any religious philosophy that denies God's sovereignty (such as finite godism, process theology, and open theism) must be false.[27] According to Christian theism, nothing competes with God's sovereign reign over all things.

10. *God is both transcendent (distinct from the world in being) and personally immanent (present within the world).* Therefore, religious systems that view God as being wholly transcendent (such as deism and forms of Islam) must be false.[28] In Christian theology, God's immanence guarantees that his creatures can know him.

11. *God not only created the universe but also continually sustains its existence.* Worldviews that consider God as merely winding up the universe so that it then became self-sustaining (such as deism) must be false. If the biblical God removed his providential hand (so to speak), the created order would fall back into the nonexistence from whence it came.

12. *God created all things, not out of need or desperation but as an act of divine freedom (given the triune nature of the Christian God).* Religions that view God as a solitary person (such as Islam and other unitarian concepts of God) must be considered ontologically inadequate. The Triune God's plurality of personhood within the unity of essence guarantees the reality of love and community.

13. *God made the universe as a very good creation.* Therefore, religious philosophies that affirm an eternal and intrinsic evil as a metaphysical part of the universe (such as Manichaeism and Zoroastrianism) must be rejected as false.[29] Christian theism, by contrast, is recognized as being world- and life-affirming.

14. *A creation out of nothing excludes any preexistent or chaotic contingent entities.* Thus any philosophy (such as Platonism) or religion (such as Mormonism) that supports preexistence must be false (contra creation *ex materia*).[30]

15. *The world was created by God with rich natural and living resources to be used wisely by human beings for the purpose of sustaining and enhancing human life.* Radical environmental views that fail to recognize humankind's proper role of dominion over nature should be rejected as false. The Bible warns of replacing the true worship of God with devotion to nature.

16. *Creation out of nothing does not imply some kind of time before time.* Therefore, exotic theories of modern physics proposed by naturalists to posit a pre-time are at odds with the historic Christian view of creation.

The creation of the cosmos involved the beginning of time itself. Therefore, only the eternal God preceded time.

17. *Creation out of nothing does not imply that* nothing *actually made* something. Only something or someone can cause something to exist. Christian theism affirms that the divine Someone caused the universe to exist. Therefore, speculations that some yet-to-be-understood principle of nature allows something to come from actual nothingness is at odds with the Christian view of creation.

18. *Creation out of nothing does not imply that* nothing *is* something. Contrary to the exotic speculations of some modern theorists, *nothing* should not be thought of as an invisible, immaterial *something*. Rather, the Christian doctrine of creation affirms that someone (God) made something from nothing.

19. *Creation out of nothing is actually a positive way of stating a negative concept.* Contrary to those who question its logical meaning, *creation out of nothing* means that God created all things but not out of something.

20. *Creation out of nothing means that something can be created* from *nothing but not* by *nothing.* Christian theology teaches that someone (God) made something (the created order) from nothing (literally no thing). Creation *ex nihilo* therefore stands at odds with both creation *ex materia* and creation *ex Deo*.

In the field of modern cosmology, the creation implication seems inescapable. According to prevailing scientific theory, the universe had a singular beginning nearly 14 billion years ago. All matter, energy, time, and space exploded into existence (in a carefully controlled and fine-tuned manner) from nothing (no preexisting materials). This standard big-bang cosmological model, embraced by the vast majority of research scientists because it has withstood extensive scientific testing, uniquely corresponds to the biblical teaching of creation *ex nihilo*. A book written a couple thousand years ago contains a view of cosmology that stunningly corresponds to the latest and best scientific findings.

German mathematician and philosopher Gottfried Wilhelm Leibniz (1646–1716) asked the ultimate cosmological question: "Why is there something rather than nothing?"[31] His question—though many have attempted a reply—seems to reverberate through the cosmos in search of a satisfying answer.

Why did God create? Tackling that question may be treading on dangerous territory, but it will be helpful to explore the implications of the Creator's purposes in creation. We will discuss this in the next chapter.

6

Divine Providence and the Emergence of Science

> Who could make all of this? Who could make it out of nothing? Who could sustain it day after day for endless years? Such infinite power, such intricate skill, is completely beyond our comprehension. When we meditate on it, we give glory to God.
>
> Wayne Grudem, *Systematic Theology*

On December 26, 2004, an undersea megathrust earthquake struck off the west coast of Sumatra, Indonesia. The quake unleashed a series of devastating tsunamis that were recorded on tide gauges all over the world and inundated coastal communities, killing almost 230,000 people in fourteen countries. It was the deadliest tsunami in recorded history.[1]

Such a confluence of nature's powerful forces requires explanation. (See chapters 13 and 14 for a discussion about the problem of evil.) If chance governs the universe, there is no explanation. If the God of Christianity controls the creation and nothing happens by chance, then there's a purpose for the earthquake and resulting tsunamis. Speaking strictly of the physical forces, Christian theism holds that God not only creates but providentially sustains his creation. He moves. He acts. Many events are difficult providences to be sure, but human beings derive greater satisfaction in a purposeful rather than a chance creation.

Why Did God Create?

The physical realm displays God's sheer delight in creating. Why else would he create a universe that contains hundreds of millions of galaxies? In manufacturing an exquisite home for humanity, he spared no expense. Here his creatures can play out their destiny on a stage as the drama of God's redemption of fallen human beings unfolds. So with a clear desire to promote human welfare (especially that of those who are his very own), God created for the primary purpose of manifesting his glory. In Isaiah, Yahweh reveals this intent: "Whom I created for my glory, whom I formed and made" (Isa. 43:7).

Theologian Millard Erickson explains further, "Humans alone are capable of obeying God consciously and willingly, and thus glorify God most fully."[2] All of creation testifies to God's awesome majesty. King David proclaimed, "The heavens declare the glory of God; the skies proclaim the work of his hands" (Ps. 19:1).

The last book of the Bible summarizes an appropriate response to God's wondrous work of creation *ex nihilo*: "You are worthy, our Lord and God, to receive glory and honor and power, for you created all things, and by your will they were created and have their being" (Rev. 4:11).

The Importance of Divine Providence

The doctrines of creation and providence are closely connected in Christian theology. Not only did God call the universe into existence from nothing, but he also has been continually involved with all of creation since its inception. He reveals himself as both transcendent (above) and immanent (within) in his work. Evangelical theologian John Jefferson Davis defines the doctrine of providence this way: "Providence is that sovereign activity of God whereby he sustains, preserves, and governs all his creatures, and guides all events toward their appointed ends."[3]

The Creator actively and continually sustains the universe. He is never idle. His supernatural power keeps the created order in place and all his creatures alive.

The doctrine of providence is usually divided into three theological categories: preservation, concurrence, and government.[4]

Providential Preservation

God continuously upholds (Greek, *pherō*, "carry" or "bear") all things in their existence and sustains the natural properties of those created things (see Neh. 9:6; Pss. 136:25; 145:15; Acts 17:28; Col. 1:17; Heb. 1:3). The apostle Paul identifies Jesus Christ as personally active in this work of preservation, steadfastly maintaining all creation in being and in action. "He [Christ] is before all things, and in him all things hold together" (Col. 1:17).

Providential Concurrence

God continuously acts within the created order and causes his creatures to act in precisely the manner that they do, though people nevertheless remain responsible for their actions (Deut. 8:18; Ps. 104:20–21, 30; Amos 3:6; Matt. 5:45; 10:29; Acts 14:17; Phil. 2:13). Real secondary causes are at work in the world (e.g., nature and human effort), but they do not operate apart from God's power at work in his creation and creatures. Paul describes how God stimulates the actions of his people: "For it is God who works in you to will and to act in order to fulfill his good purpose" (Phil. 2:13).

Providential Government

As the supreme authority over all things, God continually directs the course of all actions and events toward accomplishing his sovereign purposes (see Gen. 50:20; Ps. 103:19; Prov. 16:33; Dan. 4:34–35; Matt. 10:29–31; Acts 14:16; Eph. 1:11). His providential will reigns over all things, including the events of nature and the choices of human beings. Paul describes God's overruling plan: "In him we were also chosen, having been predestined according to the plan of him who works out everything in conformity with the purpose of his will" (Eph. 1:11).

Scripture reveals God's all-encompassing authority:

- God sovereignly controls the entire universe. "The Lord has established his throne in heaven, and his kingdom rules over all" (Ps. 103:19; see also Dan. 4:35; Eph. 1:11).
- God sovereignly controls the natural events of the world. "The Lord does whatever pleases him, in the heavens and on the earth, in the seas and all their depths" (Ps. 135:6; see also Ps. 104:14; Matt. 5:45).
- God sovereignly controls the events of world history. "For dominion belongs to the Lord and he rules over the nations" (Ps. 22:28; see also Job 12:23–24; Acts 4:27–28).
- God sovereignly controls a human being's birth, life, and death. "All the days ordained for me were written in your book before one of them came to be" (Ps. 139:16; see also Job 14:5; Gal. 1:15–16).
- God sovereignly controls the details of a person's life. "And even the very hairs of your head are all numbered. So don't be afraid" (Matt. 10:30–31; see also Prov. 16:33; Rom. 8:28).
- God sovereignly meets all the needs of his people. "And my God will meet all your needs according to the riches of his glory in Christ Jesus" (Phil. 4:19; see also Gen. 22:8; 2 Cor. 9:8).

- God sovereignly controls the answers to his people's prayers. "And will not God bring about justice for his chosen ones, who cry out to him day and night?" (Luke 18:7; see also 2 Chron. 33:13; Matt. 7:7).[5]

The doctrine of providence goes hand in hand with the doctrine of creation (see table 3). God's deliberate attention and ongoing actions underscore his sovereign rule over all heaven and Earth. This intimate involvement with the time-space world is laden with worldview implications.

Table 3. God's Actions in Creation and Providence

In Creation	In Providence
Source	Preserver
Creator	Operator
Maker	Holder
Originator	Provider
Producer	Conserver

World- and Life-View Implications

The dangerous doctrine of divine providence validates the concept that people aren't at the mercy of arbitrary, impersonal forces such as luck, fate, or chance. Rather, God firmly holds all human affairs in his hands and is working all things together for good for his people (Rom. 8:28). Providence can be a great source of comfort, assurance, and security when God's people inevitably face difficult times. This belief should lead to devotion, commitment, gratitude, and loyalty. Erickson explains:

> Providence in certain ways is central to the conduct of the Christian life. It means that we are able to live in the assurance that God is present and active in our lives. We are in his care and can therefore face the future confidently, knowing that things are not happening merely by chance. We can pray, knowing that God hears and acts upon our prayers. We can face danger, knowing that he is not unaware and uninvolved.[6]

The doctrine of providence should not be taken as a basis for human apathy or fatalism. Rather, the Bible teaches *both* that God is sovereign *and* that human beings are morally responsible agents. Sometimes these paradoxical truths appear in the same verse of Scripture (see Luke 22:22; Acts 2:23).

People bear responsibility for their actions. Yet God's providential actions guarantee meaning and significance in life. While divine providence is mysterious to finite creatures, recognition of this truth should produce humility and thankfulness.

What about Divine Providence and the Existence of Evil?

Divine concurrence (a point of God's providence) makes evil actions and events possible. Though evil, to some degree, remains a mystery, nevertheless God's relationship to it can be inferred from Scripture.

1. God permits evil for his sovereign purposes (Gen. 50:20; Job 1:1–12).
2. God uses evil (or calamity and disaster) to restrain the evil actions of his creatures (Ps. 81:11–12; Rom. 1:26–32).
3. God uses evil (or calamity and disaster) to test and discipline those whom he loves (Matt. 4:1–11; Heb. 12:4–14).
4. God always brings good out of evil. This goodness is especially true for those who belong to God through faith (Gen. 50:20; Acts 2:23; Rom. 8:28).
5. God has defeated the powers of evil in and through the life, death, and resurrection of Jesus Christ (Eph. 1:21; Col. 2:15).
6. God will redeem his people from the power and presence of evil completely in the future (Rev. 21:27; 22:14–15).[7]

God does not commit evil (Ps. 5:4), and he does not coerce any creature to participate in evil acts (James 1:13). God is not ultimately accountable for the moral evil expressed by the creatures he has made.

Creator and Sustainer

The dangerous doctrines of creation and providence set Christianity apart from other worldviews and other religious systems. The sovereign God of the Bible has created all things, and he sustains, controls, and directs them all toward his appointed ends. Ideas such as creation and providence, once grasped, have yielded remarkable results.

How Historic Christianity's Most Far-Reaching Dangerous Idea Changed the World: The Invention of Science

God's providential hand in his creation supplies a solid foundation for science. Given God's work as transcendent Creator and immanent Sustainer of the universe, nature's order, regularity, and uniformity can be expected and accounted for. In fact, their belief in such things as creation *ex nihilo* and continued divine providence led early theological naturalists (scientists) to pursue research. This effort led to the birth and flourishing of science as an esteemed enterprise in (Christian) Europe during the seventeenth century.[8]

Not only were virtually all of the founding fathers of science themselves devout Christians (including Copernicus, Kepler, Galileo, Brahe, Steno, Newton, Boyle, Pascal, Faraday, Agassiz, Kelvin, Mendel, Pasteur, Maxwell, and Ramsey), but the Christian worldview provided a context in which modern science could emerge and ultimately flourish.

Christian theism affirms that an infinite, eternal, and personal God created the world *ex nihilo*. As a reflection of the rational nature of its Creator, the natural realm is orderly, uniform, and divinely pronounced as *good*. Further, humankind was uniquely created in God's image (Gen. 1:26–27), thus capable of reasoning and discovering the intelligibility of the created order. In effect, the Christian worldview supported the underlying principles that made scientific inquiry possible and desirable.

The Bible itself played a role in the development of the scientific method. The principles undergirding the scientific method (testability, verification, falsification) are uniquely compatible with the intellectual virtues affirmed in the Judeo-Christian Scriptures. In truth, the experimental method was nurtured by Christian doctrine.[9] Because the Christian founders of modern science believed that the heavens genuinely declare the glory of God (Ps. 19:1), they possessed both the necessary conceptual framework and the spiritual incentive to explore nature's mysteries. According to Christian theism, God has disclosed himself not only in the *special revelation*—the Bible, God's Word—but also through the *general revelation* of God's creative actions discoverable through nature—God's world (see table 4). This point is amply illustrated by the pious Puritan scientists in England and in America who viewed the study of science as a sacred attempt to *think God's thoughts after him*.

Table 4. Historic Christianity's Two Books Model

Figurative Book	Literal Book
Nature	Scripture
General Revelation	Special Revelation
God's World	God's Word
Creator	Redeemer

What Kind of World Is Necessary for Science to Work?

Secular scientists are fond of saying that one of science's fundamental features is that it *works*. The operation of science, however, presupposes certain foundational truths that are not wholly derived from science itself. In order for the experimental venture to work and thrive, certain nonempirical assumptions about the world must be true. In other words, it takes a certain kind of world even for valid scientific study to be possible.[10] The scientific process simply cannot work in every conceivable world.

One reason modern science was so late getting started was that the philosophical views (conceptual framework) of earlier cultures were inadequate to justify and sustain the necessary preconditions for research. Science was birthed, nurtured, and flourished within the European culture because the predominantly Christian vision of reality invoked all the necessary presuppositions to undergird the scientific enterprise. The following points reflect twelve ways in which the Christian worldview anticipated, shaped, encouraged, justified, and sustained the general character and presuppositions of modern science.[11]

1. *The cosmos is a distinct, objective reality.* By his incalculable wisdom and awesome power, the God of the Bible created the universe. It therefore has a distinct existence of its own (apart from the mind and will of the human observer) though it remains contingent *on* the creative and sustaining power of God. If, as suggested by other cultures and philosophical-religious traditions, the cosmos were somehow less than an objective reality, science would be superfluous. The transcendent God revealed in Scripture is the necessary causal agent of the contingent universe.

2. *The laws of nature exhibit order, patterns, and regularity.* Because a personal God designed the universe to reflect his inherent rationality, the world exhibits elegant order, detectable patterns, and dependable regularity. These teleological qualities are essential to the nature of science because they make self-consistent scientific theories possible. Since it mirrors the mind of its Creator, the cosmos reflects clarity and coherence. Philosopher of science Del Ratzsch comments, "And given that cosmos precludes fundamental chaos, we insist on self-consistent theories, and since we expect the patterns to be broad and unified, we expect that theories which are even approximately true will mesh with each other."[12]

3. *The laws of nature are uniform throughout the physical universe.* Because of God's providential ordering and governance of the universe, the orderliness and regularities of nature hold throughout the entire universe. This is critical to the scientific enterprise, for the universal nature of these laws guarantees predictability and the possibility of duplicating scientific outcomes. The uniformity of nature assures the scientist that causal relationships yesterday and tomorrow will correspond with those of today. The inductive method and inferential reasoning are dependent on the uniformity of nature's laws, and that universality corresponds to what one would expect when looking through the lens of the Christian, theistic worldview.

4. *The physical cosmos is (in large measure) intelligible.* Since God designed the world by means of his infinite wisdom, the order and patterns of the universe are capable of (at least partially) being understood. The physical world can serve

as the object of study, thus making science conceivable. The world's amazing intelligibility led British physicist John Polkinghorne to note the following:

> We are so familiar with the fact that we can understand the world that, most of the time, we take it for granted. It is what makes science possible. Yet it could have been otherwise. The universe might have been a disorderly chaos, rather than an orderly cosmos.[13]

5. *The world is good, valuable, and worthy of careful study.* In the book of Genesis, God calls his creation "very good" (Gen. 1:31). The created order testifies to God's existence, power, wisdom, majesty, righteousness, and glory. Therefore, studying nature reveals truth about God. The world is also the place where human beings are to play out their destiny. The study of nature holds great benefit (medical, technological, economical) for humanity, and as the crown of creation, humankind has a divine imperative to manage or "rule over" nature (Gen. 1:28).

6. *Because the world is not divine and therefore not a proper object of worship, it can serve as an object of rational study.* The Judeo-Christian Scriptures condemn as idolatrous all belief systems that deify the natural realm (e.g., animism, pantheism, paganism). Christianity's curbing of pagan superstition regarding nature allowed science to be viewed as an appropriate discipline. Historian Rodney Stark notes, "Christianity depicted God as a rational, responsive, dependable, and omnipotent being and the universe as his personal creation, thus having a rational, lawful, stable structure, awaiting human comprehension."[14]

7. *Human beings possess the basic ability to discover the universe's intelligibility.* God created human beings with cognitive and sensory faculties capable of discovering the intelligibility of the created order. People can know and discern truth. Humans also enjoy intellectual interaction and are able to check each others' inferences (making the scientific practice of peer review possible). God, as the designer of both the world and the human mind, has made possible the congruence between the two, thus guaranteeing the validity of truths in mathematics, logic, and language.

This correspondence between the physical universe and the human mind is a powerful witness to the truth of divine design as set forth in historic Christianity. Scientist and theologian Alister McGrath explains the significance of this connection:

> There is a deep-seated congruence between the rationality present in our minds, and the rationality—the orderedness—which we observe as present in the world. Thus the abstract structures of pure mathematics—a free creation of the human mind—provide important clues to understanding the world.[15]

8. *God created human beings with the ability to hunt and gather data and to recognize the importance of testing truth-claims.* Human beings are made

in God's image with the necessary intellectual capacities to distinguish truth from falsehood. Scripture implores believers to make such distinction by subjecting assertions to rigorous examination and testing (Acts 17:11; 1 Cor. 14:29; 1 Thess. 5:21). The scientific principle of verification-falsification inherent in the broader scientific method was first used by theological naturalists (early scientists) who were familiar with such biblical principles.

9. *The free agency of the Creator makes the empirical method necessary.* God's creative patterns could have taken a variety of pathways. Since human beings have no prior knowledge of those set patterns, the empirical method with its experimental process is necessary. The creation illustrates that God is both a reliable engineer and also a playful artist.

10. *God encourages science through his imperative that humans take dominion over nature.* God created human beings not only with the ability to study the natural world but also with a command to do just that. Adam's caring for the garden and naming the animals involved a necessary mastery and classification of nature. God's imperative to "subdue" nature (Gen. 1:28) justifies and encourages the scientific enterprise.

11. *The intellectual virtues necessary to carry out the scientific enterprise are part of God's moral law in Scripture.* In order for science to flourish, it must be practiced in a particular way. Good science involves such intellectual virtues as honesty, integrity, discernment, humility, and courage.[16] These moral qualities are part of God's intended moral law for humankind. And moral principles need to be grounded in something objective in nature.

12. *The devotional basis of pursuing the life of the mind to the glory of God led to the educational advancements that helped usher in the study of science.* The Christian worldview values logic and rationality, which find their source in God. Accordingly, Christian civilization spread literacy and founded the great universities of Western Europe, which offered the first formal courses in the natural sciences. Integrating the truth of God found in the book of nature and the book of Scripture was a mandate of the Christian world- and life-view.

Rodney Stark explains the Christian motivation for the scientific enterprise: "In contrast with the dominant religious and philosophical doctrines in the non-Christian world, Christians developed science because they *believed* it *could* be done, and *should* be done."[17] If the world had been left with only pagan influences, there would have been major impediments to establishing science:

- a cyclical view of time
- astrology and superstition
- deification of nature
- denial of nature
- arbitrary and whimsical nature of the gods

Creation: A Personal Reflection

I distinctly remember the first time I heard the cosmological argument. The argument gripped me and led to an enduring interest in the study of cosmology.

This formal argument involves a distinction between a *contingent* reality and a *necessary* reality. A contingent reality is something that is caused (begins), is dependent (an effect), and lacks an explanation in itself (is unexplained). A contingent reality could either exist or not exist, but it certainly could not bring itself into existence.

A necessary reality, on the other hand, is uncaused, independent, and self-explanatory. A necessary reality cannot *not* exist (must exist). So how does this distinction relate to God and the universe?

The universe appears to be a contingent reality. Big-bang cosmology gives powerful evidence that the universe is contingent. As we saw earlier, this prevailing scientific view of cosmology asserts that the space-time-matter-energy universe had a distinct and singular beginning nearly 14 billion years ago. Therefore, the universe appears to be an *effect*—dependent on something outside of and beyond itself (a transcendent causal agent)—unless one affirms the incredible claim that something can come from sheer and utter nothingness.

The second law of thermodynamics (principle of entropy) seems to lend further support for the conclusion that the universe had a beginning and is a contingent reality. Physicists argue that if nature takes its course, the universe will ultimately dissipate all of its energy and suffer a heat death. If the universe had not been in existence for a certain finite period of time, this eventuality would have already happened.

To sum it up, a contingent reality by definition cannot bring itself into existence. Because the universe came into existence (had a singular beginning), then some other reality must have caused or created it from nonexistence.

It is also critical to understand that a contingent reality cannot be explained by appealing to another contingent reality. For example, it would be incoherent to argue that the universe was created by the big-bang explosion that was, in turn, created by an earlier big bang that was, in turn, created by a still earlier big bang, and so on (multiverse). As Aristotle cogently argued, there must be a reality that causes but is itself uncaused (in Aristotle's words, a being that moves but is itself unmoved). Why? Because if there were an infinite regression of contingent causes, then by definition the whole process could never begin.

To conclude then, the universe appears to be a contingent entity and therefore cannot stand on its own without a causal explanation. For many Christian thinkers through the centuries, the contingent universe (a creation) requires a necessary reality (an eternally existent Creator) who by definition needs no causal explanation (is a necessary being).

Two Forms of the Cosmological Argument

Here are two versions of the cosmological argument set forth in their simple logical form (syllogism).

Kalam cosmological argument:

1. Whatever begins to exist has a cause for its coming into being.
2. The universe began to exist.
3. Therefore, the universe has a cause for its coming into being.

Contingency cosmological argument:

1. All contingent realities depend for their existence on a noncontingent or necessary reality.
2. The universe is a contingent reality.
3. Therefore, the universe depends for its existence on a noncontingent or necessary reality.

Though it has been more than thirty years since I first heard this argument in a college philosophy class, I still find this basic reasoning compelling and too dangerous to be ignored. In light of big-bang cosmology, it seems all the more probative.

At night when I look at the starry heavens above, I am reminded of Gottfried Leibniz's ultimate metaphysical question: "Why is there something rather than nothing?"[18]

May the dangerousness of these historic Christian ideas—creation *ex nihilo* and providence—enrich your life and cause you to glorify your Creator, in whose image you were created and who invites inquiry into his wondrous creation.

Further Suggested Reading

Collins, C. John. *Science and Faith*. Wheaton: Crossway, 2003.

Copan, Paul, and William Lane Craig. *Creation Out of Nothing*. Grand Rapids: Baker, 2004.

Hannam, James. *The Genesis of Science*. Washington, DC: Regenery, 2011.

Jaki, Stanley L. *The Savior of Science*. Grand Rapids: Eerdmans, 2000.

Pearcey, Nancy R., and Charles B. Thaxton. *The Soul of Science*. Wheaton: Crossway, 1994.

Poythress, Vern S. *Redeeming Science*. Wheaton: Crossway, 2006.

Ratzsch, Delvin Lee. *Science and Its Limits*. 2nd edition. Downers Grove, IL: InterVarsity, 2000.

Ross, Hugh. *The Creator and the Cosmos*. 3rd edition. Colorado Springs: NavPress, 2001.

Discussion Questions

1. How have the scientific discoveries of the twentieth century in astronomy and cosmology differed with the expectations of secular scientists?

2. What does the historic Christian doctrine of creation *ex nihilo* teach about the origin of the cosmos and about God's nature?

3. How does creation *ex nihilo* differ from creation *ex materia* and creation *ex Deo*?

4. What does the historic Christian doctrine of providence reveal about God and his relationship to the cosmos?

5. How did the Christian worldview influence the development and presuppositions of science?

CLEAR POINTERS TO GOD

7

The Explanatory Power of Atheism versus Christian Theism

> Does the skeptic's outlook do a *better* job of explaining things than the Jewish-Christian one? We're wiser to accept a more robust, wider-ranging, less-contrived explanation—since it's more likely to be true—than rely on *it-could-have-happened-this-way* scenarios and other thin reeds.
>
> Paul Copan, *Loving Wisdom*

They arrived in 2007 with books in hand, heralding an animated, strident form of nonbelief. The *four horsemen of the new atheism* topped best-sellers lists with *The God Delusion*, by Richard Dawkins; *Letter to a Christian Nation*, by Sam Harris; *God Is Not Great*, by Christopher Hitchens; and *Breaking the Spell*, by Daniel C. Dennett. These authors warn of global apocalypse if Christianity and other religions continue to guide people's ideas and actions.

If nothing else, their considerable influence has galvanized people of faith—especially in light of these new atheists' unapologetically caustic statements. Dawkins likens belief in God to a type of "mental virus" and describes parents giving their child religious instruction as a form of child abuse.[1]

Ironically, the new atheists seem preoccupied with the being they adamantly insist does not exist. If the atheists are correct and God does not exist, then how does a person justify such meaningful realities of life as the cosmos, science, mathematics, logic, moral values, and religious experience?

Historic Christianity's Fourth Dangerous Idea: God Makes Sense of Reality

Do the most meaningful realities of life correspond better with God being real (in this case, the God of Christian theism) or with God not being real (atheistic naturalism)? Surely God's existence or nonexistence impacts every area of human life and thought, including conceptions of what is real, what is true, what is rational, what is right, what is valuable, and what is meaningful. Because one's view of God (either as real or not real) is the context of one's overall worldview, the atheistic naturalist and the Christian theist therefore view all of reality in essentially different ways. In other words, the Christian theist thinks he or she lives in a God-created and sustained universe, while the atheistic naturalist thinks he or she lives in a godless world.

This chapter and the next argue that it makes good sense to believe in the existence of the God of the Bible. Evidence and reason combine to suggest that the biblical God of historic Christianity *best* explains the many fundamental and profound realities we all encounter in life.

How Theists and Atheists Reason About God

Theists and atheists do reason differently about God and the world. A common skeptical objection to the enterprise of Christian apologetics is that believers engage in a god-of-the-gaps form of reasoning. This charge means that the believer in God typically attributes gaps in knowledge—especially scientific knowledge—to something God has done. For example, when science can't explain how the universe came into being or how life originated on Earth, the Christian apologist is quick to point to God as the cause or explanation. Thus the skeptic's accusation is that Christians do nothing more than give their ignorance a name: God. No real and adequate explanation, says the skeptic, is provided by simply appealing to God as a cause or source.

The atheistic naturalist (a person who believes that the physical cosmos is the ultimate reality) assumes that, given enough time, scientific exploration will discover a naturalistic explanation for whatever is now inexplicable. Dawkins responded this way to intelligent design advocate Michael Behe's argument based on irreducible complexity—the idea that the complexity of some life-forms cannot be accounted for through gradual, evolutionary steps. Dawkins and other naturalists say that attributing scientific mysteries to God is illegitimate and even stifles scientific discovery.

One cannot help but notice how entrenched naturalists are in their own worldview. When it comes to science, only physical and material explanations are allowable (called methodological naturalism); the supernatural is ruled out a priori (without examination). Also, some naturalists express excessive confidence that future discoveries will explain reality. Because they don't live in the future, however, it is illegitimate to appeal to expectations of evidence in the future to explain present reality. This faulty form of reasoning constitutes the *argumentum ad futurus* fallacy—in other words, accepting a conclusion because future evidence will support it. Ironically, this could be called naturalism-of-the-gaps reasoning.

While modern science has been successful in explaining many aspects of the universe, some observers of the scientific enterprise acknowledge that it may have reached its limits when explaining the biggest questions of existence.[2] Those boundaries may not allow answers to profound questions regarding the origin of the universe, the origin of life, and the origin of consciousness. If this contested perspective is close to being true, then the grand natural explanations of science may have been exhausted. If so, naturalism as a worldview has been unable to adequately explain reality. Given this pessimistic scenario (from a naturalist's perspective), perhaps appealing to the supernatural to explain reality can be legitimate after all.

Regardless of the course taken by naturalists, most sophisticated Christian theists refrain from dependence on a god-of-the-gaps form of reasoning. Rather, Christian scholars tend to appeal to God as an *inference to the best explanation* (see chapter 4 for a description of abductive reasoning). This form of logical reasoning resembles the way detectives, lawyers, historians, and scientists reason. For example, scientists sometimes postulate ideas that are unobservable in order to explain the data that is observed (consider, for example, dark matter and dark energy). This approach posits the biblical God as the best explanation for all the significant realities in life.

Christian thinkers do not naively assume divine activity or intervention as an explanation for whatever humans cannot yet explain. Instead they offer a genuine explanatory theory for the nature of life's realities. For many, inference to the best explanation (abduction) serves as the most powerful and cogent approach to explaining reality.

Explanatory Power and Scope Test

How well does a belief system explain the facts of reality (power), and how wide is the range of its explanation (scope)? A viable belief system explains the phenomena of the material realm and of life in sufficient detail. This description should account for what can be observed externally (in the physical universe) and internally (in hopes, desires, and aspirations). An adequate belief system explains a broad range of data. The more profound the explanatory power, the greater the assurance that one is encountering a truthful vision of reality. Thus the best explanation has both specificity of detail (power) and satisfying breadth (scope).

Robert A. Harris provides a helpful illustration of this test for worldview thinking:

> When detectives examine a crime scene, their goal is to develop a narrative of events—a story—that explains as many of the details of evidence as possible in as plausible a way as possible. In other words, they develop a hypothesis that covers the facts. Similarly, a worldview might be seen as a hypothesis that aims to take into account as many of the observed phenomena of the world, life, and experience as possible in a coherent, unified way. The more phenomena that can be reasonably and plausibly explained by a given hypothesis, the greater is that hypothesis's explanatory power.[3]

Given such criteria as depth and breadth, the God of historic Christianity provides a solid and consistent metaphysical foundation for explaining the world we live in.[4] Consider six examples:

1. The existence of the God of the Bible provides a rationally plausible explanation for the existence of the universe.

Consider the following form of the cosmological argument.[5] (In a logical argument the *premises* provide the support while the *conclusion* makes the central claim.)

Premise 1: Everything that exists requires an explanation of its existence either in the necessity of its own nature or in an external cause.

Premise 2: If the physical (unnecessary) universe has an explanation of its existence, that explanation is an external cause (God).

Premise 3: The universe exists.

Conclusion: Therefore, the explanation of the universe's existence is God.

For an argument like this to be acceptable, two things are required: (1) The premises must logically entail the conclusion, and (2) the premises must all be true or acceptable (each premise must stand on its own ground as viably true). In analyzing this argument, a solid inferential connection exists between the premises and the conclusion—so the argument employs proper reasoning. The question then remains whether all the premises are true.

Premise 1 appears more rationally plausible than deniable. Philosopher Richard Taylor suggests that discovering a large, translucent ball lying on the ground while one is walking in the forest requires an adequate explanation. Proposing that the ball just exists inexplicably as a brute reality is rationally unacceptable. Moreover, Taylor proposes that even if the ball were the size of the universe, that fact does not eliminate the need for an adequate explanation of its existence.[6]

It seems logically convoluted to propose—as some atheists do—that every aspect of the universe requires an adequate explanation except for the cosmos as a whole. And the universe shows no sign of being a *necessary reality*, which is by definition uncaused, independent, and self-explanatory. In other words, a necessary reality cannot *not* exist (in other words, it must exist). Instead, the cosmos exhibits clear signs of being a *contingent reality*. A contingent reality by definition is something that is caused (begins), is dependent (an effect), and lacks an explanation in itself (is left unexplained). A contingent reality could either exist or not exist, but it certainly could not bring itself into existence from nothing.

Premise 2 likewise appears to be rationally plausible for two basic reasons: (1) This premise is consistent with the common claim that if God doesn't exist then the universe's existence is left unexplained. (2) The premise can stand on its own ground as viably true. As philosopher William Lane Craig notes, "An external cause of the universe must be beyond space and time and therefore cannot be physical or material."[7] Moreover, Craig points out that only two kinds of realities can serve as transcendent, nonphysical causal agents—namely, either abstract entities (such as mathematical equations) or an intelligent mind. But abstract entities by their very nature are causally powerless. Only personal agents possess the power to will things into existence. Thus Craig states in light of premise 2, "It follows that the explanation of the universe is an external, transcendent, personal mind that created the universe—which is what most people have traditionally meant by 'God.'"[8]

Premise 3 stands as a self-evident truth for all who aren't pantheistic monists or solipsists of some type. Therefore, the conclusion that "the explanation of the universe's existence is God" stands as a rationally plausible explanation.

2. The existence of the God of the Bible provides a rationally plausible explanation for the universe's beginning.

Two powerful lines of scientific evidence attest to the universe's beginning.[9]

First, according to accepted scientific theory on the origin of the universe (big-bang cosmology), the universe had a singular beginning roughly 14 billion years ago. All matter, energy, time, and space emerged in a cataclysmic but controlled explosion of extreme heat and light. The basic big-bang cosmological model, embraced by nearly all research scientists and based on extensive astronomical evidence and testing,[10] demonstrates that the universe is not eternal but instead had a specific beginning a finite period of time ago.

Leading astrophysicists John Barrow and Joseph Silk speak of the beginning of the universe in striking philosophical (if not biblical) terms: "Our new picture is more akin to the traditional metaphysical picture of creation out of nothing, for it predicts a definite beginning to events in time, indeed a definite beginning to time itself."[11]

Second, the concept of *entropy* (a key part of the second law of thermo-dynamics) provides further confirmation that the universe had a beginning. This well-established principle indicates that the energy in the universe is being gradually and equally distributed in all places. (For example, heat flows from hot bodies to cold bodies.) Thus, there will come a time (if nature takes its course) when "thermal equilibrium" (all locations in the universe manifest the same temperature)[12] will result and all physical activity will come to a halt. Yet if the universe is eternal, this would, by necessity, already have happened. Therefore, the principle of entropy supports the view that the universe has only been in existence a finite period of time.

There are also philosophical reasons for doubting that the universe has existed eternally. If the universe had no beginning, then the number of past events in the history of the cosmos is truly infinite in number. But this conclusion leads to paradoxical, if not absurd, consequences. How could the present event ever come to pass if an infinite number of prior events had to precede it? Arriving at the end of an actual infinite raises serious questions about logical coherence.[13]

Knowing that the universe had a singular beginning a finite period of time ago, one cannot easily sidestep the simple but compelling logic set forth in another version of the cosmological argument know as the *Kalam*:[14]

Premise 1: Whatever begins to exist has a cause for its coming into being.

Premise 2: The universe began to exist.

Conclusion: Therefore, the universe has a cause for its coming into being.

Premise 1 simply reflects the standard principle of scientific causality. The old scientific and philosophical maxim *ex nihilo nihil fit* asserts: from nothing, nothing comes. And as previously discussed, premise 2 is well-supported by both scientific consensus and philosophical reasoning.

Since the premises of the Kalam cosmological argument appear to be true and reasonable, then the conclusion should be regarded as a rationally plausible explanation for the origin of the universe. Abductively speaking, God appears to be the best explanation as to why the universe had a beginning.

POSSIBLE LOOPHOLES FOR THE UNIVERSE'S BEGINNING

Throughout history people have proposed explanations that don't require a divine creator. But these naturalistic options are limited, lacking in both evidence and coherence. Let's consider a few.

A first option is to look to the East. What we discover is that the cosmologies of Eastern religion break down in two basic ways. In the pantheistic monistic tradition the cosmos is either described as being an illusory reality (*maya* in Hinduism) or as an emanation from the being of God. This religious, mystical view that combines God and the cosmos offers no way to sort truth on rational and scientific grounds. Also, the basic cosmologies of Hinduism and

Buddhism affirm that the universe is without beginning or end[15]—a cosmological perspective that simply does not comport with the best scientific evidence concerning the origin of the universe.

The second option suggests that the universe somehow caused or created itself. This, however, is immediately recognized as an irrational conclusion because to create itself, the universe would have to exist before it existed—a clear absurdity. Something cannot both exist and not exist at the same time and in the same way.

A third option is that the universe just popped into existence from nothing and by nothing (or from no one). This, however, is also irrational because something cannot be derived from absolute nothingness (no energy, no matter, no space, no time, no power, no mind, no reason, no potential, etc.). An effect cannot be greater than its cause, and in this case the cause is nothing. To conclude otherwise is to violate one of the foundational principles of logic and of the scientific enterprise: causality.

A fourth, exotic, quasi-scientific option is to conclude that there are multiple universes (called the multiverse[16] or the many-worlds hypothesis). This idea postulates that a nearly infinite number of universes may have burst into existence, triggered by a universe-generating mechanism that stands beyond the physics of the known universe. According to its advocates, human beings have *won the cosmic lottery* by emerging from natural processes in what may be the only universe that has all the narrowly drawn physical characteristics necessary to permit complex life.

This exotic theory, while having some basis in speculative (yet to be verified) mathematics, nevertheless must overcome serious obstacles. Let's consider seven such problems:

1. As yet no direct, empirical data supports the existence of these multiple universes or of the mechanism that supposedly brings them forth. Therefore, the multiverse principle currently can be neither verified nor falsified—a defining factor in the scientific enterprise.
2. Atheistic naturalists, usually quick to invoke the Ockham's razor principle,[17] must consider whether this exotic theory multiplies entities beyond necessity or is possibly ad hoc in nature.
3. Presuming that this multiverse exists may amount to a type of infinite regression fallacy. In other words, how did the multiverse (or the meta-laws) begin and what is its source?
4. Are naturalists willing to bet their destiny on an unseen and unverified (likely unverifiable), speculative theory when they chastise Christians for considering such arguments as Pascal's wager?[18]
5. The multiverse appears to be virtually metaphysical (beyond the physical) in nature. So can this theory be solely naturalistic when it employs a mechanism that exists outside the physical realm?

6. Some of the leading advocates of the multiverse theory have admitted that any universe in the state of cosmic expansion must have had an absolute beginning.[19] Thus the multiverse theory is unable to dodge philosophical and scientific questions about a beginning and a cause.
7. If some version of the multiverse is somehow shown to be true, the theory in general is not incompatible with Christian theism. The Bible teaches that God created at least one other realm of reality besides the time-space world (Col. 1:16).

Therefore, as a highly speculative and nonfalsifiable hypothesis, the multiverse view cannot serve as a viable challenge to the notion that the universe had a beginning and a beginner.

Hawking Says There Is No Need for God

What if someone of the stature of Stephen Hawking says, "God may exist, but science can explain the universe without the need for a creator"? So said the famed theoretical physicist on CNN's *Larry King Live* in 2010.[20] And in their popular-science book *The Grand Design*,[21] Hawking and fellow physicist Leonard Mlodinow argue that invoking God is not necessary to explain the origin of the universe and that the big bang is the consequence of the laws of physics alone.

The authors categorically state:

Because there is a law such as gravity, the universe can and will create itself from nothing. Spontaneous creation is the reason there is something rather than nothing, why the universe exists, why we exist. It is not necessary to invoke God to light the blue touch paper and set the universe going.[22]

A few questions seem appropriate in light of Hawking and Mlodinow's bold, unsubstantiated metaphysical claim:

- If there are multiple universes and a universe-generating mechanism beyond space and time that triggers them, then what is the best explanation for the origin of this phenomenon?
- If there is a set of sweeping metalaws that stand beyond the multiverse, are these laws best explained as the product of a mind or as the product of a nonmind?
- If this law of gravity that Hawking and Mlodinow speak of is some overarching metareality, then how is its origin best explained if not by God?
- If the ultimate causal agent behind everything (including the multiverse) is an impersonal principle or law, then how is it possible for such an impersonal principle to adequately account for such personal realities as consciousness, personhood, mind, rationality, morality, beauty, and meaning?

- If human beings are a random collection of molecules and the product of an unguided, mindless process, then how is it possible to trust human rationality in studying science and to have confidence that the human mind produces true beliefs about reality?

Eliminating God's involvement in the creation of the universe appears to be as challenging as accounting for children apart from the existence of parents.

3. The existence of the God of the Bible provides a rationally plausible explanation for the complex order, design, and elegance evident in the universe.

Even the staunchest atheist would have to admit that the universe exhibits amazing order, regularity, complexity, and intelligibility. Eminent physicist and cosmologist Paul Davies comments on the striking elegance evident in the cosmos:

> All science proceeds on the assumption that nature is ordered in a rational and intelligible way. You couldn't be a scientist if you thought the universe was a meaningless jumble of odds and ends haphazardly juxtaposed. When physicists probe to a deeper level of subatomic structure, or astronomers extend the reach of their instruments, they expect to encounter additional elegant mathematical order. And so far this faith has been justified.[23]

The general acceptance by the scientific community of the *anthropic principle*—the view that nature's laws appear to be fine-tuned to allow for the existence of human life—has heightened the intuition that the universe is the product of a cosmic designer.[24] The astonishing intricacy, harmony, and organization of the cosmos in allowing for human life is evidenced from the fine-tuning of the fundamental constants of physics, to the just-right nature of the galaxy and solar system, to the information-laden building blocks known as the genetic code, to perhaps the crowning teleological achievement: the incredible complexity of the human brain-mind relationship.

Physicists often speak of nature's four fundamental forces—gravity, electromagnetism, strong and weak nuclear forces—as having a very narrow range of life-permitting values. If these forces were even slightly altered, this balance would be ruined and life would not be possible. Amazingly, the vast universe exhibits all the precise characteristics to be hospitable to life (representing the *Goldilocks Effect*). Philosopher of science Robin Collins comments on the extent and balance of design in the cosmos to allow for life: "Almost everything about the basic structure of the universe—for example, the fundamental laws and parameters of physics and the initial distribution of matter and energy—is balanced on a razor's edge for life to occur."[25]

The many fine-tuned elements in the universe needed to allow for the emergence of human beings led physicist Freeman Dyson to make the following provocative statement: "The more I examine the universe and study the details of its architecture, the more evidence I find that the universe in some sense must have known that we were coming."[26]

In thinking about this life-friendly, orderly universe, consider the following form of the fine-tuning or teleological argument (from the Greek word *telos*—"end," "purpose," "completeness") that purports to demonstrate God's existence from the design evident in the universe:[27]

> *Premise 1*: The fine-tuning of the universe must result from physical necessity, chance, or design.
>
> *Premise 2*: It does not result from physical necessity or chance.
>
> *Conclusion*: Therefore, it results from design.

The basic reasoning of this argument appears to be sound. So to take the next step we must look at the truth of the premises.

The first premise is uncontroversial. It merely provides the range of options to account for the universe's extraordinary fine-tuning.

The second premise carries the real weight of the argument by rejecting both physical necessity (the universe must have the qualities that it does) and chance (the qualities of the universe are the result of luck or accident). Many preeminent scientists give reasons for rejecting both of these naturalistic options.

Regarding necessity, Davies insists that the universe is not the inevitable outworking of nature's fixed laws and initial conditions. Instead the cosmos could have followed a vast variety of potential contingent outcomes. He writes, "It seems, then, that the physical universe does not have to be the way it is: it could have been otherwise."[28] It appears that the consensus of the scientific community now agrees with Davies that the laws of physics do not necessitate a universe that is hospitable to human life.

Concerning chance being responsible for the universe's fine-tuning, physicist Roger Penrose has calculated the chance, or undirected, formation of our universe to be one part in $10^{10(123)}$. This number (to the degree that it can be comprehended) is so wildly improbable that it makes chance not even a rationally plausible consideration.[29] But regardless of whether one accepts Penrose's calculation, the scientific community recognizes the incredible improbability of a chance explanation of the universe's fine-tuning.

Given that physical necessity and chance are not rationally plausible explanations, it seems that design is the best, if not the only, reasonable explanation. Philosopher Paul Copan makes this observation: "*Design* seems the preferable option given its greater explanatory power. If God exists, a delicately balanced universe *isn't* surprising at all. If God doesn't exist, shock is appropriate."[30]

But something more than improbability makes the naturalistic position rationally untenable. If one embraces the evolutionary view that the sensory organs and cognitive faculties of human beings are the result of strictly natural processes, then how can one trust that the things one observes correspond with reality?[31] As a matter of reasonable practice, one doesn't typically accept the idea that information, knowledge, and truth can come from a random, accidental source. How can one, then, reasonably justify such rational enterprises as logic, mathematics, and science if the human brain and mind are the result of a nonrational, mindless accident? Naturalism, in effect, purports that life, the mind, personhood, and reason came from a source that lacked all of these qualities. This effect would certainly be much greater than its cause!

4. The existence of the God of the Bible provides a rationally plausible explanation for the cosmos's susceptibility to rational investigation.

Physicists study the universe through the prism of mathematics. Recognizing the role mathematical constructs play in understanding the cosmos raises a critical philosophical question: Why do the conceptual principles present in the human mind correspond to the structure of the cosmos itself? In other words, how is it possible that Albert Einstein's famous equation ($E = mc^2$) corresponds to the very nature of the universe? Or put more simply: Why is mathematics valid?

This astonishing affinity between the mathematical thoughts of human beings' minds, in the form of equations, with the objective cosmos corresponds well with the Christian worldview. According to Scripture, God created both the universe and the human mind. And because people were created in the image of God, they possess the necessary cognitive faculties and sensory organs to recognize and study the intelligible order of the universe. In effect, God *networked* the graspable cosmos and rational structures within human minds together with himself. So the enterprises of logic, mathematics, and science become expected features of a universe made by a perfectly rational Creator. Given these theological presuppositions, it is easy to see why a universe created by God is open to rational investigation.

Philosopher Gregory E. Ganssle comments further about this *expected congruence* within the Christian theistic world- and life-view: "The fact that the universe is made by a mind for reasons leads us to expect that it can be grasped rationally. It makes sense that stable laws would allow predictions to be made and inferences to be drawn."[32]

By comparison, how does an atheistic perspective stack up? Does a universe that conforms to rational investigation comport well with a naturalistic point of view? In answering this question, it is important to recall Davies's point that the developing cosmos was potentially open to a variety of possible outcomes. Ganssle notes again:

> A naturalistic universe, however, would not have to be susceptible to rational investigation. It fits perfectly well with a naturalistic universe that it be wildly chaotic.

Of course, being susceptible to rational investigation is not incompatible with a universe without God, but the theory that God does not exist allows the universe to exhibit any one of a wide variety of descriptions as far as order is concerned.[33]

In terms of abductive explanatory power, the Christian theistic worldview is able to account for a broad range of phenomena observable in the cosmos.

5. The existence of the God of the Bible provides a rationally plausible explanation for the reality of abstract, nonphysical entities.

Some of the most wondrous realities of life are things that cannot be observed by the human senses. These abstract, intangible realities are conceptual in nature, in such entities as numbers, propositions, sets, properties, in the laws of logic, in moral values, and in universals. These conceptual realities are considered by many to be objective, universal, and, of course, invisible. They are nonphysical in nature and not reducible or explainable in terms of physical matter and its processes. Materialism as a metaphysical theory faces insurmountable logical problems in accounting for abstractions like these.[34] Such conceptual entities appear to be more than the product of mere human convention (invention). Consider two brief examples.

First, it is very difficult to account for truth by postulating that it is merely the result of human intellectual activity. Humans' apprehension of necessary truths seems to extend beyond their temporal existence. But if truth existed prior to the first human mind, then as a concept it needs a foundation. Christian philosopher Augustine of Hippo (AD 354–430) argued that the human mind apprehends universal, objective, unchanging, and necessary truths that are superior to the mind itself.[35] Since truth must reside in a mind, Augustine argued that these eternal truths are grounded in the eternal mind of God. Thus an eternal God's existence explains these eternal truths.

Second, the fundamental laws of logic (e.g., the laws of noncontradiction, excluded middle, and identity) are not merely a product of human convention. The principle of noncontradiction—nothing can both be and not be at the same time and in the same way—is not only cognitively necessary and irrefutable but also ontologically true. In other words, it defines the very nature of reality itself.[36] Logic too appears to require a foundation beyond the mind of man.

Since mathematics and logic (the foundations of science) have validity and provide human beings with real knowledge about the world, then these two conceptual realities cannot arise from subjective, manmade notions; they must be concerned with objective realities. But if these abstract entities are invisible, nonphysical, objective realities, then how are we to account for them appropriately?

Surely the naturalistic worldview, which says that the physical and material is all that exists, cannot adequately account for them. It is more than difficult to conceive of how abstractions could arise in a world strictly defined by such physicalism.

The Christian theistic worldview, however, grounds these conceptual realities in the mind of an infinite, eternal, and personal spiritual being. God is the Creator of both the visible and the invisible, the source of both the sensible and the intelligible (Ps. 148:2–5; Col. 1:16–17). In a Christian conceptual framework, God serves as the metaphysical foundation that adequately accounts for these critical conceptual and epistemological entities.[37]

6. The existence of the God of the Bible provides a rationally plausible explanation for the presence of conscious beings in the universe.

If we adopt the worldview of atheistic naturalism, then we must conclude that the conscious mind of human beings (with capacities such as personal mental states and intentionality) ultimately came from a source that is (in and of itself) mindless and nonconscious. So given naturalism, the natural cause of humans' mind, personhood, reason, and conscious awareness itself *lacked* all of these profound qualities. In other words, we, the personally conscious effect, can reflect back on the nonpersonal, nonconscious universe, but it cannot reflect on us. Thus we can know the cosmos in a way that it cannot know us. This effect would be exponentially greater than its cause.

One can see why the attempt to explain personal self-awareness from a naturalistic perspective has been called "the intractable problem of consciousness."[38] Naturalistic philosophers of mind candidly admit they have no idea how personal consciousness emerged from nonconscious matter. Therefore, it is safe to say that consciousness is not an easy fit in the world of naturalism.

Does the Christian theistic worldview better account for consciousness? Ganssle explains:

> If God exists, then the primary thing that exists is itself a conscious mind of unlimited power and intellect. This mind has its own first-person perspective, and it can think about things. The notion that such a mind, if it creates anything, would create other conscious minds that have their own first-person perspectives and can think about things is not a great mystery.[39]

Thus while naturalism faces what is called "the hard problem of consciousness,"[40] in a theistic world, self-conscious awareness is an anticipated and common feature. And it is important to recognize that this reasoning constitutes something more substantial than a god-of-the-gaps conclusion. Rather, it is an inference drawn from the worldview that has the better fit with the available and sufficient data, and thus, the greater explanatory power.

At this point, we can pause to ask whether either of two belief systems—atheistic naturalism or historic Christianity—has demonstrated adequate specificity of detail (power) and acceptable breadth (scope) to pass this truth-gathering test and warrant our trust. The evidence seems to point in one direction.

You'll find six more clear pointers to God in the next chapter.

8

More Signposts to the Almighty

> At least four major elements of our universe fit significantly
> better with a universe in which God exists than in the atheistic
> universe. These elements are: (1) the universe is ordered and
> susceptible to rational investigation; (2) it is a world with
> consciousness; (3) it is a world with significant free agency;
> and (4) it is a world with objective moral obligations. Each
> of these aspects fits neatly into a theistic world but is not at
> home in a naturalistic world.
>
> Gregory E. Ganssle,
> "Dawkins's Best Argument against God's Existence"

You're driving late at night on a paved rural road far away from city lights. You take a wrong turn somewhere but have no navigation system. There's nothing out here—not even cars coming the other way. You have plenty of gas, so you decide to keep going, but the help you really need just is not available. No signs, no reflectors on the highway—don't they maintain roads around here? What you need are clear pointers to your way.

Indicators of God from the Human Condition

Adopting a worldview can come down to *clear pointers* as well. Is there enough evidence to point the way either to the God of historic Christianity or to the worldview of atheistic naturalism? We examined six such indicators in favor of Christian theism (in light of recent assaults on faith by the new atheists) in the preceding chapter, and we will continue with six more in this chapter. Remember that a trustworthy belief system must demonstrate specificity of detail and acceptable breadth (the explanatory power and scope test) as it explains the realities of the world.

But an acceptable worldview must also illuminate the critical human condition. This chapter contains more pointers to God from the perspective of human beings living on planet Earth. It also addresses the historical record of the Messiah who visited Earth to save lost human beings.

1. The existence of the God of the Bible provides a rationally plausible explanation for the reality of objective moral values.

Moral values are a fundamental part of human life every bit as real as the law of gravity, and people are generally intuitively cognizant of their moral obligations. In their heart, people experience the pull of moral duty. This sense of moral *oughtness* is prescriptive in nature, and it transcends mere subjective feelings. Individuals may deny, rationalize, or even violate their moral obligations, but those obligations remain a necessary part of human life. Moral intuitions such as, "It is always wrong to murder," or, "It is right to be loving, truthful, courageous, and compassionate," testify to the reality of objective moral values. These values stand as distinct from, and independent of, the human mind. In other words, they are discovered, not invented.

How, then, does one account for the existence of objective, universal, unchanging moral principles? What guarantees their validity? And what is their foundation?

Let's consider a version of the Moral Argument—an argument that seeks to demonstrate God's existence by showing that God is the source of morality.[1]

Premise 1: If God does not exist, objective moral values and duties do not exist.

Premise 2: Objective moral values and duties do exist.

Conclusion: Therefore, God exists.

In terms of logical analysis, this argument employs correct reasoning. Therefore, what is left to determine is whether the premises are true and acceptable.

Premise 1 is affirmed by many within the camps of both atheism and theism. For example, one of the most robust defenses of atheism comes from Oxford philosopher J. L. Mackie. He argues that there are no objective moral values because moral properties constitute so odd a cluster of qualities and relations that they are most unlikely to have arisen in the ordinary course of events, without an all-powerful god to create them. If, then, there are such intrinsically prescriptive objective values, they make the existence of a god more probable than it would have been without them.[2]

Mackie, on that basis, chooses to deny the existence of objective moral values and duties.

Premise 2 is also commonly affirmed. But atheists who recognize the existence of objective values and duties must ground them in something outside of God. One may rightfully ask: How can human beings possess inherent dignity and moral worth if they are the product of blind, valueless, natural processes? Given atheism and naturalistic evolutionary theory, one is hard-pressed to justify the existence of an objective moral realm. The truth is that objective moral values seem logically incompatible with all forms of ethical relativism, including nontheistic evolutionary theory.

In the absence of a morally perfect, personal God, morality appears to be conventional, arbitrary, and subjective. Without God, where is the unchanging anchor by which objective ethics must be securely grounded? Objective ethical principles do exist, but they cannot exist in a metaphysical vacuum. What is morally good (ethics) cannot be separated from what is real (metaphysics) and what is true (epistemology).

In light of the fact that objective moral values and duties do not fit easily in a naturalistic world, it seems reasonable to come to the conclusion that God exists as their source.

Unlike secular attempts to account for morality, the ethics of Christian theism are grounded in the morally perfect nature of God, who has revealed his will to humankind in the Judeo-Christian Scriptures. God's existence and nature provide a source and foundation for objective moral values. Absolute moral law extends from the cosmic, moral law giver.

2. The existence of the God of the Bible provides a rationally plausible explanation for the purpose and significance that human beings yearn for in their lives.

If God doesn't exist and the universe is merely the product of blind, purposeless, natural processes, then from a logical standpoint there can be no objective meaning to life. Given a nontheistic perspective, the fact that people exist becomes simply an amazing accident of evolution. Human beings live on this planet for a very short time and then inevitably die (permanent extinction). Given this forlorn naturalistic outlook, the only meaning and purpose that humans can possibly enjoy is what they create for themselves.

In view of each person's imminent, personal death, along with the extinction of the human species and the death of the entire cosmos (due to entropy—the loss of available energy), can there be any meaning, purpose, significance, and value in life, even in a temporary way apart from God's reality? After all, nothing anyone thinks, says, or does will change the grim naturalistic scenario that each person will die, the race as a whole will become extinct, and the universe will one day grow lifeless and cold. Reflection on this fate rightfully leaves many with the sense of utter hopelessness.

Handed such a predicament, atheists tend to be divided into two camps: optimistic and pessimistic. The more optimistic camp simply proclaims that while there is no intrinsic meaning *to* life, meaning *in* life may be derived through individual choice. On the other hand, atheistic existential philosophers such as Jean-Paul Sartre (1905–80) and Albert Camus (1913–60) say that contemplation on this personal and cosmic scenario leads to philosophical angst, despair, and dread.[3] According to the atheistic existentialist, each man or woman is alone to face his or her existential predicament.

Nevertheless, three observations about human beings seem to conflict with this latter pessimistic and nihilistic perspective:

1. *Most people intuitively sense that their lives have real meaning and purpose.* It may be true that people don't seriously reflect on their condition in life, but even if they are not happy with the content of their individual lives, people in general live with the sense that there is something worth living for, something meaningful going on behind the scenes.

2. *Virtually all people yearn for a purpose that extends beyond the grave.* For most people, this pursuit of ultimate meaning leads to a belief in life after death, or immortality, usually involving belief in God. While skeptics may dismiss this tendency as a cosmic form of wishful thinking, studies in anthropology and sociology reveal that humans have possessed a deep religious-immortality impulse virtually from day one of their existence. It is fair to say that the search for meaning and purpose is one of the defining characteristics of our species.

American philosophical theologian Paul Tillich suggests that everyone, including atheists, seeks an ultimate cause or concern in life. We may rightfully ask if these profound, internal yearnings that seem universal point to some external potential for fulfillment (God, immortality, redemption).

3. *If the world is actually meaningless and human life is equally meaningless, what explanation can be given for the fact that people living in a meaningless world come to the amazingly meaningful recognition that the world has no meaning?* Christian writer and apologist C. S. Lewis points out that meaningless creatures would never have discovered the truth of their own meaninglessness.[4] Is the unique ability of humans to reflect about the meaning of life a strong hint that there is indeed something deeper to life?

Humanity's deep sense of and need for meaning comports well with the Christian truth-claim that God created human beings in his image (Gen. 1:26–27) and that their greatest need is to be reconciled to God and enjoy fellowship with him forever. The Christian theistic worldview, with its unique gospel of gracious redemption in Christ, offers genuine meaning, purpose, and significance to sinners estranged from God and from their destiny.

3. The existence of the God of the Bible provides a rationally plausible explanation for humankind's innate sense of the divine.

Scripture reveals that human beings at their core know there is a God. God created human beings in the expressed image of himself with a built-in awareness of the Creator. God also created an environment that triggers and supports humans' inner sense of God. This divine consciousness is therefore evident to people based on powerful external and internal factors. Externally, God's existence, power, glory, and wisdom are evident to humankind, being manifest in the cosmic cathedral that surrounds him—namely, the world and the universe (Ps. 19:1–4). Internally, human beings are intimately aware of their moral accountability to their Maker through their conscience (Rom. 2:14–15).

Biblically speaking, although people see, understand, and know that there is a God to whom they are directly morally accountable (based on these external and internal factors), nevertheless in their state of sin they tend to suppress the truth of this awareness (Rom. 1:18). Sinful human beings thus suffer from what one may call an intellectual and spiritual schizophrenia, both desiring and resisting God at the same time. Humans were made for the specific purpose of fellowshiping with their Creator, but because of sin they refuse to acknowledge the true God or accept moral responsibility. God intends to judge every human on the basis of this powerful external and internal revelation (Rom. 1:20). The greatest need of every man and woman, therefore, is redemption—reconciliation with God.

If true, this inherent sense of the divine explains a lot about humanity. It accounts for a deep-seated religious and moral impulse as well as the overall phenomenon of religious experience. (Some philosophers have referred to humans as *Homo religiosus* because of their basic religious tendencies and nature.) In general, atheism appears to be contrary to human nature, while the biblical view of humankind's sense of the divine matches up well with human religious experience.

4. The existence of the God of the Bible provides a rationally plausible explanation for the enigma of man.

One of the chief realities a belief system must explain before gaining acceptance involves the enigmatic nature of human beings. Christian thinker Blaise Pascal (1623–62) describes humans in his classic Christian work *Pensées* as an unusual mixture of greatness and wretchedness, being at the same time both the "glory and refuse of the universe."[5] Human nature poses a paradox: humans are capable of greatness in mathematics, science, technology, philosophy, the arts, compassion, and generosity; yet humans are equally capable of such shameful and evil acts as rape, robbery, racism, slavery, murder, and genocide. Explaining human nature apart from the reality of God represents an extraordinary philosophical, psychological, and spiritual feat.

The Bible seems to hold the secret to unraveling the enigma of humans and the paradox of human nature. The Christian theistic worldview asserts that the greatness of humans is a direct result of the *imago Dei*. As creatures made in the image and likeness of God, humans reflect the glory of their Maker, thus making us virtually God-like in many respects and unique when compared with other animals (see chapter 12). Our wretchedness, on the other hand, can be traced to the first human beings' fall into sin (Gen. 3). Adam misused his freedom by rebelling against God, and as a result he suffered alienation from his Creator and became pervasively sinful. Adam's sin, however, affected more than just himself; Adam's sinful condition has been passed on to all humanity. Original sin is the biblical doctrine that the entire human race has inherited guilt, moral corruption, and spiritual alienation from the first human (Pss. 51:5; 58:3; Rom. 5:12, 18–19; 1 Cor. 15:22).

In the present state of sin, humans are capable of using certain of their gifted qualities for evil purposes. Thus it's no surprise to see both great humanitarianism and great inhumanity in the regular course of human events. The sinful condition of spiritual beings also explains individual hypocrisy.

Neither the naturalistic worldview nor the alternative religions of the world provide satisfactory answers for the world's greatest riddle: humans.

5. The existence of the God of the Bible provides a rationally plausible explanation for the extraordinary life, death, and resurrection of Jesus Christ.

According to the historically reliable documents of the New Testament,[6] Jesus of Nazareth made unparalleled claims of divine authority during his public ministry (see chapters 3 and 4 for evidence of his claims of deity). Jesus's divine credentials deserve a few more thoughts.

Jesus fulfilled dozens of very specific Old Testament prophecies concerning the identity, mission, and message of the coming Messiah.[7] These prophecies, which give precise details about the birth, heritage, life, and death of the long-awaited Messiah, were amazingly fulfilled by Jesus even though written hundreds of years before his birth. Many of these prophecies lay beyond Jesus's natural, human ability to fulfill intentionally, and the chance probability of all of these prophecies coming true in the life of one man is utterly staggering.

Also, according to the well-attested Gospel records, Jesus was a prolific miracle worker.[8] He healed incurable diseases, restored sight to the blind, multiplied small amounts of food to feed thousands of people, calmed a storm, walked on water, and even raised the dead. Yet even Jesus's enemies didn't question the authenticity of his miraculous acts. While an antisupernatural bias often keeps modern skeptics from even considering the factuality of Jesus's life and actions, such prejudice should not stand in the way of accepting remarkable events as true if those events are well established historically. It seems reasonable to conclude that if a theistic God exists (certainly a rational viewpoint), then he would perform miracles if he came to Earth.

In addition, Jesus exhibited a matchless moral character during his three-year public ministry that changed the world. Both Jesus's intimate friends and staunch foes could find no moral fault with him. Not only did his teachings contain incredible ethical insight, but he also perfectly fulfilled his lofty moral ideals. Jesus's pristine moral example and profound teachings laid the foundation for much of the ethical theory embraced throughout Western civilization. He is widely considered even by non-Christians as the ideal blueprint of moral virtue and the only perfect life ever lived.

A compelling reason for seriously considering that Jesus was indeed God in human form is that he was so fundamentally different from every other person who has ever walked the earth. Even the world's great philosophers and religious leaders—Socrates, the Buddha, Confucius, Moses, and Solomon—pale in comparison to him. In fact, human goodness is measured according to the life, character, and teachings of Jesus Christ. Jesus has had an incalculable influence on human history. Western civilization in particular is inconceivable apart from him. No one has impacted the world for good as did Jesus of Nazareth.

The New Testament documents record in great detail firsthand testimony of Jesus's resurrection from the dead (again, see evidence for the resurrection in chapters 1 and 2). Support for the resurrection is found in the fact of Jesus's empty tomb, his many postcrucifixion appearances, the transformation of the disciples from cowards to apostles and martyrs (in light of Christ's resurrection), the dramatic conversion of Saul of Tarsus into the apostle Paul, the historic emergence of the Christian church, the change in the official day of worship to Sunday to commemorate the day of Jesus's resurrection, and the fact that all alternative naturalistic explanations for the resurrection fail miserably.

According to historic Christianity, humans need not live in doubt about God's existence; he has made himself known in Jesus Christ. In fact, God came to Earth looking for us. Thus, the most reasonable explanation for the historical life, death, and resurrection of Jesus is that he was God in human flesh. Christianity's most distinctive dangerous idea is that in the historical person of Jesus Christ, God has climactically and decisively made himself known to humanity.

6. *The existence of the God of the Bible provides a rationally plausible explanation for the meaningful realities of life by means of a cumulative case for God's existence.*

Just as a detective builds a case by adding evidence, or a physician arrives at a diagnosis by considering multiple symptoms and tests, anyone can arrive at a meaningful conclusion based on a cumulative case. One of the strongest evidences that Christian theism's truth-claims are correct rests in its ability to account for and justify the many diverse and undeniable realities of life. The arguments in these last two chapters appeal to the existence of the God of the Bible as a means of explaining reality (reasoning to the best explanatory hypothesis). These arguments present a cumulative case of compelling evidence for the God of the Bible; that is, while each of the individual arguments has a certain logical or evidential force of its own, it is also true that the arguments taken collectively offer a formidable case in favor of the existence of the God of the Bible.

Historic Christianity's Explanatory Scope

One of Christian theism's greatest worldview strengths is the scope of its explanatory power. The historic Christian viewpoint accounts for the array of realities in nature and in human experience, including:

> *The Universe*: its source and singular beginning, order, regularity, and fine-tuning
>
> *Abstract Entities*: the existence and validity of mathematics; the laws of logic; and scientific models (which include their correspondence to the time-space universe as conceived in the mind of human beings)
>
> *Ethics*: the existence of universal, objective, and prescriptive moral values
>
> *Human Beings*: our existence, consciousness, rationality, free agency, enigmatic nature, moral and aesthetic impulse, and our need for meaning and purpose in life
>
> *Religious Phenomena*: humankind's spiritual nature and religious experience, the miraculous events of Christianity, and the unique character, claims, and credentials of Jesus Christ[9]

A viable worldview must be supported by multiple lines of converging evidence that together add support for its truth-claims and extend the breadth of its explanatory power—a cumulative test. An assortment of data from various fields of inquiry illustrates the historic Christian worldview's explanatory power and makes a case for its truthfulness even stronger. Table 5 lists a few examples that corroborate this position.

Table 5. Cumulative Case for Christian Theism's Explanatory Power

Field	Data
Cosmology	A singular beginning to the universe (big-bang cosmology); beginning of time

Field	Data
Astrophysics	Nature's laws appear fine-tuned to allow for human life (anthropic principle); so do the universe's content and systems (galaxy, stars, planets, etc.)
Biology/Chemistry	Life systems yield evidence of having been intelligently designed
Anthropology/Psychology	Human beings are richly endowed intellectually but morally flawed
Neuroscience	Humans possess consciousness and a capacity for intentionality and rational reflection
Math	Mathematical theories correspond with physical reality
Logic	As abstract entities, the laws of logic are universal, invariant, and independent of human conventions
Ethics	Moral absolutes seem intuitively authentic, and moral relativism is self-defeating
Religion	Religion is a universal phenomenon, and religious experience seems intuitively real and consistent with biblical revelation
History	Credible historical reports corroborate the life, death, and resurrection of Jesus Christ
Philosophy	Human beings crave meaning, purpose, and immortality

These multiple lines of converging evidence support and verify the Christian worldview's basic truth-claims.

How Historic Christianity's Most Comprehensive Dangerous Idea Changed the World

Human history is inconceivable apart from the idea of God. And the biblical conception of God—in particular—is arguably the most majestic and certainly the most popular of all religious perspectives. In fact, more than half the people of the world follow one of the three Middle Eastern monotheistic religions that claim (in greater or lesser ways) to take their lead from "The Book." Thus one may argue that belief in the biblical God is either the greatest truth of all time or the greatest delusion to ever enter the minds of human beings.

Christians simply argue that believing in the Triune God of the Bible makes sense. The prism of Christian revelation serves to illumine life and the world itself. In other words, all of the meaningful realities of existence find their grounding, justification, and validity in the Creator-Redeemer-Sanctifier God of historic Christianity. The Christian worldview lens uniquely allows people to see and understand the nature of truth, reality, and goodness. Thus, philosophically speaking, the Christian faith explains reality in both its detail and breadth.

The truth that there is an infinite, eternal, and personal mind behind the realities of the universe that can be detected through human reflection is the most transformative Christian apologetics idea in history. Christianity's explosive explanatory power and scope extends to such human enterprises as philosophy, psychology, science, religion, the arts, history, law, education, labor, economics, and medicine.

A Worldview Exercise

Of all the areas in our home, my family and I congregate most often in our family room. My wife and I and our three children have many conversations in that room. We even eat some of our meals there, especially when we watch movies together. Unfortunately, the carpet in that room reflects the fact that it receives the most traffic in the house.

For me, some of the furniture in the room is essential, especially our big-screen television and my favorite reclining chair, perfect for watching World War II documentaries and Los Angeles Lakers basketball games. I also appreciate the couch: an ideal spot for naps on Sunday afternoons after busy mornings of teaching and preaching at church. Large lamps provide bright light that makes the family room an ideal place to read late in the evening.

With this example of a well-used family space in mind, will you try a mental experiment with me? Using analogical reasoning, instead of a physical family room, think of a *conceptual* worldview room. A worldview consists of a cluster of beliefs that a person holds about the big questions of life (such as God, the cosmos, knowledge, morality). This abstract room represents the place where a person lives in terms of beliefs and ideas—in other words, it represents the conceptual life of the mind.

Once you have conceived of this mental family room—a very busy place where conceptual entities reign supreme—ask yourself a necessary question: What sort of *furniture* is needed to fill this worldview room?

Some of the furniture undoubtedly includes such realities as the laws of logic, mathematical principles, universals, reflections, inferences, propositions, and ethical ideals. Just as a physical family room is often occupied with various activities of family life, a nonempirical worldview room also echoes with vigorous intellectual action.

Does the furnishing of your conceptual worldview room, with all of its nonphysical, intangible entities, best comport with atheism or theism? Put another way, does it best fit with the view that there is a mind behind the universe or that there is not a mind behind the universe?

Science writer Paul Davies conveyed in a recent article that when scientists explore the universe, they uncover "elegant mathematical order" and "tidy mathematical relationships." Davies, though skeptical about religion, goes on to state, "The idea that the laws [of physics] exist reasonlessly is deeply antirational. After all, the very essence of a scientific explanation of some phenomenon is that the world is ordered logically and that there are reasons things are as they are."[10]

The purpose of this worldview thought experiment is to ask how these abstract areas can best be accounted for. For example, although Albert Einstein didn't believe in a personal God, he did believe that the universe corresponded amazingly to a rational-mathematical order. One must ask: Why order rather than chaos? Why such logical and mathematical elegance? And why is it that human beings can, to an extraordinary degree, comprehend this intelligibility that appears to be built into the nature of the cosmos?

Can the critical abstract areas of life be sufficiently explained through natural processes alone (atheistic naturalism)? Or does an appeal (inference to the best explanation) to the theistic God of the Bible better explain these invisible entities?

Logic and evidence combine to confirm that the conceptual world of ideas best comports with a worldview that can account for mind, consciousness, and abstract, intangible entities. The theistic worldview, and Christian theism in particular, asserts that the finite minds of human beings are derived from the infinite mind of God. Thus the greater and ultimate mind causes the lesser and limited minds. In this case the cause is magnitudes or exponentially greater than the effect, which is in accord with the scientific principle of causality.

When it comes to the atheistic naturalistic worldview, however, finite human minds somehow come from a nonrational, nonpersonal, and therefore non-mindful mechanism (evolution). According to this worldview, the effect is magnitudes or exponentially greater than the cause—an idea that runs counter to the principle of causality.

The conceptual room we have described seems to comport with a mindful, rather than mindless, source. The conceptual furniture in a theistic worldview room is an expected and normal set of features (mind to mind, God to man). On the other hand, the conceptual furniture in an atheistic worldview (logic, math, science, ethics, etc.) renders these furnishings coincidental, out of place, dissonant, and ultimately unexplained (mind from nonmind).

I encourage you to spend more time reflecting on your conceptual worldview room. This analogy may help more people see the importance of evaluating worldviews to determine their coherence and explanatory power and scope. A viable worldview must account for both the world we can see and, maybe more so, the world we cannot see.

The idea that God explains the various and monumental realities of life is historic Christianity's most comprehensive dangerous idea.

Further Suggested Reading

Boa, Kenneth D., and Robert M. Bowman Jr. *20 Compelling Evidences That God Exists*. Tulsa: River-Oak, 2002.

Copan, Paul. *Loving Wisdom*. St. Louis: Chalice, 2007.

————, and William Lane Craig, eds. *Contending with Christianity's Critics*. Nashville: B & H Publishing Group, 2009.

Craig, William Lane. *Reasonable Faith*. 3rd edition. Wheaton: Crossway, 2008.

————, and Chad Meister, eds. *God Is Great, God Is Good*. Downers Grove, IL: InterVarsity, 2009.

Miller, Edward L. *God and Reason*. 2nd edition. Upper Saddle River, NJ: Prentice-Hall, 1995.

Moreland, J. P., and William Lane Craig. *Philosophical Foundations for a Christian Worldview*. Downers Grove, IL: InterVarsity, 2003.

Taylor, Richard. *Metaphysics*. 4th edition. Englewood Cliffs, NJ: Prentice Hall, 1992.

Discussion Questions

1. What specific aspects about the physical cosmos fit better with a Christian theistic worldview than with an atheistic naturalistic worldview?

2. How does abductive reasoning differ from a god-of-the-gaps approach?

3. How should one respond to the multiverse challenge from a historic Christian perspective?

4. What specific insights does Christian theism offer in explaining human nature?

5. What credentials does Jesus Christ possess in supporting his claims to deity?

NOT BY WORKS

9

Moral Goodness and the Human Condition

> The message of justification is difficult to accept because it seems too good to be true. It says: Stop trying to justify yourself. You do not need to. There is no way to buy or deserve God's love or acceptance. You are already being offered God's love on the cross without having to jump hoops or pass tests. You are already there, where you think you are not.
>
> Thomas C. Oden, *The Justification Reader*

You survive the death of your body and awake to a conscious existence in the next life. You now anticipate an imminent, face-to-face meeting with the Almighty. Filled with incredible angst, you wonder how your tête-à-tête with God will go. Questions grip your mind: How will God evaluate the life I've lived? Will I be assigned to heaven or to hell? What is God's basis for granting people either eternal life or eternal damnation in the hereafter? Is there any hope of a good outcome?

From informal polling data, we learn that people are more confident of their chances of heaven than of any other place. The idea that heaven is reserved for people who *try* to live good, decent, moral lives and that hell is just punishment for really evil people seems an extremely common belief. It is a belief held by many within the institutional religions of the world and by people who identify themselves as nonreligious per se but rather as *spiritual* in self-designation.

Let's explore this commonly held view that people who try their best to live decent lives go to heaven and only the absolutely worst people go to hell. Understanding this religious viewpoint will put us in a good position to contrast it with historic Christianity's most hopeful dangerous idea: the Gospel teaching that God freely saves sinful people by his grace alone through faith.

Islam: A Religion of Submissive Obedience

From an institutional perspective, Islam, now the second largest[1] and arguably the most controversial of all the religions in the world today, clearly teaches that paradise is an earned reward and damnation is a just punishment.

Estimated to be the fastest-growing religion in the world, Islam[2] declares itself the only straight path to God.[3] At the center of the Islamic religion is the belief that there is one and only one God. This single, sovereign, and personal God—Allah—is said to have uniquely revealed his will for humankind through his prophet Muhammad (AD 570–632). The specific content of this divine revelation was set forth in the holy book known as the Qur'an. It calls all people everywhere to worship the one true God, who is the creator and judge of humanity and is supreme over all. People, therefore, need to submit their lives to Allah's expressed will.

The Arabic term *Islam* incorporates the meanings of *peace* and *surrender*. The religion of Islam teaches that human beings will find true peace, both in this life and in the hereafter, only by surrendering their will to the will of Allah. The word *Muslim* means one who *submits* his life and seeks to follow the straight path of God. Islam, similar to modern Judaism, is a religion that stresses what an individual practices more than what he or she believes (devotion over doctrine, law over theology).

The basis of divine judgment in Islam comes from the view that human beings are fully responsible for their actions and God is all-knowing and completely just. This belief system rejects the idea of original or inherited sin and instead teaches that human beings are born good. Self-discipline and divine guidance make them capable of morally acceptable living.

Muslims do not believe, as historic Christians do, that sin is a state of being. Rather, they insist that sin is merely the momentary expression of willful disobedience. In Islam, humans are limited, weak, and generally forgetful of spiritual realities, but they are not fallen sinners who remain trapped in that state. Allah, though spoken of in the Qur'an as merciful, does not offer redemption to humankind but instead offers fair and impartial justice. An introductory article on the website Islam.com notes the following: "Islam believes that each person is born pure. The Holy Quran tells us that God has given human beings a choice between good and evil and to seek God's pleasure through faith, prayer and charity."[4]

Though claiming to be heirs of the biblical tradition, Islam is not a religion of grace and redemption. Muslims believe that paradise is a just reward and hell is a rightful punishment.

For Muslims, judgment day or the Day of Reckoning is a future cataclysmic event, its time known only to Allah. According to Islam, this day will begin with the sound of a trumpet followed by a general resurrection of the dead. Then all people will appear before God to be judged based on their actions, which have been perfectly recorded in the Book of Deeds.

It is a common Islamic belief that two angels follow each Muslim throughout life. The angel on the person's right records his or her good deeds, while the angel on the left records his or her bad deeds. A Muslim's destiny hinges on the preponderance of his actions as measured on a scale. Generally speaking, Muslims have no assurance that they will earn paradise, but this dilemma is often understood as an incentive to strive for greater submission to Allah's requirements.

Paradise involves both spiritual and physical pleasures (often described in sensual terms for men), whereas hell consists of eternal banishment from Allah's presence accompanied by despair and physical punishment. While this judgment seems based solely on a person's actions, Muslims also believe that Allah can consign people to paradise or hell based on his sovereign or arbitrary will.

Islam.com describes what Muslims are taught to believe concerning the afterlife:

> They believe that life after death is not a new phenomenon; in that all it's [sic] manifestations will be reflections of what one does in this life. They believe that each soul will be held accountable for what it has done and that God will punish and reward accordingly. They believe life as we know it is only transitory and that life after death is a permanent state.[5]

In this manner, this influential world religion affirms what many religions teach: that paradise is a reward for moral goodness expressed in this life and that hell is punishment for a lack of sufficient ethical accomplishment.

The Spiritual Man in the Street's View

How does Islam compare with the beliefs of those who claim no association with organized religion but prefer a type of *personal spirituality*? Common expressions reveal an echo:

"God helps those who help themselves."

"God knows I'm only human."

"I'm trying my best; God will understand."

The view that heaven is reserved for people who *try* to live good, decent, moral lives and hell is set aside only for the worst possible people is pervasive. Even people with some vague connection to Christianity express these beliefs.

Many people think God will grade on a curve and cut the virtuous among us some slack when it comes to assigning heaven or hell. Why? Because current culture says that at their core, most people are good. In other words, if their life's deeds were placed on a scale, the good would outweigh the bad.

The flip side of this popular sentiment about human nature is that hell is reserved for only the truly evil people. That includes iconic despots, mass murderers, and heinous criminals such as Adolf Hitler, Joseph Stalin, Mao Zedong, Charles Manson, Jeffrey Dahmer, and Ted Bundy. These evil monsters are thought to be clear exceptions or distortions to the general rule concerning humankind's basic moral goodness.

The typical person on the street apparently thinks that while most people are not as kind and compassionate as Mother Teresa, they clearly are not as evil as Saddam Hussein. Therefore, the vast majority of people in the moral middle will get a passing score on God's graded curve. So whether as the tenet of a formal, non-Christian religion or a facet of personal spirituality, people commonly view heaven as a reward for being a fairly decent person and hell as a punishment for being a truly terrible human being.

Against the backdrop of a near-global consensus that God sees humankind as being basically good and, therefore, worthy of heaven stands historic Christianity's fifth dangerous idea—a revolutionary notion that brings with it both profoundly *bad news* and profoundly *good news* for humanity. According to historic Christianity, in the eyes of God no one is or becomes morally acceptable by his or her own merit. In fact, it is fair to say that sin (moral transgression) is a much bigger problem than most people (including many Christians) realize. But the *good news* (Gospel) is that God's grace is deeper and Jesus Christ is a much greater Savior than most people (including Christians) realize.

According to the biblically derived faith expressed in historic Christianity, salvation is not achieved through human moral merit; rather, salvation is the free gift of a loving and forgiving God that comes through faith in Jesus Christ. To be clear, Scripture does teach that God will judge humanity in the *eschaton*—the last or final day (Ps. 96:13; Eccles. 12:14; Matt. 25:32–33, 46; Acts 17:31; Rom. 14:11–12; Heb. 9:27). But God's Word also teaches that all those who by grace embrace the glorious gospel of Jesus Christ will escape the wrath of God, receive forgiveness for all their sins, and enjoy God's loving presence forever (Isa. 53:11; Acts 13:39; Rom. 3:23–24; 5:1; Eph. 2:4–5; Titus 3:5–7).

Historic Christianity's Fifth Dangerous Idea Explained: Salvation by Grace

Christianity at its heart is a religion not of self-help but of divine rescue. According to the Gospels, what human beings need most is not moral guidance but rather a Savior. In fact, the central message of the New Testament is that God the Son has come to Earth in the person of Jesus Christ to rescue sinful human beings from God the Father's deserved wrath. The Gospel reveals that we are saved *by* God (the Son) *from* God (the Father) *through* God (the Holy Spirit) and *for* God (the three in one). The Triune God accomplishes the whole salvation process, and justification comes specifically through the death of Jesus Christ on the cross. The Latin word for *cross* is *crux*, but in English *crux* means "central point." So, to use a play on words, the *crux* of Christ is the crux of Christianity.

The next chapter will briefly explore the significance of Jesus's death on the cross. Before examining what is referred to as the *atonement*, however, it is critical to consider both the sinful condition of humanity and God's righteous wrath against sin. For without sin there is no divine wrath, and without divine wrath there is no need for salvation.[6]

Sin Uncovered

According to Scripture, humanity's need for salvation stems from the fact that we are sinners. But this notion immediately raises several important questions about sin, such as what it is and where it came from. What follows offers a biblical examination of the issue by briefly answering six critical questions on sin.[7]

1. What is sin?

In Scripture, sin is something committed primarily against God (Ps. 51:2–4), though it is also committed against human beings. The Bible uses a number of Hebrew and Greek terms to describe the various aspects and shades of sin.[8] The most prominent terms are the Hebrew *hata'* and the Greek *hamartia*, both of which generally depict sin as missing the mark set by God, going astray from God, and actively rebelling against God. This willful stance often takes the specific form of violating God's expressed commands. Thus sin is usually defined in terms of violations or transgressions of God's law (Rom. 2:12–14; 4:15; 5:13; James 2:9–10; 1 John 3:4). Because the moral law revealed in Scripture is the extension of God's holy and righteous character, to break God's law is a direct affront to God himself. In light of this, sin can be defined as anything (including actions, attitudes, and nature) that is contrary to the moral character and commands of God.[9] Other ways of referring to sin include unrighteousness, godlessness, and lawlessness.

> Wash away all my iniquity
>> and cleanse me from my sin.
> For I know my transgressions,
>> and my sin is always before me.
> Against you, you only, have I sinned
>> and done what is evil in your sight;
> so that you are proved right when you speak
>> and justified when you judge. (Ps. 51:2–4 NIV 1984)

The sinful mind is hostile to God. It does not submit to God's law, nor can it do so. (Rom. 8:7 NIV 1984)

Everyone who sins breaks the law; in fact, sin is lawlessness. (1 John 3:4)

The English Standard Version gives us ten terms used for sin in the Bible:[10]

1. Disobedience (Rom. 5:19)
2. Evil (Judg. 2:11)
3. Iniquity (Lev. 26:40)
4. Lawlessness (Titus 2:14)
5. Transgression (Exod. 23:21)
6. Trespass (Eph. 2:1)
7. Ungodliness (1 Peter 4:18)
8. Unholiness (1 Tim. 1:9)
9. Unrighteousness (1 John 1:9)
10. Wickedness (Prov. 11:31)

2. Where did sin come from?

Sin finds its origin in the will of the creature. The Bible reveals that sin entered the world when the first humans, Adam and Eve, rebelled against God while they lived in the Garden of Eden (Gen. 3). They transgressed God's expressed command not to eat of the tree of the knowledge of good and evil (Gen. 2:17). Satan—who had led an earlier angelic revolt against God (Isa. 14:12–20)—appeared as the serpent in the Garden, tempted Eve to doubt God's word, and exposed Adam's choice to defy God (Gen. 3:1–5). The first humans therefore misused their God-given freedom by willfully rebelling against their Creator. Adam and Eve sinned by going their own way. They chose to find truth and goodness outside of God and his expressed commands.

And the Lord God commanded the man, "You are free to eat from any tree in the garden; but you must not eat from the tree of the knowledge of good and evil, for when you eat from it you will certainly die." (Gen. 2:16–17)

When the woman saw that the fruit of the tree was good for food and pleasing to the eye, and also desirable for gaining wisdom, she took some and ate it. She also gave some to her husband, who was with her, and he ate it. (Gen. 3:6)

3. What are the two types of sin?

We are frequently reminded of the many kinds of sins people commit. But these sins flow from the sin nature we inherited from Adam.

ORIGINAL SIN

While there are some important differences concerning the doctrine of original sin among the various theological traditions within Christendom,[11] the following discussion reflects a widely accepted perspective. Biblically speaking, one cannot think of Adam in his relationship to God as a private, isolated individual. He was not only the *first* man but also the *representative* man.[12] Adam represents all of humanity via the covenant God made with him (this is usually referred to as the Covenant of Works).[13] God decided as part of his covenant with humans that he would treat all of humanity based on the actions of Adam (either in obedience or disobedience). In other words, when Adam was placed in the Garden he was on probation (so to speak) before God on behalf of all humankind.

Therefore, when Adam disobeyed God, it wasn't just Adam who incurred divine disfavor but all of Adam's descendants as well. As a result of Adam's fall, sin and guilt were transferred from Adam to all of humanity that would follow (Rom. 5:12, 18–19). Thus, through Adam all people have sinned and are morally accountable to God. Accordingly, original sin, as theologian John Jefferson Davis defines it, refers to "the sinfulness, guilt, and susceptibility to death inherited by all human beings (Christ excepted) from Adam"[14] (Pss. 51:5; 58:3; 1 Cor. 15:22; Eph. 2:3).

The doctrine of original sin also implies that all of Adam's progeny are conceived in sin and have inherited a sin nature, which is a severely debilitating force permeating the core of each person's being (Pss. 51:5; 58:3; Prov. 20:9). Consequently, humans are not sinners because they happen to sin; rather, they sin because they are sinners. The underlying sin nature produces specific sins.

> Surely I was sinful from birth,
>   sinful from the time my mother conceived me. (Ps. 51:5)

> Even from birth the wicked go astray;
>   from the womb they are wayward and speak lies. (Ps. 58:3)

> Therefore, just as sin entered the world through one man, and death through sin, and in this way death came to all people, because all sinned. (Rom. 5:12)

PERSONAL SIN

This type of sin refers to the vast variety of sins committed by people. These sins are distinct from but nevertheless flow from the inherited sin nature stemming from Adam's original sin (1 Kings 8:46; Prov. 20:9; Rom. 3:23; 1 John 1:8). All people frequently commit such sins in thought, word, and deed (in omission as well as commission). That human beings sin is an undeniable and inexorable fact.

Who can say, "I have kept my heart pure; I am clean and without sin"? (Prov. 20:9)

If we claim to be without sin, we deceive ourselves and the truth is not in us. (1 John 1:8)

By describing human beings as fallen sinners, Scripture possesses explanatory power and scope that other holy books and secular philosophies of life clearly lack. In other words, historic Christianity's description of human nature and actions corresponds to reality. The Bible accurately pegs the person in the mirror.

4. What are the effects of sin?

First and foremost, according to Scripture, sin negatively affects one's relationship with God. It produces discord and disconnection. But sin also impacts one's relationship with other people, with oneself, and to some extent even with nature. Sin is not merely a bad habit. Rather, it is, as theologian John Stott describes it, "a deep-seated inward corruption."[15] The sinful nature produces such horrendous effects as spiritual blindness, enslavement to moral corruption, hardness of heart, lawlessness, spiritual death, and eventual physical death (Rom. 1:18–22; 5:10; 6:17; 8:7; 2 Cor. 4:4; Eph. 2:1–3; 4:11–19). Sin has alienated men and women from God, resulting in each person's hostile relationship with the Creator. In the state of sin, humans stand in the precarious and dangerous position of being the objects of God's holy wrath.

We know that the law is spiritual; but I am unspiritual, sold as a slave to sin. I do not understand what I do. For what I want to do I do not do, but what I hate I do. (Rom. 7:14–15)

So I tell you this, and insist on it in the Lord, that you must no longer live as the Gentiles do, in the futility of their thinking. They are darkened in their understanding and separated from the life of God because of the ignorance that is in them due to the hardening of their hearts. (Eph. 4:17–18)

5. What is the extent of sin?

Sin is universal, affecting each and every human being (Ps. 143:2; Eccles. 7:20; Jer. 17:9; Gal. 3:22; James 3:2; 4:4). This sin nature that was inherited from Adam resides at the heart (inner being) of humankind (Jer. 17:9; Matt. 15:19) and affects the entire person—including the mind, will, affections, and body (Eph. 2:3; 4:17–19). Human beings are thus *totally depraved*.[16]

The doctrine of total depravity doesn't mean that people are completely or utterly evil, but it does mean that people are pervasively sinful (sin has affected their total being). This condition has also made it impossible for human beings to merit God's favor (Jer. 17:9; John 5:42; 6:44; Rom. 7:18; 1 Cor. 2:14; Titus 1:15). While fallen human beings are still capable of doing certain morally good acts, the sin nature renders us incapable of living in a way that is pleasing to God. The tendency to overestimate our moral goodness is a sure sign of sin's firm grip.

> There is no one on earth who is righteous,
>   no one who does what is right and never sins. (Eccles. 7:20)

For all have sinned and fall short of the glory of God. (Rom. 3:23)

For out of the heart come evil thoughts—murder, adultery, sexual immorality, theft, false testimony, slander. (Matt. 15:19)

6. What is the sin nature?

The human problem with sin should be thought of as a condition or a state of being (nature) rather than as a problem with specific acts of sin. The nature all people inherit from Adam is in bondage (slavery, captivity) to sin. Human beings, in effect, cannot *not* sin. That doesn't mean that people have no volitional control; rather it means that humans cannot rid themselves of sinful attitudes and expression. Scripture describes human beings as sinners by *nature* (from the Greek *physis*), thus implying that the sinful state of men and women is a *congenital* (present at birth) condition rather than an acquired one.[17] "All of us also lived among them at one time, gratifying the cravings of our sinful nature and following its desires and thoughts. Like the rest, we were by nature objects of wrath" (Eph. 2:3 NIV 1984).

Hamartiology (the doctrine of sin) provides a summary of sin:

Definition: anything contrary to the moral character and commands of God

Origin: found in the volitional will of the creature

Types: original and personal sin

Effects: alienation from God; physical and spiritual death

Extent: universal (total) depravity

Nature: fallen human nature is held in bondage to sin

Given our sinful condition and God's holy and righteous character (Deut. 32:4; Ps. 98:9; Isa. 6:3), all people must face the just wrath of God (Rom. 1:18; Eph. 2:3). A just God must punish the responsible sinner.

Thus historic Christianity asserts that the problem with sin is much worse for humanity than most people recognize. No one will be able to achieve God's true standards of goodness. In God's perfectly righteous eyes, no one is found morally acceptable. From a human perspective, many, if not most, people seem decent enough. But before God, no human being stands as truly benevolent and ethically sound. And a perfectly moral God cannot grade on a curve. God's perfect justice requires that he condemn sin and evil. Thus the bad news about the sinful condition of men and women is bleak and, upon true reflection, naturally leads a person to despair.

Yet in the midst of the desperate circumstance of humans, God has intervened and provided a way of escaping divine judgment through divinely bestowed forgiveness. That forgiveness comes in and through the life, death, and resurrection of the God-man, Jesus Christ. In the next chapter we turn to the gospel (Good News) of Jesus Christ. God's saving grace, with its transforming power, is truly a shocking and dangerous idea.

10

God to the Rescue

People do not merit salvation but receive it as a free gift from
God on the basis of what Christ's death accomplished.

Leon Morris, *The Atonement*

The world watched in anxiety and hope over the summer and fall of 2010 as thirty-three Chilean miners remained trapped in darkness for sixty-nine days. Early reports that they survived the collapse provided an initial boost, and gradually, hopes were buoyed as communication, food, and supplies sustained them under dreadful circumstances. Thanks to the Herculean efforts of many heroes, their emotional rescues were witnessed on live television by an estimated one billion people around the world.[1]

Their story helps illustrate God's divine rescue of sinners: helpless, residing in darkness, in certain peril. God's deliverance has been accomplished by means of a cross. It was not broadcast on any media, but nonetheless the message has been powerfully communicated for centuries and continues to rescue people unfailingly.

Divine Rescue

The bad news about sin (chapter 9) is dire, but God in his infinite love and compassion has provided a way of salvation for sinful human beings. That way comes exclusively through Jesus Christ (John 14:6; Acts 4:12). Salvation can be attained by repenting of (turning away from) one's sins and believing (having confident trust) that Jesus Christ is the divine Messiah, that he died on the cross as a sacrifice for one's sins, and that he rose bodily from the dead (1 Cor. 15:3–4). Salvation is a direct, exclusive gift of God's grace (unmerited kindness), apprehended through faith alone, and totally on the account of Jesus Christ (Eph. 2:8–9).

Salvation by Grace

Christianity's distinctively dangerous idea stands at odds with all other religions of the world and with the so-called spiritual consensus of humanity. The New Testament explicitly teaches that salvation is not earned by human moral effort but is a divinely imparted gift or endowment. Though the three major branches of Christendom have hotly debated the exact meaning of "salvation by grace through faith in Jesus Christ" over several centuries, there remains powerful agreement. Historic Christianity affirms that salvation comes by God's grace alone, solely through faith in Jesus Christ's unique life, death, and resurrection.[2]

The apostle Paul summarizes the gracious formula of salvation:

> For it is by grace you have been saved, through faith—and this not from your-
> selves, it is the gift of God—not by works, so that no one can boast. For we
> are God's workmanship, created in Christ Jesus to do good works, which God
> prepared in advance for us to do. (Eph. 2:8–10 NIV 1984)

This short soteriological passage is so treasure-laden that it is worthy of further exploration.

"By grace you have been saved"

Grace refers to the kindness, unmerited favor, and forgiving love of God. The New Testament Greek word for "grace" is *charis*, and theologian Thomas Oden notes that this word can be "variously nuanced as graciousness, free giving, favor, help, benefaction, an act of good will, a sign of favor."[3] Thus it is God's benevolence that secures salvation. This undeserved blessing is freely bestowed on human beings. God's grace stands as the true, abiding, and unearned cause of human salvation. And the grammar of this verse clearly indicates that salvation is an objectively completed act (thus "you have *been* saved").

"Through faith"

The principal words for "faith" in the New Testament are *pisteuō* (verb) and *pistis* (noun). Faith can be defined as confident trust in and reliance on the person of Jesus Christ as Lord and Savior. Faith is the means or instrument through which salvation is obtained. God's grace in Jesus Christ's life, death, and resurrection has accomplished salvation, and it is through *faith* that a person is made right with God. *Grace* is the cause and *faith* is the means of salvation.

"And this not from yourselves, it is the gift of God"

Contextually, does the phrase beginning with "and this" refer to faith or grace? Which is to be understood as being "not from yourselves"? The grammar of the passage is best understood to mean that the entire *grace through faith process* of salvation is not a human accomplishment.[4] Therefore, even the human *contribution* of faith, while necessary, is nevertheless a gift of God (Rom. 10:17). Human faith is not meritorious in salvation. Theologian Benjamin Warfield explains, "It is not, strictly speaking, even faith in Christ that saves, but Christ that saves through faith. The saving power resides exclusively, not in the act of faith or the attitude of faith or the nature of faith, but in the object of faith."[5]

"Not by works, so that no one can boast"

Because salvation is uniquely the gift of God, no human effort can contribute to it. If human works accomplished salvation, then human beings could take the credit. And if human effort combined with grace to attain salvation, then God would have to share some of the glory with his creatures. But the totally *sola gratia* (Latin, "grace alone") nature of salvation rules out all human boasting.

"We are God's workmanship, created in Christ Jesus to do good works, which God prepared in advance for us to do"

The Greek behind the English word *workmanship* carries with it the idea that the life of the saved person in Christ is a divine *work of art*. Thus good works are not the basis of salvation but are the inevitable result of saving grace. In other words, human good works are the *fruit*, not the *root* of salvation. Or as the Protestant Reformers generally stated, "Faith alone saves, but saving faith is never alone." That saving faith, however, is always *pregnant with good works*. The apostle Paul confirms that idea in one of his other New Testament letters, noting that grace naturally produces a saving "faith expressing itself through love" (Gal. 5:6).

An important parallel passage in Paul's writings that restates the biblical formula of "salvation by grace through faith in Jesus Christ" is found in the pastoral epistle of Titus.

But when the kindness and love of God our Savior appeared, he saved us, not because of righteous things we had done, but because of his mercy. He saved us through the washing of rebirth and renewal by the Holy Spirit, whom he poured out on us generously through Jesus Christ our Savior, so that, having been justified by his grace, we might become heirs having the hope of eternal life. (Titus 3:4–7)

In this summary statement Paul does these three things:

1. He reminds Titus that the gracious nature of salvation ("kindness and love of God") is found in the historical incarnation ("appeared") of the Savior Jesus Christ.
2. Paul underscores again his constant affirmation that salvation is not the result of human righteous acts. Rather, salvation is the result of God's grace and mercy: grace gives people what they don't deserve (salvation), and mercy doesn't give them what they do deserve (judgment).
3. Paul states that salvation comes through the spiritual rebirth of the soul that is carried out by the third person of the Trinity—the Holy Spirit.

Why does the apostle repeat the critical formula of "salvation by grace through faith in Jesus Christ" in his writings to the church? No doubt the reason is that people find it so difficult to accept salvation as a divine gift. The natural human impulse always wants to make works a requirement.

It is clear in Scripture that salvation is by grace:

For all have sinned and fall short of the glory of God, and all are justified freely by his grace through the redemption that came by Christ Jesus. (Rom. 3:23–24)

For he says, "In the time of my favor I heard you, and in the day of salvation I helped you." I tell you, now is the time of God's favor, now is the day of salvation. (2 Cor. 6:2)

But because of his great love for us, God, who is rich in mercy, made us alive with Christ even when we were dead in transgressions—it is by grace you have been saved. (Eph. 2:4–5)

May our Lord Jesus Christ himself and God our Father, who loved us and by his grace gave us eternal encouragement and good hope, encourage your hearts. (2 Thess. 2:16–17)

And salvation is not by works:

Therefore no one will be declared righteous in God's sight by the works of the law; rather, through the law we become conscious of our sin. (Rom. 3:20)

For we maintain that a person is justified by faith apart from the works of the law. (Rom. 3:28)

Know that a person is not justified by the works of the law, but by faith in Jesus Christ. So we, too, have put our faith in Christ Jesus that we may be justified by faith in Christ and not by the works of the law, because by the works of the law no one will be justified. (Gal. 2:16)

You who are trying to be justified by the law have been alienated from Christ; you have fallen away from grace. (Gal. 5:4)

The Work of Jesus Christ on the Cross

Having defined (biblically) the dangerous historic Christian idea of salvation by grace through faith in Jesus Christ, we can now probe the details of the doctrine of the atonement (the redemptive work of Christ on the cross).[6]

What Was the Atonement, and Why Was It Necessary?

As we have seen, God's perfectly holy, righteous, and just character demanded that he punish sinners. So he could not just simply pardon them in a word, because his infinite justice had to be genuinely satisfied. Yet God in his loving-kindness and wisdom chose to punish a substitute instead, thus allowing the sinners to receive mercy. The divinely appointed substitute, who suffered divine wrath in the place of sinners, was none other than God's own incarnate Son, Jesus Christ. God's incredible love is manifest in his decision to punish not the disobedient creatures but his own Son. Our redemption came at great expense for God. On the cross, Jesus Christ the willing substitute became the object of God's just wrath against sin. Through this incredible, atoning sacrifice, God's justice was fully satisfied and his love was fully manifest in granting fallen human beings the privilege of forgiveness.

Seven Specific Word Pictures of Christ's Atoning Work

Like many Christian doctrines, the atonement contains considerable divine mystery. Human reflection on the truth of Christ's sacrifice on the cross is inexhaustible. Seven biblical metaphors help explain this grand work of Christ:[7]

1. SALVATION

As noted previously, *salvation* is a key word, especially in the apostle Paul's explanation of how Jesus Christ's actions on the cross restore a person's relationship with God. The notion of salvation carries with it the idea of being *healed* or *liberated*. It also conveys the concept of being *freed from danger* or *released from captivity*. Thus the person who places his or her faith in Jesus

Christ as Savior and Lord is rescued from the just wrath of God as well as liberated from the dominion of sin and the consequential power of death (Rom. 1:18; 3:9; 5:21).

But believers are also saved into a life of loving and serving God as well as neighbor (1 John 4:19–21). Theologian Alister McGrath describes the dynamic nature of salvation as reflected in the Pauline Epistles: "Paul sees salvation as having past (e.g., Rom. 8:24), present (e.g., 1 Cor. 1:18), and future (e.g., Rom. 13:11) dimensions. It is a process that has begun, but has yet to reach its fulfillment."[8]

> For the grace of God has appeared that offers salvation to all people. It teaches us to say "No" to ungodliness and worldly passions, and to live self-controlled, upright and godly lives in this present age, while we wait for the blessed hope—the appearing of the glory of our great God and Savior, Jesus Christ. (Titus 2:11–13)

> Salvation is found in no one else, for there is no other name under heaven given to mankind by which we must be saved. (Acts 4:12)

2. Legal Substitutionary Sacrifice

Demonstrating the very essence of the gospel, Jesus Christ assumed the identity of sinners and died as their substitute sin-bearer (suffering alienation from God in their stead). Yet in the process of his sacrifice on the cross, he also exchanged his righteousness (derived from his perfect law-keeping) for their sin. Therefore, as heirs of salvation, Christians enjoy both the forgiveness of their sin and the imputed righteousness of Christ that is credited to them through faith.

Martin Luther called the substitutionary death of Christ the *great exchange*. Theologian John Jefferson Davis describes the importance of Christ's penal substitutionary sacrifice: "The Atonement is at the very heart of the Christian faith. Christ died in our place, becoming the object of the wrath of God and the curse of the law, and purchased salvation for all believers."[9]

> God made him who had no sin to be sin for us, so that in him we might become the righteousness of God. (2 Cor. 5:21)

> For Christ died for sins once for all, the righteous for the unrighteous, to bring you to God. (1 Peter 3:18 NIV 1984)

The New Testament uses an ancient bookkeeping analogy in describing how Jesus Christ saves sinners through the *great exchange*—imputing or crediting something (debit or credit) to another's account.

- The sinner's debit account (guilt) is charged to Christ's account.
- Christ's credit account (righteousness) is charged to the believers' account.

Through faith in Jesus Christ's sacrificial death on the cross, believers receive a double benefit:

1. In a negative sense, believers are acquitted or pardoned of all their sin before God because Christ took their sin and guilt upon himself.
2. In a positive sense, the believer's account before God is credited with Christ's perfect law-keeping (righteousness).

3. PROPITIATION

The basic redemptive theme in the Old Testament centers on the idea of *propitiation*—the averting of God's holy wrath against people when they sin. This idea is expressed primarily in two ways:

1. *Israelites who flagrantly violated God's law angered him and deserved death*. In some cases, especially in the wilderness, God killed some of the people (e.g., Num. 11:1, 10; 25:3–4), though he spared the nation as a whole in response to Moses's mediation (Exod. 32:10–14, 30–35). These incidents underscore the point that ultimately human sin must be punished.

2. *God provided for* atonement *(covering) of his people's sins through the blood sacrifice of ritually clean animals* (Lev. 4–6; 16:1–34; 23:26–32). These Old Testament sacrifices did not actually avert God's wrath; rather, they prefigured the final atonement offered by the Messiah, Jesus (Heb. 9:11–14, 28; 10:1–14). By shedding his own blood on the cross of Calvary, Jesus Christ extinguished the wrath of God that was intended for the sinner.

Theologian John Murray explicates the meaning of propitiation: "To propitiate means to 'placate,' 'pacify,' 'appease,' 'conciliate.' And it is this idea that is applied to the atonement accomplished by Christ."[10] The understanding that Christ's death on the cross quenched the wrath of God illustrates that God is indeed good, but not safe.

> My dear children, I write this to you so that you will not sin. But if anybody does sin, we have an advocate with the Father—Jesus Christ, the Righteous One. He is the atoning sacrifice for our sins, and not only for ours but also for the sins of the whole world. (1 John 2:1–2)

> God presented Christ as a sacrifice of atonement, through the shedding of his blood. (Rom. 3:25)

4. RECONCILIATION

Sin has created a real barrier between God and man. One may say that humans, in their state of sin, are completely alienated from God. The relationship, particularly on God's part, is characterized by hostility. Scripture even refers to sinners as enemies of God and objects of his holy wrath. But the death of Christ has assuaged God's wrath and has broken down the wall. God's attitude toward sinners is completely changed because Jesus Christ's sacrifice has removed the source of enmity (human sin). God's love for human beings was manifest even when they were sinners. And the reconciliation of humans with God was motivated by God's incomprehensible love. The dangerous idea of the Gospel is that God loves and saves sinners through Jesus Christ's work on the cross.

> Since we have now been justified by his blood, how much more shall we be saved from God's wrath through him! For if, while we were God's enemies, we were reconciled to him through the death of his Son, how much more, having been reconciled, shall we be saved through his life! (Rom. 5:9–10)

> God was reconciling the world to himself in Christ, not counting people's sins against them. (2 Cor. 5:19)

5. Redemption

The word *redemption* entails the notion of securing the release of someone held in captivity by paying for his or her discharge. According to Scripture, sin is a potent force that has clenched us in its unrelenting grip. Human beings are *held hostage* or enslaved by sin and cannot (of themselves) break free. As in a kidnapping case, Jesus Christ's death on the cross has paid a ransom to set human beings free from sin and death and from the devil. Christ has liberated his people from the bondage caused by sin. His atoning sacrifice has secured a full release for those taken captive by sin. He has freed his people from the dire consequences of their sins. Jesus Christ's death on the cross is thus seen as an act of divine intervention. Christ accomplished on the cross what he and only he could achieve: rescue.

> For even the Son of Man did not come to be served, but to serve, and to give his life as a ransom for many. (Mark 10:45)

> Christ redeemed us from the curse of the law by becoming a curse for us, for it is written: "Cursed is everyone who is hung on a pole." (Gal. 3:13)

> He has died as a ransom to set them free from the sins committed under the first covenant. (Heb. 9:15)

6. Justification

As confirmed sinners, human beings stand guilty before their holy Creator for specifically violating his law. The divine Judge, however, has made a ruling in light of Jesus Christ's atoning death. Justification refers to the judicial (legal) act of God whereby he acquits the believer of wrongdoing and accepts the person as righteous in his sight based on the perfect, imputed (forensic and alien) righteousness of Jesus Christ (Luke 18:14; Acts 13:39; Rom. 3:20, 23–24, 28; 5:1–2; Gal. 2:16; 3:24; Titus 3:5, 7). This divine declaration of justification comes exclusively by God's grace, through the means of human faith alone, and solely because of the saving merits of Christ.

Practically speaking, justification means that for those who trust in Jesus as Savior, God will not hold their sins against them ever again. In other words, God's final judgment on the last day concerning a person's destiny is brought into the present and declared here and now forevermore: not guilty!

When sinners are justified through faith in Christ, they enter into a right relationship with God and thus enjoy restored standing with their Creator-Redeemer. Again, justification not only guarantees legal acquittal in God's presence but also provides the repentant sinner with an imputed righteousness before God. Thus God views his children as if they had never sinned. Believers are both forgiven and righteous in God's eyes. Justification by grace (the cause), through faith (the means), on the account of Jesus Christ's atoning work on the cross (the object) stands at the very center of the historic Christian gospel.[11]

While justification involves a change in the legal status of a person before God (being declared righteous), by distinction, sanctification is the lifelong process of inward moral renewal (being made righteous) initiated by the Holy Spirit.

> So the law was our guardian until Christ came that we might be justified by faith. (Gal. 3:24)

> Therefore, since we have been justified through faith, we have peace with God through our Lord Jesus Christ, through whom we have gained access by faith into this grace in which we now stand. (Rom. 5:1–2)

> Through him everyone who believes is justified from everything you could not be justified from by the law of Moses. (Acts 13:39 NIV 1984)

In his book *The Justification Reader*, Thomas Oden provides a formula on the doctrine of justification:

Source: God
Nature: gracious act
Elements: pardon and acceptance
Scope: all believers
Ground: imputed righteousness of Jesus Christ
Condition: faith alone[12]

7. Adoption

Because sin has severed one's relationship with God (alienation), in a sense, that person has been orphaned. Scripture indicates, however, that building on the gift of justification (legal standing before God), God further grants the privileged status of sonship. Through trusting in Jesus Christ, a person is adopted into the family of God (John 1:12; Rom. 8:15–16; Gal. 4:6; 1 John 3:1). God grants the redeemed the full status and inheritance of being his children and hence they enjoy all the privileges of being sons and daughters of the Most High God. Adoption provides an important familial perspective on God's gracious gift of salvation. Scripture refers to believers as "heirs of God and co-heirs with Christ" who call on God using the intimate Aramaic word *Abba*: "my father" or "daddy" (see Rom. 8:15–17). Salvation results in strangers and slaves becoming part of the family. By God's grace and mercy, the lost have indeed found their way to the family home.

> But when the set time had fully come, God sent his Son, born of a woman, born under the law, to redeem those under the law, that we might receive adoption to sonship. Because you are his sons, God sent the Spirit of his Son into our hearts, the Spirit who calls out, "Abba, Father." So you are no longer a slave, but God's child; and since you are his child, God has made you also an heir. (Gal. 4:4–7)

> Yet to all who received him, to those who believed in his name, he gave the right to become children of God—children born not of natural descent, nor of human decision or a husband's will, but born of God. (John 1:12–13)

Perspectives on the Atonement

The seven powerful word pictures discussed above are used in Scripture to help describe God's gracious gift of salvation; but there's more. Among the historic Christian theological traditions, the cross of Christ has been understood to reflect a variety of perspectives on the overall work of redemption.[13] Some of them include:

1. *Christ's death on the cross as sacrifice*: The atoning death of Christ on Calvary's cross has been interpreted as the *perfect sacrifice* that the various Old Testament sacrifices could only point to and suggest but never accomplish (Heb. 10). Yet Jesus's sacrificial death was unique in that it consisted of a "once for all" atonement (Heb. 10:10) that effectively brought about the forgiveness of human sin. Moreover, in submitting himself on the cross, Christ served as both priest (he officiated) and sacrifice (he offered himself). In light of Christ's crucifixion at the hands of Pontius Pilate in AD 30, there is no other sacrifice for sin available or needed. In this act, sin's staggering cost required the perfect sacrifice: the death of God's one and only Son.

2. *Christ's death on the cross as forgiveness*: The cross of Christ is God's way of dealing finally and fully with the problem of human sin. Jesus Christ's atonement took away sin (John 1:29) and brought about full access to God and pardon and remission from all transgressions. God's forgiveness via the cross results in the complete removal of all estrangement between God and the sinner. God's pardon restores people to a state of favor and he remembers their sin no more. This ability to forgive fully and forever is rooted in God's gracious and merciful nature and separates Christianity from all other religions. Calvary's atonement cleanses a person from all sin, thus providing true forgiveness, peace, and restoration of spiritual union with God (2 Cor. 5:19).

3. *Christ's death on the cross as love*: Jesus Christ's death on the cross stands as a spectacle of God's love for human beings. Though God was justly angered and grieved by human rebellion, he nonetheless responded by providing a way for sinners to escape from his wrath. The Father sent his Son into the world to die in the place of sinners (John 3:16). The incarnate Son of God showed his devotion by leaving his heavenly abode and taking to himself a human nature in order to ultimately lay down his life on a Roman cross. The Savior accepted humiliation, pain, death, and ultimately separation from the Father to accomplish redemption.

The cross shows the profound and costly investment that God made on behalf of humanity. Christ's atoning death is the ultimate demonstration of his special (*agape*) love for his flawed creatures (Rom. 5:8). Theologian Louis Berkhof describes the atonement as being deeply grounded in two of God's attributes: "It is best to say that the Atonement is rooted in the love and justice of God: love offered sinners a way of escape, and justice demanded that the requirements of the law should be met."[14]

4. *Christ's death on the cross as victory*: Jesus Christ has won the ultimate victory. His death on the cross defeated the hidden, hostile forces that enslaved and harassed humanity. The Lord's atoning death and bodily resurrection from the grave permanently defeated such colossal worldly powers as sin, death, and the devil. The Lord Jesus liberated those who had been taken captive (Eph. 4:8). The divine Messiah emerged as the conquering hero who broke the bonds of captivity. Jesus is the Lamb of God who defeated the one who stalks about like a roaring lion seeking to devour our souls (1 Peter 5:8). Christians celebrate a new VE-Day—Victory upon the Earth—through the cross of the Lord and Savior Jesus Christ. The cross as victory demonstrates that God's power in salvation is the most dangerous force of all.

Historic Christianity's Classic Debate on Sin, Grace, and Salvation

The gracious nature of the gospel message—"salvation by grace through faith in Jesus Christ"—sets Christianity apart from all other religions. When it comes to their particular conceptions of salvation, the religions of the world offer very little grace. Yet it should be noted that even Christianity went through a vexing theological controversy regarding the exact nature of sin and grace in relation to salvation. Let's investigate that controversy and note its critical theological outcome for the Christian faith.

The Pelagian Controversy

In the early part of the fifth century, a dispute broke out over the nature of human sin and the necessity of divine grace in salvation. Pelagius, a British lay monk of the late fourth and early fifth centuries, sought to bring about moral reform in the church. He began teaching that human nature was not corrupted by Adam's fall (a denial of original sin) and that salvation was, in effect, an earned reward (*autosoterism*, "self-salvation"). A summary of his beliefs include:

1. Adam's sin affected no one but himself.
2. Human nature was not injured (corrupted) by the fall.
3. There is no hereditary transmission of a sinful nature or guilt from Adam to his descendants, and thus no such thing as original sin.
4. Babies are born in the same condition as Adam before the fall.
5. Adam's descendants are free from both guilt and corruption.
6. Human nature has no inclination or disposition toward evil that must inevitably result in sin (thus men and women need not sin).
7. Adam's actions constitute a bad example for his descendants.[15]

Pelagius asserted that human nature had no natural or inherent inclination toward evil that must inevitably result in sin; thus, human beings need not sin. He believed that sin resulted merely from improper education and bad examples. Theologian Robert Reymond explains the Pelagian perspective on salvation: "Men can save themselves, that is to say, that *their native powers are such that men are capable of doing everything that God requires of them for salvation.*"[16] Pelagius's views were obviously controversial and out of the theological mainstream of Christianity.

Pelagius's contemporary, Augustine of Hippo (AD 354–430), reacted to Pelagianism as a dangerous heresy of self-help salvation.[17] In summary form, Augustine responded to the Pelagian controversy by arguing vigorously that Adam's fallen nature, including both guilt and corruption, had been transmitted to his progeny. Augustine contended that fallen humans, left to their own devices, could never enter into a relationship with God. He even referred to fallen humanity as *massa damnationis*, "a mass of damnation."[18] But God has graciously intervened in humankind's desperate dilemma through the life, death, and resurrection of the God-man, Jesus

Christ. Augustine saw salvation as a gift of God's grace from first to last. What human beings could not do for themselves because of sin, God has accomplished through the grace of Christ. Historical theologian Alister Mc-Grath explains:

> Augustine held "grace" to be the unmerited or undeserved gift of God, by which God voluntarily breaks the hold of sin upon humanity. Redemption is possible only as a divine gift. It is not something which we can achieve ourselves, but is something which has to be done for us. Augustine thus emphasizes that the resources of salvation are located outside of humanity, in God himself. It is God who initiates the process of salvation, not men or women.[19]

Ultimately, Pelagius and Augustine held two fundamentally different views of Christianity. When they went head-to-head theologically, something had to give. McGrath succinctly summarizes the Pelagian-Augustinian debate:

> The ethos of Pelagianism could be summed up as "salvation by merit," whereas Augustine taught "salvation by grace."
>   It will be obvious that these two different theologies involve very different understandings of human nature. For Augustine, human nature is weak, fallen, and powerless; for Pelagius, it is autonomous and self-sufficient. For Augustine, humanity must depend upon God for salvation; for Pelagius, God merely indicated what has to be done if salvation is to be attained, and then leaves men and women to meet those conditions unaided. For Augustine, salvation is an unmerited gift; for Pelagius, salvation is a justly earned reward.[20]

Augustine's view that Christianity is a religion of divine rescue finally overcame Pelagius's self-help religion. In the year AD 431, at the Council of Ephesus, Pelagianism was condemned as a heresy. Much later, the sixteenth-century Protestant Reformers were significantly influenced by Augustine's teaching about salvation by grace, in which he was deeply influenced by the apostle Paul's Epistles. Augustine later became known as the *doctor gratiae* (doctor of grace).[21] Robert Reymond describes historic Christianity's permanent connection with Augustine in the church father's Pauline proclamation of salvation solely by grace: "The church of Jesus Christ, alone among all the religions of the world in this regard, in its best creedal moments is 'supernaturalistic' or 'Augustinian' in its soteric conception."[22]

Augustinian Orthodoxy: "In Adam's Fall We Fell All"

Augustine is especially recognized as having had a profound impact on how Christian orthodoxy defined and formulated essential Christian doctrine. Since the idea of original sin is presently somewhat out of favor in some quarters of the Christian church, it may be instructive to review some of Augustine's provocative thinking on Adam's catastrophic fall into sin.[23]

According to Augustine, Adam in his original state of creation was free, but nevertheless still dependent on divine grace. Augustine saw human beings as utterly reliant on God's unmerited favor at every stage of their life and being. Though Adam was created immortal, he was not impervious to death, but he had the capacity for bodily immortality. In fact, Augustine wrote that if Adam had remained obedient and not sinned, he would have been confirmed in divine holiness. Thus Augustine saw Adam's three states as:

1. *Original State*: Adam's original state is characterized by the Latin phrase *posse non peccare et mori* ("able not to sin and die"). That is, in Adam's original state of created righteousness, he had the capacity to avoid sin and the spiritual and physical death that resulted from it.

2. *Potential State*: Adam's potential state is expressed in the Latin phrase *non posse peccare et mori* ("not able to sin and die"). That is, if Adam had remained obedient, God would have transformed him to be forever confirmed in holiness and therefore apart from sin and the resulting death that necessarily follows it. But one should not think that Augustine was in any way implying that God was taken by surprise when Adam sinned. God's sovereign nature doesn't allow for that scenario.

3. *Actual State*: Adam's actual state is reflected in the Latin phrase *non posse non peccare et mori* ("not able not to sin and die"). Because of Adam's willful act of rebellion, he became enslaved by sin and could not of his own will avoid its power and lethal consequence. Augustine viewed Adam's fallen state as pitiful and damnable before God.

Augustine contended that all humanity is connected to Adam in an organic sense and that Adam's sin nature (including both guilt and corruption) was transmitted to his progeny. Augustine believed the whole human race was germinally present in Adam and therefore actually sinned in him. Augustine also argued eloquently that the only hope for fallen and enslaved humanity is the grace of God that comes in and through the life, death, and resurrection of the God-man, Jesus Christ.

While many Protestant, evangelical theologians view Adam as being the *federal representative* of humanity (Rom. 5:12, 18–19), a sizable segment of the evangelical theological community also embraces an Augustinian view of sin and affirms the absolute necessity of grace in salvation.

Revealed early in Scripture and emanating throughout, the doctrine of original sin is a critical biblical teaching that helps Christians reflect on the great divine grace that rescues us from our enslavement to sin. Being saved by grace and not by works is a dangerous idea extraordinaire.

Jesus Christ: Lord and Savior

The solution to our greatest problem (sin that separates us from God) is found in the perfect life, sacrificial death, and glorious resurrection of the God-man, Jesus Christ. Christians can be comforted that no matter how great their sin, God's gracious gift of salvation in Christ's atoning death is both complete and permanent. His perfect love and justice meet together in the atonement for all to see. As the apostle John declared: "This is love: not that we loved God, but that he loved us and sent his Son as an atoning sacrifice for our sins" (1 John 4:10).

How Historic Christianity's Most Hopeful Dangerous Idea Changed the World

The gospel message that salvation is an exclusive gift of God's grace received only through faith in the person of Jesus Christ sets Christianity apart from all other religions. The natural human religious instinct is to believe that God accepts people on the basis of their own good works. Thus, historic Christianity has challenged all people to think in a radically different way about how they find acceptance before God. This fundamental difference in orientation has changed the way untold numbers of people view religion altogether.

Yet Christianity itself over the centuries has at times had to battle against the seemingly never-say-die heresy of self-help salvation. Augustine confronted a version of it in the theology of Pelagius. The Protestant reformer Martin Luther encountered it again in the form of medieval Catholicism. But the rebirth of the gospel of grace has always succeeded in both reforming Christendom and changing the world.

The Reformation movement of the sixteenth century was at its heart a theological debate about how to define the gospel of Jesus Christ. But out of that contentious religious dispute emerged a renewed affirmation of the truth of salvation by grace alone. The Protestant Reformation was arguably the most influential movement in the history of Europe, if not the world. Not only was a new branch of Christendom birthed, but the cultural changes and reforms produced by the movement extended to all areas of society such as economics, politics, education, vocation, science, and the arts. All of this "positive upheaval" was sparked by a renewal of the gospel of grace.

Guilt, Grace, and Gratitude: A Personal Reflection

Sometimes in my heartfelt effort to lead a godly life I can become discouraged with my lack of spiritual growth and vibrancy. I have been a Christian for more than thirty years and have advanced training in the study of Scripture and theology, yet I still battle against such sins as anger, envy, gluttony, selfishness, lust, pride, and sloth. During tough times or in more insecure moments I even entertain the idea that my standing before God depends on my daily performance in living out the Christian life. But that mind-set creates great consternation within me because I am then tempted to think that God is pleased with me or loves me only on those days when I seem to evidence a more Christlike spirituality and devotion.

I admit this tendency because I believe this scenario plays itself out in the lives of many, if not most, Christians. For some believers, this misguided spiritual narrative becomes their constant perspective on how God views them. This way of seeing one's relationship with God, however, can make the daily Christian life deeply burdensome.

Scripture clearly teaches that saving faith will provide evidence of its genuineness in acts of loving obedience (Gal. 5:6). But the life of sanctification—being morally retransformed into the image of God—is challenging and never completed in this earthly sojourn. What has been helpful to me during times of spiritual insecurity is remembering what my Reformed theological tradition calls the three G's of salvation—Guilt, Grace, and Gratitude.[24]

1. *Guilt*: God's law shows me both the holiness of God's character and that I have failed to meet his moral standards. This awareness—made possible through God's Spirit—then leads me to confession of sin and a desire for genuine repentance.
2. *Grace*: The gospel (Good News) then teaches me that Jesus Christ died on the cross on my behalf to take away all my sins. This awareness leads to an understanding that God loves me and that he views me through the prism of Christ's perfect righteousness. I therefore stand securely pardoned of my sin and righteous in the Lord's presence.
3. *Gratitude*: Knowing that Christ has freely given me salvation that I don't deserve and could never earn motivates me to live a life that reflects sincere gratitude to God for his grace. I then seek to please God with my life, not in order to earn or retain God's love but instead because I already know God's love and forgiveness in Christ Jesus.

Living by Grace

The grace of God teaches us that when we struggle and fail in Christlikeness, God freely forgives us. All we need to do is acknowledge our sin to God and accept his ongoing forgiveness (1 John 1:9). We then start living anew, seeking to demonstrate gratitude to God for his incredible and ongoing grace. As Christians we must adopt a lifestyle of confession, repentance, and the acceptance of a renewed forgiveness before the Lord. But we must also appreciate that no believer practices perfect confession and repentance of sin before God. And yet God's forever-forgiving grace keeps us securely united with our Lord Jesus Christ.

God's grace can also be appropriately understood as a power source in the life of believers. Therefore, we can call on God's grace to empower us to face the challenges of living for him and to continue growing in faithful obedience (2 Cor. 3:18). Thus, living by grace means we need not fear that God will stop loving us or that he loves us only when we are walking in total obedience before him. God's unmerited favor and love can dispel our anxious insecurities and motivate a life of gratitude (Rom. 8:15; 1 John 4:17–18).

The gift of salvation, then, comes by grace alone, through faith alone, and in and through the person of Jesus Christ alone. But that amazing and dangerous idea is hard for us to accept, and we must constantly remind ourselves of its everlasting truth. Once grace penetrates hearts, individuals, families, communities, and civilizations can be transformed.

Further Suggested Reading

Carson, D. A. *Scandalous: The Cross and Resurrection of Jesus*. Wheaton: Crossway, 2010.

Hoekema, Anthony A. *Saved by Grace*. Grand Rapids: Eerdmans, 1989.

Morris, Leon. *The Apostolic Preaching of the Cross*. 3rd edition. 1965. Reprint, Grand Rapids: Eerdmans, 1992.

———. *The Atonement*. Downers Grove, IL: InterVarsity, 1983.

Murray, John. *Redemption Accomplished and Applied*. 1955. Reprint, Grand Rapids: Eerdmans, 1975.

Oden, Thomas C. *The Justification Reader*. Grand Rapids: Eerdmans, 2002.

Packer, J. I. *Concise Theology*. Wheaton: Tyndale, 1993.

Stott, John R. W. *The Cross of Christ*. 2nd edition. Downers Grove, IL: InterVarsity, 2006.

Discussion Questions

1. What exactly is sin and why is it so offensive to God?

2. What is *original* sin and how does it affect human beings?

3. What is it that believers are actually saved from in the death of Christ?

4. What metaphors does the Bible use in describing the meaning of Christ's death on the cross?

5. What is the saving grace of God? What is involved in the believer living the Christian life by grace?

HUMANITY'S VALUE AND DIGNITY

11

Secular Humanism and the *Imago Dei*

> That God made man in his own image, so that humans are like God as no other earthly creatures are, tells us that the special dignity of being human is that, as humans, we may reflect and reproduce at our own creaturely level the holy ways of God, and thus act as his direct representatives on earth. This is what humans are made to do, and in one sense we are human only to the extent that we are doing it.
>
> J. I. Packer, *Concise Theology*

The rise of the so-called *new* atheism in the marketplace of ideas raises questions about an emerging secular world- and life-view. For example: What does a truly secular society look like? If God doesn't exist and humans are just highly evolved animals, what value and dignity would each individual person possess? And what ethical principles could a naturalistic worldview genuinely ground and justify for human civilization?

The Death of God

These questions about a secular perspective and ethic are not really new. Nineteenth-century German philosopher Friedrich Nietzsche (1844–1900) thought and wrote extensively about these issues. Nietzsche was an important forerunner of atheistic existentialism and secular postmodernism. He is probably best known, however, for his shocking proclamation: "God is dead."[1]

What Nietzsche proposed by announcing the "death" of God some two hundred years ago was that (as he saw it) the traditional view of God (Christian theism) was no longer a viable belief for most intellectuals in Western culture. Nietzsche thought that historic Christianity was in steady decline, especially among the Western world's leading thinkers, because advances in science had shown life to be the mere product of naturalistic evolution. Astronomy had revealed the earth to have no special place in the cosmos (Copernicus), and biology had shown human beings to be the product of natural forces (Darwin). Intellectuals increasingly viewed the God of the Bible as a myth.

According to Nietzsche, the problem this secular scenario poses is that the ethics of Western civilization are grounded in the Judeo-Christian concept of God. Thus God serves as the ultimate basis for morality. So a collapse of belief in God would reveal that ethics has no secure metaphysical foundation. In other words, ethics and values (the good) must be anchored in the nature of metaphysical reality (the real and true). The perceived danger is that nihilism (the view that there is no meaning, purpose, and value to life) would reign supreme.[2] Moral nihilism means that there is no objective foundation for morality. Human society would therefore lack a secure moral foundation. And without God to provide objective meaning, humankind would be cast adrift in a meaningless and valueless existence.

Christian thinker Dinesh D'Souza vividly describes how Nietzsche's declared death of the biblical God destroys the value and dignity of the very people said to be made in his image:

> Nietzsche's argument is illustrated in considering two of the central principles of Western civilization: "All men are created equal" and "Human life is precious." Nietzsche attributes both ideas to Christianity. It is because we are created equal and in the image of God that our lives have moral worth and that we share the rights to life, liberty, and the pursuit of happiness. Nietzsche's warning was that none of these values make sense without the background moral framework against which they were formulated. A post-Christian West, he argued, must go back to the ethical drawing board and reconsider its most cherished values, which include its traditional belief in the equal dignity of every human life.[3]

In response to this inevitable moral and societal collapse due to a glaring lack of metaphysical foundations, Nietzsche contends that human beings can follow one of two paths: passive acceptance or active revision. If we passively accept the breakdown of truth and values, we succumb to the ultimate meaninglessness and nothingness of life. Since God is dead, we are orphans without such meaning and purpose. This nihilistic worldview scenario carries with it incredible pessimism, angst, and existential despair.

The other path is what Nietzsche himself advocates. He calls for a "transvaluation of values"—laying the foundation for a strictly secular ethic and value system.[4] In contrast to the defeated passivist, the activist can face this inevitable nihilism by letting the old religious values pass away and in their place creating a brand-new, secular ethic through strength of will. Thus Nietzsche's concept of the "will to power"[5] rejects the *Herdenmoral* (slave morality of the religious herd) for the *Herrenmoral* (master secular morality).

Nietzsche asserted that the *Übermensch*[6] (superman or free spirit) overcomes the moral nihilism by constructing a secular meaning and value to life. The autonomous superman forges this secular life and value system as if it were a work of art. So in light of God's death, brave and forceful individuals create for themselves a purely secular meaning and value to life. Nietzsche's secular revolution of values can be stated:

1. *God Is Dead*: Intellectuals increasingly view God as a myth.
2. *Nihilism*: Without the Christian God, Western culture lacks a foundation for morality and meaning.
3. *Transvaluation of Values*: A strictly secular foundation for values can and must be laid.
4. *Will to Power*: A secular master morality must replace a religious slave morality.
5. *The Ubermensche*: The autonomous superman creates his own secular morality.

At least one prominent, contemporary person seeks to realize what Nietzsche envisioned. A probe into this ethicist's value system will put us in a good position to contrast it with historic Christianity's dangerous idea about the true nature of human beings.

Peter Singer's Brave New World

Australian philosopher Peter Singer, a bioethicist at Princeton University, seems to have picked up the baton from Friedrich Nietzsche when it comes to forging a post-Christian, secular foundation for ethics. An atheist and utilitarian ethicist, Singer argues that God does not exist and Christianity is a fictional religion. Therefore, the belief that human beings were created in the image of God is patently false and, by implication, so are such notions as *human dignity* and the *sanctity of human life*.

Singer rejects all religious foundations for ethics. In their place he promotes a utilitarian ethic: pursuit of the greatest good, or preferences, for the greatest number. He outspokenly advocates late-term abortions, infanticide in the first month of life, active euthanasia for the elderly, and even bestiality.[7] He is also a leading advocate for animal rights—affirming that some human beings are not persons (those lacking self-awareness and autonomy: the unborn, newborns, the mentally disabled, the senile aged) and that some nonhumans are indeed persons. He states:

> I have argued that the life of a fetus (and even more plainly, of an embryo) is of no greater value than the life of a nonhuman animal at a similar level of rationality, self-awareness, capacity to feel and so on, and that because no fetus is a person, no fetus has the same claim to life as a person.[8]

Singer condemns *speciesism*—the view that human beings hold a privileged ethical position above animals—and equates it with racism and sexism.[9] In his 1994 book, *Ethics*, he states his values: "Once we admit that Darwin was right when he argued that human ethics evolved from the social instincts that we inherited from our non-human ancestors, we can put aside the hypothesis of a divine origin for ethics."[10] And in a *New Yorker* article titled "The Dangerous Philosopher," Michael Specter quotes Singer as saying, "The notion that human life is sacred just because it's human life is medieval."[11]

D'Souza illustrates how Singer's secular, ethical system comports with the ideas Nietzsche expressed some two hundred years ago:

> Singer resolutely takes up a Nietzschean call for a "transvaluation of values," with a full awareness of the radical implications. He argues that we are not creations of God but rather mere Darwinian primates. We exist on an unbroken continuum with animals. Christianity, he says, arbitrarily separated man and animal, placing human life on a pedestal and consigning the animals to the status of tools for human well-being. Now, Singer says, we must remove Homo sapiens from this privileged position and restore the natural order. This translates into more rights for animals and less special treatment for human beings.[12]

Nietzsche and Singer agree that a secular ethic must replace the traditional Judeo-Christian ethic that laid the foundation for Western civilization for two millennia. They also agree that the new secular order will radically affect the position of human beings as image bearers of God. Both secular philosophers recognize that the dignity and sanctity of human life is directly tied to the biblical teaching of humans made in the image of God.

At this threshold of secularism's grand dismissal of humans' inherent dignity and the overall sanctity of human life, historic Christianity's sixth dangerous idea comes to bear. Let's explore what historic Christianity affirms about human beings made in the image of God. Then we'll be in a good position to test which view of humanity (secular or biblical) carries greater explanatory power.

Historic Christianity's Sixth Dangerous Idea

What follows is an introduction to the historic Christian doctrine of what it means to be made in the image of God. We'll trace the doctrine's biblical basis and compare how the image of God is impacted both by the fall of humanity into sin and by the redemption accomplished by Jesus Christ. Later we'll explore both the moral and apologetics implications of this truly dangerous biblical idea.

Biblical Anthropology

According to the Bible, the central defining characteristic of humans is that of divine image bearer.[13] Human beings are created in the expressed *image of God* (Latin, *imago Dei*).

From a biblical perspective, what Scripture reveals about humanity's creation and the implications of being made in God's image impact every aspect of the way Christians sees themselves and live life. The effects of both the fall and redemption on this image are critical components of the historic Christian view of anthropology (used in this sense to mean the nature of human beings).

Imago Dei: *A Divine Reflection*

The Bible reveals that of all God's creatures, *only humans* were created in the expressed image of God. While Scripture mentions the *imago Dei* several times (Gen. 5:1; 9:6; 1 Cor. 11:7; Col. 3:10; James 3:9), Genesis 1:26–27 is the most important text that describes this vital doctrinal truth:

> Then God said, "Let us make mankind in our image, in our likeness, so that they may rule over the fish in the sea and the birds in the sky, over the livestock and all the wild animals, and over all the creatures that move along the ground." So God created mankind in his own image, in the image of God he created him; male and female he created them.

A careful examination of this passage shows that Hebrew references to *image* (*tselem*) and *likeness* (*dᵉmût*) convey the idea of an object similar to or representative of something else, but not identical to it.[14] Further, the words *image* and *likeness* should not be understood as referring to two different things but rather as interchangeable terms that reflect a Hebrew form of synonymous parallelism.[15] The New Testament Greek word for *image* (*eikōn*) conveys virtually the same meaning as the Hebrew. Both languages indicate that God created humans to be similar to himself, but certainly not identical to himself. Therefore, from a biblical perspective, human beings are in some sense both *like* and *unlike* the God who made them.

What exactly does it mean for a person to be *like* God? Three qualifications must be made before examining this question further:

1. *Scripture contains an implicit rather than explicit explanation of the image of God.* A definition for *imago Dei* must come from drawing proper inferences from the biblical text, buttressed by careful reflection about the state of the human condition.

2. *A complete understanding of the meaning of* imago Dei *simply isn't possible.* To do so requires an exhaustive understanding of God's nature (in addition to that of humans), which is not possible.[16] Finite creatures by definition cannot comprehend or fully fathom the infinite nature of God; therefore, by necessity people are faced with mystery and limited knowledge.

3. *Throughout church history, different theological traditions have taken a variety of positions on the exact meaning of the divine image.* For example, Catholic, Lutheran, Reformed, and Wesleyan traditions each emphasize different aspects.[17] The various strands of Christian theology are certainly not monolithic in every detail of theology.

Nevertheless, while acknowledging these three important considerations, it's still possible to present a basic biblical description of the meaning of the *imago Dei*. Inferences drawn from Scripture and philosophical reflection about the nature of human beings bring forth a common Christian perspective.

Some theologians emphasize humans' personality in suggesting how people are most like God. Evangelical theologian Millard Erickson says, "The image is the powers of personality which make man, like God, a being capable of interacting with other persons, of thinking and reflecting, and of willing freely."[18] To some degree we mirror God and in certain respects even represent God.

Humans' Natural Image

Many evangelical theologians comfortably distinguish between the *natural image* and the *moral image*.[19] The broader of the two, the natural image, includes constituent aspects of humans' created nature—their spiritual, intellectual, volitional, relational, immortal, and powerful capacities. The moral nature involves a more restricted sense of God's image based on humans' *original* knowledge, righteousness, and holiness. Adam in the Garden of Eden possessed these qualities before his fall into sin.

Humans' natural image appears to include at least six uniquely expressed endowments or gifts:[20]

1. *Human beings are spiritual.* Although people are material creatures, their human nature includes two aspects: physical and spiritual. Having a soul or

spirit makes humans a union of both spiritual and material natures, in other words a *whole person*.

Genesis 2:7 alludes to this union by describing the man he created (Adam) as a "living being." Possessing a distinctive spiritual nature gives individuals the ability to know and relate to God through prayer, worship, repentance, and so forth. Inherent spiritual needs include a tremendous desire for a relationship with the Creator. Humans' creatureliness makes that need for companionship their most basic necessity.

2. *Human beings are personal, self-conscious, and rational.* People possess a mind, will, and emotions. They are uniquely capable of grasping thought, knowledge, and truth (propositional and nonpropositional)—especially truth about God.

Theologian Cornelius Plantinga captures the provocative thought of Reformer John Calvin on this point: "Calvin understood that God created human beings to hunt and gather truth, and that, as a matter of fact, the capacity for doing so amounts to one feature of the image of God in them (Col. 3:10)."[21] Though humans are capable of rational thought, emotion also plays an important role in their lives. People are uniquely capable of feeling, expressing, and evaluating their emotional responses.

3. *Human beings are volitional.* Humans possess free agency, making them capable of authentic deliberation and choice. Ultimately they are morally accountable to God for those choices. Humans are the only creatures aware of the moral spheres in life and are responsible for their actions.

4. *Human beings are relational.* Human beings are uniquely capable of profound interpersonal communication and relationships with other humans and with God. The inherent need to interact with others appears to be a distinctive feature of human nature. While various animal species demonstrate community interaction to some degree, human beings communicate among themselves and with God on a much deeper level.

5. *Human beings are immortal.* They possess a God-given or derived immortality.[22] Humans are unique among all physical creatures in that they face an eternal destiny either with God (redemption) or apart from him (damnation).

6. *Human beings are powerful.* People exercise dominion—control, custodianship, power—over the natural order and over Earth's living and nonliving natural resources. This environmental dominion is possible principally because of humanity's unparalleled intellectual capacities.

This natural image manifests in distinct ways how humans differ from Earth's other creatures. Human beings possess spiritual, personal, self-conscious, and rational components. Similar to God they are volitional, relational, immortal, and powerful—unlike any other creatures.

More recent theological discussions concerning the meaning of the image of God take the six endowments discussed above and subdivide them further into three categories.

1. *Resemblance view*: This position asserts that humankind possesses a formal nature that serves to resemble God. This nature then bears certain qualities, characteristics, or endowments (spiritual, rational, volitional, etc.) that make humankind like God. This position represents the basic view discussed earlier.

2. *Relational view*: This perspective, while allowing for the idea of formal traits, nevertheless insists that humans are most like God when it comes to their unique relational qualities. Thus, it is humankind's ability to engage in complex interpersonal relationships that best reflects the divine (echoing the community life among the divine persons of the Trinity).

3. *Representative view*: This viewpoint insists that being made in the image of God is more about what a person does than what a person is. Thus, when human beings perform certain functions (e.g., take dominion over nature or appropriately represent God on Earth) then the divine image is most deeply reflected.

Rightly formulated and integrated, all three positions could express the different ways that human beings reflect the natural image of their Creator.

Humans' Moral Image

As originally created, Adam possessed direct knowledge of God and an inherent righteousness and holiness (Eccles. 7:29). This moral image was evident during Adam's time in the Garden of Eden prior to his fall into sin (Gen. 1–2).

Theologian Charles Hodge notes the importance of being made in God's image and, in a certain sense, on God's level: "He [man] belongs to the same order of being as God himself, and is therefore capable of communion with his Maker."[23] It is being made in God's image that elevates humans to God's plane and makes it possible for human beings to know God at all.

Though angels have a unique relationship and access to God and are themselves pure spirit (without physical bodies), even they are not described as *divine image bearers*. Some theologians think humans bear that privilege because *image* means a physical representative and the angels are not physical. And though God made the animals out of the dust of the ground like humans, they also do not possess the distinctive divine image.

Dutch theologian Herman Bavinck marks the distinction: "While all creatures display *vestiges* of God, only a human being is the *image* of God."[24] Humanity alone is described as the crown of God's creation—the pinnacle of God's creative activity (Ps. 8:5–8). Bavinck explains further:

> The entire world is a revelation of God, a mirror of his attributes and perfections. Every creature in its own way and degree is the embodiment of a divine thought. But among creatures only man is the image of God, God's highest and richest self-revelation and consequently the head and crown of the whole creation.[25]

Both Like and Unlike the Creator

Biblical anthropology reveals that human beings are "created persons."[26] Of course this view is paradoxical, for being a *creature* implies that people are absolutely dependent on God. Yet being a *person* means that we possess a relative independence (autonomy) from God.

The Bible, without explaining it, sets humans' *personhood* (like God) and *creatureliness* (unlike God) side by side as compatible truths, introducing a scriptural mystery. God's power, wisdom, and ability to create elude the human ability to comprehend (Rom. 11:33–36). According to the historic Christian faith, however, truths of divine revelation may range above reason but not against it. Using reason can help unravel some of the mystery of how humans can be like God yet *not* like him at the same time. Exploring his communicable and incommunicable characteristics sets forth some important distinctions in the Christian position.

Like God

God created human beings with the ability to understand and imitate, at least to some degree, his *communicable* attributes (seen in the natural and moral nature of the *imago Dei*). These characteristics belong to humanity, though in a significantly limited way. Like God, people are moral beings. They display knowledge, wisdom, goodness, love, holiness, justice, and truthfulness.

These attributes in humans, however, differ in degree from those found in God. In him the same characteristics are unlimited and perfect. This difference makes people fundamentally distinct in their creaturehood.

Unlike God

God's divinity makes him differ *in kind* from people. His *incommunicable* attributes separate God completely from his creatures, and this difference is known as the Creator-creature distinction. These qualities consist of such metaphysical characteristics as self-existence (independence), immutability (changelessness), infinity (without limitation), and eternality (timelessness).

The *Imago Dei* and the Fall of Humans

Though human beings were created to reflect God's image, when Adam disobeyed God (Gen. 3) all subsequent humanity inherited sinfulness, guilt, moral corruption, and both physical and spiritual death (Rom. 5:12–21). In a state of rebellion, all people suffer from a totally depraved nature that keeps them alienated from a holy and just God. This depravity, while not making people completely evil, nevertheless corrupts our entire being, including our mind, will, body, and spirit (Pss. 51:5; 58:3; Rom. 1:18–21; 6:23; 8:7–8; Eph. 2:1–3; 4:17–19). But to what extent does this condition affect the *imago Dei*? Did sin completely erase God's image from humankind?

Humans' *original* knowledge, righteousness, and holiness—the moral image necessary for us to have a relationship with God—were eradicated by the fall. Once sin infected humanity, all human beings became unrighteous lawbreakers separated from God (Rom. 3:23; Gal. 5:19–21).

Yet the natural image—though unquestionably tarnished and obscured—was not completely lost. As a popular saying indicates, the natural image was "effaced but not erased." After the fall, human beings remain God's image bearers (Gen. 9:6; James 3:9), yet in the state of sin, people are certainly less like God than they were before.

With humanity's original righteousness gone, even the capacities of humans' natural image became out of sync (Rom. 1:18–21; Eph. 2:1–3; 4:17–19). To some degree, sin's impact disordered them.[27] Human beings became morally and spiritually obtuse, their noetic (cognitive or belief-forming) faculties dulled.

Biblical scholars and apologists disagree as to the exact nature and extent of the fall's noetic effects on man. They question whether the category of sinful effects is moral (affecting the ethical nature of man) or cognitive (affecting the intellectual nature of man) or both. And they deliberate as to the extent—is it partial or total? Regardless, it appears that the closer an individual comes to acknowledging God and accepting moral accountability before him (the spiritual and moral spheres of life), the more sin seems to impair spiritual judgment and perspective.

The total depravity of human beings makes it impossible to live a God-pleasing life. Consequently, sinful people must depend on God's saving grace to regenerate a positive relationship with him and experience salvation.

The *Imago Dei* and Redemption in Christ

While the moral image was entirely lost because of the fall, Scripture declares that a saving relationship with Jesus Christ will restore it. The apostle Paul states that through God's grace believers can "put on the new self, which is being renewed in knowledge in the image of its Creator" (Col. 3:10), be "transformed into his image" (2 Cor. 3:18), and be "conformed to the image of his Son" (Rom. 8:29). God the Holy Spirit progressively restores his moral image in the believer through the lifelong process of sanctification (being made righteous in character).

The Bible declares that when Jesus Christ returns to Earth at his second coming, "We shall be like him, for we shall see him as he is" (1 John 3:2). In other words, human beings will undergo a complete transformation of character that will result in true Christlikeness (glorification). Finally, humankind will be set free from sin's devastating effects.

According to the New Testament, the fullest expression of God's image is not seen in humanity either before or after the fall, or even in redemption. Rather, this image is found—complete and total—in the person of Jesus Christ. Scripture speaks of the God-man Jesus as "the image and glory of God" (1 Cor. 11:7), the one "who is the image of God" (2 Cor. 4:4), "the image of the invisible God" (Col. 1:15), and the Son who is "the radiance of God's glory and the exact representation of his being" (Heb. 1:3). To view and understand God's image correctly and fully one must look to the person of the incarnate Christ.

God's perfect image in Jesus ties together two Christian truths: the *imago Dei* and the incarnation.[28] While it seems difficult, if not impossible, for God to take the form of a creature with little resemblance to himself (such as an animal), making humans in the divine image at creation foreshadowed and facilitated God's decisive entrance into the world as the God-man (John 1:14; Phil. 2:6–11; Col. 2:9).

Reformed theologian Anthony Hoekema explains that "it was only because man had been created in the image of God that the Second Person of the Trinity could assume human nature."[29] God made humans in his own image because all along he planned to become one at the incarnation in order to redeem lost sinners (2 Tim. 1:9–10). That's why Jesus told his apostles that to see the Son was to see the perfect image of the Father (John 14:8–9).

The *Imago Dei* and Humanitarian Implications

Though marred by sin, all people—believers and nonbelievers—reflect the image of God. This foundational biblical teaching launches the Christian view that each individual possesses inherent dignity, moral worth, and eternal value. Evangelical theologian John Jefferson Davis states, "God's creation is immense, but man, as the crown of creation, has a dignity and grandeur that surpasses that of the cosmos."[30] Humanity's unique worth is directly tied to being made in God's special image.

The *imago Dei* lays the foundation for the sacredness of human life. This image makes human life unrepeatable and worthy of reverence. All people—regardless of race, sex, class, age, standing, health, appearance, or other distinctions—deserve respect and dignified treatment as the crown of creation.[31] Even people with limited mental capacities and various other physical handicaps are made in God's image and therefore possess immeasurable worth. Though physical conditions may keep them from reflecting all of God's endowments in the usual way, this by no means diminishes their inherent dignity and value as human beings.

In regard to our treatment of fellow human beings, the historic Christian position embraces the strong biblical prohibitions against slander and slurs. New Testament author James asserts, "With the tongue we praise our Lord and Father, and with it we curse human beings, who have been made in God's likeness" (James 3:9). Praising God and then cursing the people made in his image is morally inconsistent and sinful.

Similarly, the biblical prohibition against murder and the allowance for capital punishment stem directly from humans being made in God's image. After the great divine judgment of the flood, Noah was told, "Whoever sheds human blood, by humans shall their blood be shed; for in the image of God has God made mankind" (Gen. 9:6). Murder is reprehensible because it steals the life of the individual and thus robs family, friends, and society. But it also assaults God because the victim was made in his image.[32] As Hoekema states, "To touch the image of God is to touch God himself; to kill the image of God is to do violence to God himself."[33]

According to Scripture, the murderer's heinous action causes him to forfeit his own right to life (a right that is not absolute) and become subject to retributive justice, "a life for a life" (Exod. 21:23 NLT). The punishment must match the crime.[34] In the New Testament, God grants state authorities the right to implement the death penalty (Rom. 13:1–5). This action signifies a willingness to carry out the ultimate punishment in order to protect people. From a biblical perspective, capital punishment serves both as a retributive form of punishment and as a viable deterrent to acts of murder.

Human beings derive value and worth from being made in the image of the true and living God. Life is valuable because of its Creator's ultimate value.

Imago Dei and the Secular Culture of Death

As noted at the beginning of this chapter, some people today reject the biblical God's existence and likewise the idea that human beings are made in God's image. This secular approach of spurning the *imago Dei* has resulted in the loss of the basic sanctity of human life and has ushered in a *culture of death* when it comes to paramount moral issues such as abortion and euthanasia (to name only two).

In contrast, the historic Christian *culture of life* dramatically differs on these critical moral issues. It is built on four broad biblical principles:

1. The scriptural teaching that humans are made in the expressed image and likeness of God (Gen. 1:27) lays the foundation for the basic dignity and sacredness of human life.
2. Human life is endowed with great value in the sight of God the Creator (Matt. 16:26).

3. The biblical value system maintains the dignity and worth of each and every human being (Ps. 8:3–6), regardless of the state of development or physical dependency, from the moment of conception until the time of natural death.

4. The truths of general revelation found in God's created order serve to confirm the biblical declaration of the value and dignity of human life (Rom. 2:14–15).[35]

Application to Ethical Issues

Human beings are most vulnerable at the beginning and end of their lives. Thus abortion on demand and active euthanasia remain direct moral challenges to historic Christian ethics. Let's briefly explore how the sanctity of life ethic (via the *imago Dei*) contrasts with the common contemporary positions on abortion and euthanasia.

Abortion

Unborn human life is precious, and unborn babies' human rights should be preserved and protected by societal law. Following are several biblical implications concerning the unborn:

- The Bible declares that all innocent life is sacred in light of being made in God's image (Gen. 1:27; 5:1), and shedding the blood of innocents is condemned as murder (Gen. 9:6).
- Scripture reveals that God—not an unguided, natural biological process—is responsible for the creation of human life in the womb (Job 10:8–13; 31:13–15).
- Scripture speaks of the unborn with the same personal terms that are applied to children after they have been born (Hebrew, *yeled*; Greek, *brephos*; Exod. 21:22; Luke 1:41–44; Acts 7:19), thus connecting prenatal and postnatal human life.
- God relates to the unborn human in a personal way (Ps. 139:13–14; Jer. 1:5; Luke 1:44), thus implying that they are genuine human beings with personal rights to legal protection.
- Since God loves and values unborn human life long before that life is personally self-conscious (Ps. 139:13–16), it seems reasonable to conclude that *personhood* is a metaphysical category and that the unborn are actual humans who are undergoing development and laden with great potential.
- The modern scientific disciplines of genetics and embryology support the full humanity of unborn humans from the moment of conception.[36]

Euthanasia

When people are close to death or suffer from a terminal illness, they sometimes consider *euthanasia*. The term literally means "good or happy death." It is further defined as the "taking of a human life for some good purpose, such as to relieve suffering or pain." It is therefore sometimes referred to as "mercy killing." Ethicists have identified two basic types of euthanasia: *active* and *passive*.[37]

In *active euthanasia*, an agent intentionally and actively takes the life of a terminally ill patient. This might be done either by the patient himself or herself (suicide) or with the assistance of someone else (possibly a physician, family member, or friend). Active euthanasia produces or causes death. This means that the patient's death results not from the terminal illness itself but from the specific act of euthanasia (such as a lethal dose of medication or gunshot).

In *passive euthanasia*, an agent allows a terminally ill patient to die naturally without intervening, usually by withholding or withdrawing life-sustaining (artificial or extraordinary) treatment. Passive euthanasia permits death to take its natural course but does not actually cause death itself.

What is the traditional Christian view of euthanasia? Most theologians and ethicists affirm the active-passive distinction from both a logical and a moral standpoint. Active euthanasia, however, is viewed as morally offensive and unacceptable (virtual homicide). It is condemned because it violates the scriptural principle that prohibits the intentional taking of innocent human life (Exod. 20:13; Deut. 5:17). Many Christian ethicists believe that given the state of human sinfulness (original sin, total depravity; see Pss. 51:5; 58:3; Prov. 20:9), active euthanasia weakens respect for human life and sets a dangerous precedent for humanity.[38]

Passive euthanasia, on the other hand, has been generally accepted by traditional Christian theologians and ethicists, but with some careful qualifications. Passive euthanasia can be considered if a patient has not been denied natural life-sustaining means such as air, water, and food (though artificial measures may not be necessary), and also if the physical condition of the patient has been diagnosed as irreversible, death is imminent, and further treatment would lead only to a burdensome prolongation of death.

Theologian Davis summarizes the historic Christian perspective well when it comes to the application of the *imago Dei* to both the beginning and end of life:

> Human life is sacred because God made man in his own image and likeness. . . . This canopy of sacredness extends throughout man's life, and is not simply limited to those times and circumstances when man happens to be strong, independent, healthy, and fully conscious of his relationships to others.[39]

In the next chapter we will take up how the dangerous idea of the *imago Dei* impacts humans' search for ultimate meaning. We will also explore humankind's relationship to the animal kingdom.

12

How Human Beings Differ

> It is impossible for anyone who understands the distinction
> between difference in degree and difference in kind to assert,
> in the face of available evidence, that man differs only in
> degree from the animals.
>
> Mortimer J. Adler,
> *The Difference of Man and the Difference It Makes*

Two centuries ago naturalist philosopher Friedrich Nietzsche set forth the secular claim that "God is dead."[1] In alignment with Nietzsche's bold assertion, today's representatives of the new atheism assert that life has no ultimate meaning and human beings are just highly evolved animals. While this secular manifesto has powerfully impacted Western thought and culture, historic Christianity's dangerous idea that God created human beings in his expressed image represents the antithesis to such claims.

The *imago Dei* doctrine carries important implications regarding ultimate meaning for human beings. This chapter probes these implications and illustrates just how being made in God's image sets humans apart in *kind* from the animals. In the end we will see whether the secular or the historic Christian perspective on humans carries greater explanatory power and scope.

Imago Dei and Human Purpose, Significance, and Meaning

As creatures made in God's image, people can find fulfillment only through an intimate relationship with their Creator. But separated from him by sin—and therefore out of sync with his intentions—humans experience existential angst and estrangement from God, from others, and from themselves. A human's true knowledge of self can only be discovered in and through knowing God.

Theologian John Calvin (1509–64) said, "True and sound wisdom consists of two parts: the knowledge of God; and of ourselves."[2] Biblically speaking, we are incomplete, unexplained, and even obsolete without reference to God our Creator.

The Presbyterian confessional statement known as the *Westminster Shorter Catechism* (1647) begins with the ultimate existential inquiry: "What is the chief end of man?" The answer: "Man's chief end is to glorify God, and to enjoy him forever."[3] Apart from God, we cannot fulfill our function and purpose in life because we were specifically created through the *imago Dei* to know, love, and serve our Creator.

Christian philosopher Augustine of Hippo (AD 354–430), in his classic work *Confessions*, conveys to God this prayer: "Man is one of your creatures, Lord, and his instinct is to praise you. . . . The thought of you stirs him so deeply that he cannot be content unless he praises you, because you made us for yourself and our hearts find no peace until they rest in you."[4]

Augustine, a wayward soul for the first half of his life, illustrates this truth by reflecting about his own misspent youth: "But my sin was this, that I looked for pleasure, beauty, and truth not in him but in myself and his other creatures, and the search led me instead to pain, confusion, and error."[5] Many people, just like Augustine, occupy their life with various diversions (affluence, hedonism, romance, sports, drugs, and so on) to escape this haunting existential reality.

Human beings were made for God, but due to sin and the fall, human beings sense that something is amiss.[6] Because of their sinful condition, people think they need various things to fulfill their desperate longings. Yet the apprehending of genuine, lasting meaning and purpose in life remains elusive.

But when people rise above their alienated state, they discover that what they really want and need is God himself. Cornelius Plantinga Jr. explains, "Our sense of God runs in us like a stream, even though we divert it toward other objects. We human beings want God even when we think that what we really want is a green valley, or a good time from our past, or a loved one."[7]

Confusion over what will satisfy human longings factors into the equation. Reflective human beings know that something is wrong or missing but cannot identify it. This fallen and out-of-sync condition has led to the creation of whole fields of study such as psychology and psychiatry. Yet in the Christian worldview, the answer to human beings' estranged and desperate condition is not far off. Jesus Christ—the way, the truth, and the life—graciously responds, "I have come that they may have life, and have it to the full" (John 10:10).

Human beings were originally made in the image of God for the very purpose of serving and glorifying their Creator. Placing faith in the life, death, and resurrection of the God-man Jesus Christ is the way to fulfill our yearning for meaning.

In his famous work *Pensées*, the great philosopher and writer Blaise Pascal (1623–62) discusses the God-shaped hole human beings have inside of them:

> What else does this craving, and this helplessness, proclaim but that there was once in man a true happiness, of which all that now remains is the empty print and trace? This he tries in vain to fill with everything around him, seeking in things that are not there the help he cannot find in those that are, though none can help, since this infinite abyss can be filled only with an infinite and immutable object; in other words by God himself.[8]

The message of historic Christianity is that this God-shaped vacuum can only be filled with the God-shaped person of Jesus Christ. Christianity, if authentically embraced, holds the answer to the desperate search for purpose, meaning, and significance. Pascal explains the Christian perspective further:

> Not only do we only know God through Jesus Christ, but we only know ourselves through Jesus Christ; we only know life and death through Jesus Christ. Apart from Jesus Christ we cannot know the meaning of our life or our death, of God or of ourselves.[9]

Pascal and Augustine's writings show that they believe that people find both themselves and God through their redemptive encounters with Jesus Christ. They demonstrate how Christianity not only explains the puzzle of human nature but also provides the solution for a person's existential estrangement from God and from himself or herself. A redemptive relationship with Christ fills the previously empty person.

Augustine elaborates, "Who will grant me to rest content in you? To whom shall I turn for the gift of your coming into my heart and filling it to the brim?"[10]

The Uniqueness and Enigma of Humans

If the biblical vision of human beings is true, what difference does being created in God's image make compared to being the product of unguided evolution? How well does the Christian worldview's basic anthropology correspond with what is known experientially about human nature? Is there a way to put anthropological theories to the test?

In assessing the viability of the historic Christian view of humans, we must explore the relationship between human beings and animals. How are people like and unlike the animals? Is there a mere difference of *degree* or a profound difference of *kind*? Secular evolutionary theory and historic Christianity are clearly at odds on this important issue, but which has the most explanatory power?

Are Humans Different from Animals?

Human beings are similar to animals in some very important ways. But if the Bible is true, this likeness can be expected. For example, Scripture indicates that the body of the first man was created from the same "dust of the ground" that God used to create the animals:

> The LORD God formed a man from the dust of the ground and breathed into his nostrils the breath of life, and the man became a living being. (Gen. 2:7)

> Now the LORD God had formed out of the ground all the wild animals and all the birds in the sky. (Gen. 2:19)

The Hebrew verbs used in Genesis for "make" (1:26), "create" (1:27), and "form" (2:7, 19) imply a divinely created physiological affinity between man and animals.[11] Genesis makes this similarity evident in other ways as well. For example, human beings eat much the same food as the land animals (Gen. 1:29–30), and the Hebrew word for first human is also applied to animals (Gen. 2:19). Therefore, from a biblical perspective certain physical similarities (anatomical, physiological, biochemical, genetic) between humans and other primates, for instance, should not be surprising.

The raw genetics of humans and chimpanzees are amazingly alike—in fact, they are over 90 percent similar.[12] While this affinity is often presented as strong support for naturalistic evolution, in reality the Genesis creation account anticipates this finding and others like it. There may well be a number of important ways that humans and animals differ only in degree.

According to Genesis, however, the *imago Dei* specifically makes humans *different in kind* from the animals. If the biblical view of humanity is correct, then we should share certain physiological characteristics with the animals but also manifest profound differences.

How Do Human Beings Differ from Animals?

Specific qualities and traits set people apart from all other creatures. According to historic Christianity, and specifically in light of the *imago Dei*, these acute differences are expected. Philosophers have noted at least seven ways in which humans differ dramatically and significantly from animals.[13]

1. HUMAN BEINGS HAVE AN INHERENT SPIRITUAL AND RELIGIOUS NATURE.

Nearly everyone pursues some form of spiritual truth. People generally have deep-seated religious beliefs and engage in intricate rituals. Common practices such as prayer and worship demonstrate their pursuit of God or the transcendental. This defining characteristic of humankind is so apparent that some have designated humans as *homo religiosus* (religious person).

Formal atheism appears largely inconsistent with the overall history of human nature and practice. Even professed nonbelievers (atheists, skeptics) ask questions about life's meaning and purpose and are drawn to whatever they consider of paramount importance and value. American philosopher of religion Paul Tillich suggests that there are no true atheists because all people have an "ultimate concern."[14] And philosopher Harold H. Titus says that even agnostics and atheists "tend to replace a personal god with an impersonal one—the state, race, some process in nature, or devotion to the search for truth or some other ideal."[15]

Ancient Greek philosopher Socrates (ca. 470–399 BC) stated, "The unexamined life is not worth living."[16] Humans alone contemplate what philosophers call *the big questions of life*. Though animals can be intelligent, they show no sign of spirituality or of concern with ultimate issues.

Only people are cognizant of their imminent death. This awareness generates personal angst and contemplation of God and the possibility of immortality.

2. HUMAN BEINGS POSSESS UNIQUE INTELLECTUAL, CULTURAL, AND COMMUNICATIVE ABILITIES.

Humans are thinkers capable of abstract reasoning and able to recognize, apply, and communicate the foundational principles of logic. Only human minds develop propositions, formulate arguments, draw inferences, recognize universal principles, and value logical validity, coherence, and truth. Only people wonder about, recognize, and appreciate such things as why the physical universe corresponds to abstract mathematical theorems.

Human beings communicate their conceptual apprehension of truth through complex symbols (language). Propositional language is intricate, complex, and flexible (verbal, written). Language networks humanity and is a necessary vehicle in establishing human culture and societal institutions. People sense a deep need to communicate with each other, and they accomplish that interaction through a sophisticated, intellectual process.

In contrast, while animals can be taught (by humans) to count and to use a vocabulary of human words, they apparently lack any ability to work with abstractions and to ask philosophical questions.

3. HUMAN BEINGS ARE CONSCIOUS OF TIME, REALITY, AND TRUTH.

Humans alone recollect the past, recognize the present, and anticipate the future. They live their entire lives within and aware of the constraints of time. Yet human beings also desire to transcend time; they think about living forever.

Reflective people wonder whether their perception of reality matches reality. Only human beings pursue truth, which has led to the founding and development of philosophy, science, mathematics, logic, the arts, and a religious worldview. What is real (metaphysics), what is true (epistemology), and what is rational (logic) are paramount questions, but again, just for humans.

Although animals can have a keen intuitive sense of concrete time—even surpassing that of a human's (e.g., some birds are more attuned to the changes of seasons)—animals lack any capacity for abstractions about time (for instance, they don't ponder history). Likewise, they may seem aware of reality in its concrete particulars but do not inquire into metaphysical, epistemological, and logical questions.

4. HUMAN BEINGS POSSESS A CONSCIENCE, IDENTIFY A VALUE SYSTEM, AND LEGISLATE MORAL LAWS FOR SOCIETY.

People have an inner sense of moral right and wrong or good and bad (conscience). They deliberate about moral choices, feel the pull of prescriptive moral obligation, and conform their lives according to a system of ethical conduct.

Individuals also know the reality of violating their own moral standards. Most people believe that universal, objective, and unchanging moral principles exist; and even those who reject absolute standards find it difficult to live that way.[17] Human society, by necessity, legislates morality and punishes the violators.

Christian philosopher Alvin Plantinga bluntly states, "It is extremely difficult to be a normal human being and not think that some actions are wrong and some are right."[18] Questions of what is good (ethics) and what is of genuine worth (values) lie solely in humankind's domain.

Animals are certainly capable of doing good, even heroic acts, but they are not capable of making morally reflective judgments. For example, a dog can sniff out cancer or save its master from a burning house or guide soldiers through dangerous obstacles during combat, but it cannot debate the merits of risking its life to save another.

5. HUMAN BEINGS ARE UNIQUELY INVENTIVE AND TECHNOLOGICAL.

Philosopher J. P. Moreland notes that in terms of technology, people living at the time of the American Civil War had more in common with the Old Testament patriarch Abraham (ca. 2000 BC) than with people living today.[19] Technological advancement in the twentieth century alone was breathtaking—to say nothing of what is already happening in the twenty-first century.

In less than a century, military technology advanced from the trench warfare of World War I, to the *blitzkrieg* and atomic bomb of World War II, to the intercontinental ballistic missiles of the Cold War, and finally to the stealth aircraft, smart bombs, unmanned vehicles, and robots of today. Inconceivable just decades before, during the past twenty years the speed of technological breakthroughs has allowed for instant, personal, global communication and access to data on ever-shrinking mobile devices. Imagine searching the archives of the Library of Congress while sitting on your couch.

Though human technology is constantly progressive, it is also a double-edged sword. Human innovation has not only lengthened the human lifespan but also brought the world to the brink of nuclear destruction. In this sobering and humbling fact, people once again prove themselves unique among all living creatures.

Animals show limited capacity for using objects in nature as tools, lacking entirely the creativity of human beings. While often powerful and instinctive creatures, animals have never had the ability to take dominion over nature with inventive ideas.

6. HUMAN BEINGS POSSESS AN INTENSE CURIOSITY TO EXPLORE AND UNDERSTAND THE ENTIRE CREATED REALM.

Human beings seek out the most desolate and dangerous places on Earth and even beyond. Though animals explore their immediate habitats, such investigations appear related to furthering their survival or enhancing their fun.

Whereas animals may play with a pretty stone or twig, human beings want to understand the smallest fundamental entities that make up the stone or twig and how those entities arise and interact. Birds may look to the star patterns in the sky to guide them in their migrations, but humans seek to comprehend the source of starlight and what lies beyond it.

The desire of animals to explore and understand their immediate environment appears to be constrained by their body size. Humans, by contrast, seek to probe the full range of existing entities in the universe down to the very smallest (e.g., strings that measure less than a trillionth of a trillionth of a trillionth of a meter across). Likewise, they are not content to just explore and understand their immediate environment. Their curiosity ranges from the core of the earth to that which lies beyond the most distant galaxy.

Stephen Hawking summarizes humanity's insatiable curiosity about the created realm in his bestselling book *A Brief History of Time*. According to Hawking, no human being can be content until he or she has received complete answers to the following questions: "What is the nature of the universe? What is our place in it and where did it and we come from? Why is it the way it is?" Hawking indicates that he will remain dissatisfied until he "would know the mind of God."[20]

7. HUMAN BEINGS POSSESS AESTHETIC TASTE AND APPRECIATION FOR MORE THAN JUST PRACTICAL PURPOSES.

People distinctly create, recognize, and appreciate beauty. This aesthetic taste and value extend to art, music, film, literature, and the natural world itself. Humans often create because they are moved by a deep and mysterious sense of the beautiful. Many people place aesthetic concerns at the level of basic needs for survival. Anthropological finds have shown that humanity's aesthetic expression dates virtually from the very beginning of its existence.

The creative capacities of animals, however, are of a lower order and are apparently motivated by practical necessity (e.g., birds make nests and beavers build dams). They do not seem to create for sheer pleasure.

Different in Kind

These seven characteristics clearly place human beings in a different category from the rest of Earth's creatures. In many respects humans are different in *kind*, not just in *degree*, from the animals. And the distinct attributes of humankind comport well with what Scripture reveals concerning the *imago Dei*.

Can a Theory of Human Nature Be Put to the Test?

So far the Christian worldview corresponds well to the real world, but to be worthy of belief, a religion or philosophy must also account for the meaningful realities a person encounters in life. And the enigma of humanity itself poses one of the most complex challenges.

Can Christianity account for the mysterious and enigmatic nature of humans? How does this worldview explain what one famous observer called humankind's "greatness and wretchedness"?

The Greatest Enigma: Humans

The French scientist and apologist Blaise Pascal described human beings as an enigmatic mixture of greatness and wretchedness, thus being at the same time the "glory and refuse of the universe."[21] Part of the nobility of humans is demonstrated in their unique ability to recognize their own wretchedness. Pascal thought only the Christian faith could account for this schizophrenic condition. Christian philosopher Thomas V. Morris explains:

> One of the greatest mysteries is in us. How is the naked ape capable of grasping the mathematical structure of matter? How can one species produce both unspeakable wickedness and nearly inexplicable goodness? How can we be responsible both for the most disgusting squalor and for the most breathtaking

beauty? How can grand aspirations and self-destructive impulses, kindness and cruelty, be interwoven in one life? The human enigma cries out for explanation. Pascal believed that only the tenets of the Christian faith can adequately account for both the greatness and wretchedness of humanity. And he was convinced that this in itself is an important piece of evidence that Christianity embraces truth.[22]

Just how does Christianity explain humanity's paradoxical nature? The Christian worldview asserts that human greatness is a direct result of the *imago Dei*. As creatures made in the image and likeness of God, human beings reflect the glory of their Maker.

Wretchedness, on the other hand, can be traced to Adam. The first human plunged all humanity into sin and corruption (Gen. 3). From a biblical perspective, any understanding of human behavior must include recognition of the sin nature.[23]

Adam's fall transmitted sin and guilt from him to all human beings (Rom. 5:12, 18–19). So through Adam all people have sinned and are morally accountable to God. The doctrine of original sin also means that all of Adam's progeny are conceived in sin and inherit a sin nature. This severely incapacitating force permeates the heart of every individual (Pss. 51:5; 58:3; Prov. 20:9). Consequently, human beings are not sinners simply because they happen to sin; rather, they sin because they are sinners by nature (review chapter 9).

Humanity's problem, therefore, should be thought of more as a condition than a struggle with specific acts. As a universal phenomenon, sin affects each and every person (Ps. 143:2; Eccles. 7:20; Gal. 3:22; James 3:2; 4:4) with Jesus Christ being the only exception (2 Cor. 5:21; Heb. 4:15; 1 Peter 2:22; 1 John 3:5). Our human nature—inherited from Adam—resides at the very core (inner being) of each person (Jer. 17:9; Matt. 15:19) and affects the entire person—including the mind, will, affections, and body (Eph. 2:3; 4:17–19).

Given God's holy and righteous moral character (Deut. 32:4; Ps. 98:9; Isa. 6:3), humans in their sinful state must face God's just wrath (Rom. 1:18; Eph. 2:3). By necessity God must punish the sinner. Yet in the midst of humanity's despairing circumstance, God graciously intervened and provided the guilty a way of escaping judgment through divinely imparted forgiveness (review chapter 10). That forgiveness comes in and through the life, death, and resurrection of the divine Messiah, Jesus Christ.[24]

A result of being simultaneously great and wretched means that humans can paint the Sistine Chapel and write the plays of Shakespeare, but they are also capable of creating Auschwitz and the Gulag. The astonishing moral dissonance evident in the life of the high-ranking Nazi leader Reinhard Heydrich demonstrates the depth of the problem. He was considered a highly educated and cultured individual who greatly appreciated the classical music of Schubert, Wagner, and Beethoven, and yet he was also deemed the mastermind behind the Nazi plan to exterminate European Jewry (the Final Solution).[25] In the same life he displayed both brilliance and sheer, unadulterated evil.

Putting an Anthropology to the Test

According to astronomer and Christian apologist Hugh Ross, humans are far too evil for naturalistic evolution to be true.[26] Unlike animals, humans often use their intellectual endowments to commit acts of wickedness. Intelligence and creativity enhance human malevolence. Experientially speaking, people appear just as one would expect if Christianity is indeed true. Could it be that the Christian worldview accurately explains the ultimate enigma: humans? And doesn't that kind of explanatory power go a long way in substantiating the truth-claims of historic Christianity?

Consider the following argument:[27]

1. If the historic Christian worldview is true, then certain features characterize human beings—namely, greatness (*imago Dei*) and wretchedness (fallenness). Human beings are personal, spiritual, rational, volitional, relational, aesthetic, philosophical, powerful, and deeply morally flawed.
2. Those features do, in fact, characterize human beings.
3. Other worldviews (naturalism, pantheism) face extreme difficulty accounting for such human features.
4. Therefore, these features provide a level of confirmation of the historic Christian worldview's explanatory power and scope.

In summation, the historic Christian worldview supplies a depth of understanding and insight into the human condition. As Scripture predicts, humans are different in both degree and in kind from the animals. And human beings are both great and wretched, just as would be expected from a creature that is godlike in many respects but also deeply fallen.

How Historic Christianity's Most Humanitarian Dangerous Idea Changed the World: The *Imago Dei*

The biblical truth that humans are made in the image and likeness of God lays the foundation for the basic sacredness of all human life. Because people are divine image bearers, they possess inherent dignity and moral worth. All people deserve respect and dignified treatment as the crown of God's creation. It is the belief in the *imago Dei* that has motivated Christians through the centuries to combat slavery, poverty, genocide, infanticide, abortion on demand, and active euthanasia. This foundational belief about humanity also motivates Christians to promote education, science, the arts, political freedom, and social justice.[28]

George Grant reveals how the *imago Dei* impacted the actions of Christian missionaries:

As missionaries circled the globe, . . . they established hospitals. They founded orphanages. They started rescue missions. They built almshouses. They opened soup kitchens. They incorporated charitable societies. They changed laws. They demonstrated love. They lived as if people mattered.[29]

Those actions, motivated by image-bearers fully cognizant of their forgiven status and thus free to serve God and their fellow human beings, continue to drive efforts to improve our world today.

Further Suggested Reading

Augustine. *Confessions*. Translated by R. S. Pine-Coffin. New York: Penguin, 1961.

Carey, George. *I Believe in Man*. Grand Rapids: Eerdmans, 1977.

Hoekema, Anthony A. *Created in God's Image*. Grand Rapids: Eerdmans, 1986.

Lewis, C. S. *The Abolition of Man*. New York: Macmillan, 1947.

Machen, J. Gresham. *The Christian View of Man*. New York: Macmillan, 1937.

Morris, Thomas V. *Making Sense of It All*. Grand Rapids: Eerdmans, 1992.

Pascal, Blaise. *Pensées*. Translated by A. J. Krailsheimer. Revised edition. New York: Penguin, 1995.

Rana, Fazale, and Hugh Ross. *Who Was Adam?* Colorado Springs: NavPress, 2005.

Discussion Questions

1. What does it mean to be made in the image of God? Theologically speaking, how are human beings like and unlike God?

2. What are the humanitarian implications of the *imago Dei*?

3. How does the fact that a person is made in the image of God affect that individual's pursuit of meaning, purpose, and significance?

4. What does it mean that humans differ from the animals in both degree and kind? How does the Bible present these differences? In what specific ways do humans differ from the animals?

5. What did Pascal mean when he said humans are both *great* and *wretched*?

THE GOOD IN SUFFERING

13

Squaring Evil with God's Goodness

> Evil isn't something we easily "explain" or "deal with"—let
> alone "solve." Yet, as opposed to its theological and philo-
> sophical competitors, the good news of the gospel offers not
> only the most adequate explanatory context for respond-
> ing to evil, but presents the best hope for fully and finally
> overcoming it.
>
> Paul Copan, *Loving Wisdom*

I've come face-to-face with two very different types of evil and suffering in my life. I battled both and, by God's extraordinary grace, I survived. And yet I'm aware that many people in similar situations have not fared so well. Both encounters were extremely difficult and painful in different ways and exacted a heavy toll. But on reflection, I'd say both experiences served to transform my character for the good.

Philosophers categorize evil in two ways: moral evil and natural evil. *Moral evil* results from a deliberate human action. It includes such horrific acts as rape, murder, kidnapping, torture, and untold other ways in which human beings inflict intentional and unjustified harm on their fellow humans. *Natural evil*, on the other hand, is natural disasters that result from the dangerous and sometimes deadly events in nature. It includes such calamities as earthquakes, hurricanes, floods, and diseases. Obviously these two types of evil and the suffering they cause can overlap one another. For example, the calamity of a natural disaster can be exacerbated by the moral irresponsibility of people.

My Encounter with Moral Evil: Violent Crime

Just before Easter in 1988 my wife and I were in for the shock of our lives. After working a late shift at the hospital, my wife made her way home and parked her car in the parking lot of our apartment building. Our apartment wasn't far from the lot, and on that night I heard what sounded like a muffled scream. Expecting my wife to get home from work at any moment, I decided to investigate.

Upon entering the parking lot I found my wife fighting an attacker who had accosted her as she was getting out of her car. I confronted the man and knocked him to the ground. We wrestled on the pavement while my wife ran into our apartment to call the police. I wasn't sure whether this man was armed with a weapon, but I knew I was in a potentially life-and-death struggle. As I fought this man I was filled with adrenaline and rage and was determined to take this man out at all costs. My mind-set was that it was either him or me, and it wasn't going to be me.

The man was arrested and ultimately prosecuted for assault. Fortunately, my wife was not physically harmed though she was obviously mentally and emotionally distraught from the experience. I also came through the event without injury. The perpetrator, however, was quite badly beaten up.

Being victims of a violent crime was an emotionally jarring event, even though things could have been much worse. My wife and I had encountered evil in an up-close and personal way, and I had seen the person I love most in the world physically attacked. I came to understand that my family and I are not immune to the effects of evil simply because we are Christians. Believers in Christ routinely undergo suffering of various types. Yet over time, both my wife and I came to see that God was with us during our perilous experience.

My Encounter with Natural Evil: Suffering through Illness

Just before Thanksgiving in 2003 I came down with a mysterious illness that caused me to be hospitalized for almost a month. The team of doctors who treated me were initially baffled by my condition. Tests ultimately revealed that I had a large lesion in my right lung and six in my brain. My wife was told initially that I might have stage-four brain cancer.

Lung surgery revealed that I didn't have cancer but rather a rare and life-threatening bacterial infection known as Nocardia. My medical prognosis remained bleak. After many months of treatment with heavy doses of antibiotics, the lesions shrank and I was finally cured of the disease (though I still have some lingering physical effects caused by the illness).

During this incredibly difficult physical ordeal, a number of doctors and brain specialists commented that they found my full recovery surprising and even rather extraordinary. They had seen other patients in similar conditions die quickly. They told me that I was lucky and that someone must be watching over me. Two physicians in particular, while cautious in drawing direct cause-and-effect relationships, nevertheless confided to me privately that they thought I had been the recipient of a healing touch from providence.

When I shared what the doctors had told me with a skeptical friend, the friend dismissed the providential component and said I was merely the recipient of good medicine. I responded by saying that I thought there was something more going on behind the scenes of my illness. I also noted that from the historic Christian worldview, good medicine is also a gift of providence.

I faced natural evil (in this case a rare disease) in a direct and personal way. This life-threatening illness was extremely difficult and pushed me to my physical, mental, and spiritual limits. But my family and I again came to discover that God was with us during our trial of uncertainty and danger.

As a reserved and somewhat introverted person, I find it difficult to write about the personal, distressing circumstances that have transpired in my life and in the life of my family. But I share these stories about encountering evil and suffering in order to assure you (the reader) that I write about this topic from a first-person perspective. Thus, this discussion of evil and suffering reflects more than just an academic philosophical and theological treatment. Though I wouldn't want my family and me to go through those difficult times again, the experience of God's grace and mercy during the tough times has impacted my spiritual growth and outlook remarkably.

My experiences with suffering have caused me to appreciate even more the great historic Christian truth-claim that Jesus Christ took on human flesh in order to suffer *with* human beings and *for* us redemptively on the cross. God, therefore, is acquainted with evil, pain, and suffering and has a greater good to accomplish through them. And historic Christianity also affirms that Jesus Christ has achieved victory over evil and suffering through his life, death, and resurrection. The application of that final victory, however, awaits a later time: the Lord's glorious second coming.

Worldview Perspectives on Evil and Suffering

To be considered viable, any worldview (a comprehensive view of reality) must provide some explanation for the reality of evil and suffering in the world. Historically, three major worldview perspectives have vied for acceptance: (1) *pantheistic monism*—comprised largely of the Eastern mystical religions,

(2) *naturalism*—comprised largely of those who affirm atheism and skepticism, and (3) *theism*—comprised largely of the monotheistic religions of Judaism, Christianity, and Islam. So how do these worldviews explain evil and suffering?

Pantheistic Monism

The Eastern mystical religious traditions say either that life by its very nature is suffering (reflected in Buddhism's concept of *dukkha*) or that evil and suffering are essentially an illusion (reflected in Hinduism's concept of *maya*). Simply put, mysticism tends to passively ignore or outright deny the reality of evil and suffering.

Naturalism

Those who affirm a strictly physical universe say that the collective natural forces (random and blind) seem to hurt some people and help others. These purely arbitrary natural forces tend to leave some lucky and others unlucky. So naturalists struggle to define and condemn evil and suffering simply because secularism struggles to ground objective goodness.

Theism

The Middle Eastern monotheistic religious traditions tend to explain evil and suffering in terms of free agents expressing their volitional choices. The principal argument is that God has greater goods that necessarily accompany malevolence and sorrow. The challenge that all theistic religions face is the attempt to justify God's goodness in light of evil and suffering (*theodicy*).

Once again, it is at this vortex of the various worldviews struggling to explain the universal problem of evil and suffering that historic Christianity's seventh dangerous idea comes to bear. Unlike pantheistic monism and naturalism, Christian theism does not find it difficult to define evil nor does it attempt to dodge its reality. And while the historic Christian viewpoint shares much in common with the other theistic religions, it's only Christianity that asserts that God is uniquely acquainted with evil and suffering in the world.

Historic Christianity's Seventh Dangerous Idea: God's Greater Good in Suffering

The Christian apologetics enterprise seeks to provide rational justification for the central truth-claims of Christianity (1 Peter 3:15). A critical part of defending the faith consists of responding to difficult objections raised against it. Perhaps the greatest challenge to the truth of Christianity lies with the perennial problem of evil.[1] The existence of evil raises questions about whether the

Christian concept of God can be considered coherent. That's why some people cite the problem of evil and suffering as the number one reason for rejecting belief in the Christian God. This challenge, therefore, deserves careful reflection.

We must first briefly define the complex problem of evil. Much more could and should be said about this topic, but this section of the book will provide some guidance in thinking through the issues involved. We will examine some non-Christian viewpoints concerning the question of evil and provide a basic Christian response to this formidable apologetic challenge. While it is true that the issue of evil and suffering raises difficult questions, it is also true that historic Christianity supplies unique and powerful answers to those questions. Christianity's response to the problem of evil constitutes a philosophically dangerous idea about physical danger itself.

Is There Really Evil in the World?

Amazing as it may seem, some people deny the reality of evil in the world. Two examples immediately come to mind:

1. *There are some mental health professionals who label evil, especially as it relates to human beings, as an outdated and misguided concept.* To this way of thinking, human beings are basically good, or at worst neutral, and therefore any negative or violent behavior results from physiological or environmental influences. Thus, some psychologists and psychiatrists assert that heinous crimes are not committed by evil people but rather by mentally ill people. In their view, violent crime has a basic pathological cause, not a moral one.

In fact, much of modern secular psychology and psychiatry have outright rejected the view that sin and moral evil actively influence human nature. And yet while questioning the existence of evil, these same people are forced to believe in human suffering, for it is evident all around them.

2. *Some forms of Eastern religion view evil as a mere illusion.* The more philosophic strands of Hinduism[2] embrace the metaphysical views of monism, idealism, and pantheism. *Monism* is the view that all reality is one, whereas *idealism* asserts that the one reality is mind, idea, or spirit. According to one school of interpretation of the Hindu writings known as the *Upanishads*, the physical world is an illusion and all reality is ultimately spirit or god. Thus they teach pantheism: "all is god and god is all."

According to this Hindu philosophy, once a person achieves the right state of mystical consciousness, evil is absent because ultimate reality not only is beyond the appearance of the physical but also is beyond the rational and moral categories of good and evil. In Hinduism, evil is part of the broader principle called *maya*, in which mere appearance and illusion stand in the way of apprehending the deeper reality or truth.

Groups such as Christian Science and Religious Science embrace a similar viewpoint, and it is seen in popular New Age spirituality as well. Hindu thinking has influenced all three of these Western groups (or expressions of spirituality). In Eastern mystical philosophy and religion, the principal problem human beings face is ignorance or lack of enlightenment, not sin or moral evil.

On what realistic basis can evil be so easily dismissed? One of the reasons for rejecting the conclusions of much of modern secular psychology as well as Eastern mysticism is that their views about human nature do not comport with most people's real-life moral experiences in the world. Evil and suffering are stark realities of life, and they cannot be merely reduced to or neatly explained away in terms of either pathological or mystical categories. Too often modern psychological theories tend to undermine the truth that each person has a basic moral responsibility.[3] And Hinduism's concept of maya fails to explain where the so-called illusion originated or why evil remains such a powerful and universal human experience. Maya is also a principle that under logical scrutiny reduces to absurdity.[4]

The history of the twentieth century alone illustrates the reality of evil and suffering. The totalitarian regimes of Adolf Hitler and Joseph Stalin (and countless tyrants after them) have provided ample objective evidence that unadulterated evil exists—as demonstrated in the Nazi death camps and the Soviet Gulags. It should be noted that of the estimated six million Jews systematically exterminated by the Nazis during World War II, one and a half million of those innocent people were children. And the number of people murdered in Stalin's purges in the Soviet Union is estimated to range into the tens of millions. World War II, with its resulting sixty to seventy million deaths, has been called the greatest catastrophe in history.[5] Surely the global conflicts of the twentieth century make it impossible to take seriously the view that evil is an illusion. Dismissing evil as an illusion in itself represents a serious departure from reality.

Evil is real, ugly, painful, and often devastating. The reality of evil in the world and specifically in human beings, however, raises serious questions about its relationship to God, particularly the Christian vision of an infinitely loving and powerful God. Some have argued that evil and the Christian God cannot logically coexist. For some, the existence of evil inevitably leads to a denial of God's existence.

Is God's Existence Incompatible with Evil?

To disprove God is an extremely difficult epistemological task because there are limits to disproof (standards governing both proof and its opposite). Some concepts of God, however, may be considered false if they are logically incoherent. Whatever is genuinely incoherent (irrational) cannot be true (e.g., a circle can't be square). Some skeptics and atheists assert that the problem of evil creates a problem of coherence for the Christian concept of God. Consider the words of the eighteenth-century Scottish skeptic David Hume as he relates the problem of evil to God: "Is he willing to prevent evil, but not able? Then is he impotent. Is he able, but not willing? Then is he malevolent. Is he both able and willing? Whence then is evil?"[6]

Evil is a multifaceted, multiple-layered apologetics issue. Some aspects are logical-philosophical in nature while others can be characterized as psychological-practical. Therefore, we must address the problem(s) of evil. Hume raised what is known as the logical or deductive form of the problem of evil. Some skeptics call it the "inconsistent triad." Christians believe, based on Scripture, that God is omnibenevolent (perfectly good) and omnipotent (completely powerful). Yet when these two divine attributes are combined with the reality of evil in the world, an alleged logical incompatibility arises. The reasoning often follows this pattern:

1. An omnibenevolent God *would want* to eliminate evil.
2. An omnipotent God *could* eliminate evil.
3. Yet evil conspicuously *still* exists.

The logical tension is clear in these three statements. How could evil exist in the world if God has both the desire and the power to eliminate it? In light of this allegedly inconsistent triad, the only possible, reasonable conclusions—at least in the mind of some skeptics and atheists—are the following:

1. God is willing to eliminate evil but not able. Therefore, God is impotent (lacking power); or
2. God is able to eliminate evil but not willing. Therefore, God is malevolent (lacking goodness); or
3. An omnibenevolent and omnipotent God does not exist.

In light of these statements, some skeptics and atheists accept the following argument: Since omnibenevolence, omnipotence, and evil are logically incompatible, and since all three must be affirmed if one is to accept the Christian God, then the Christian concept of God is logically incoherent and therefore cannot be true.

Over the last several centuries this so-called logical problem of evil has been used as a powerful weapon in the arsenal of atheists against Christian theism. Although very few people have been willing to accept the option that God is actually malevolent, this argument has driven some religious philosophers to acquiesce to a limited view of God—agreeing that he is willing to eliminate evil but not totally capable of doing so on his own. In this view, God desires that human beings support him in attempting to overcome evil. This basic position has been given various names, including *finite godism* and *limited theism*, but the defining characteristic is that *god* is finite (limited), especially in terms of his power. Such distinguished philosophers as John Stuart Mill, William James, and Edgar Brightman embraced this position roughly a century ago. Rabbi Harold Kushner reflects a similar position today in his popular book *When Bad Things Happen to Good People*.[7]

At least three basic problems can be discerned in examining finite godism[8] and other similar viewpoints: (1) If adopted, such a view provides no guarantee that evil will ever be defeated. If this god doesn't have the ability to overcome evil and must rely on the help of human beings, then the world is in a dreadful predicament. (2) This finite god, who has created a world he cannot control, is neither omnipotent nor omniscient and is therefore an unlikely candidate for human worship. (3) The need to adopt a finite view of God does not exist in the first place because the so-called inconsistent triad is logically resolvable. A reexamination of the argument for atheism is therefore in order.

Is the Triad Really Inconsistent?

Consider again the initial reasoning of skeptics concerning God and evil:

1. An omnibenevolent God *would want* to eliminate evil.
2. An omnipotent God *could* eliminate evil.
3. Yet evil conspicuously *still* exists.

There is no intractable logical problem with the three points raised by skeptics concerning the theistic God's attributes and the existence of evil. The three statements are not explicitly logically contradictory (A equals A and equals non-A). Bear in mind the following critique of this argument against the God of theism.

The truth or reasonableness of the first two statements is very much open to question. First, it seems reasonable to conclude that an omnibenevolent God might not necessarily desire to eliminate all evil and suffering, at least not immediately, because evil and suffering may serve to produce greater good. Christian philosopher Richard Swinburne acknowledges that this greater good theory is the core to answering the problem of evil. He writes, "The basic solution is that all the evils we find around us are logically necessary conditions of greater goods, that is to say that greater good couldn't come about without the evil or at any rate the natural possibility of evil."[9]

Therefore, God could conceivably eradicate various forms of evil, but this elimination may also undercut the particular good of human free agency and moral development (as well as other things). The elimination could then result in a worse moral scenario. Thus, God may desire to preserve truly greater good even in the face of evil and suffering. Christian philosopher Paul Copan notes,

"Perhaps this world has the balance of the *greatest* amount of good and the *least* amount of evil."[10]

By way of analogy, conscientious human parents often allow their children to undergo difficulties and pain, though the parents could—to some degree—shield their children from it. Yet the reason parents allow their children to experience adversity is that these very challenges help produce in their children greater good—namely, virtues such as maturity, independence, perseverance, strength, courage, and wisdom. An infinitely wise, just, and loving God may similarly allow evil and suffering to exist because it serves a greater purpose for human beings and the universe and ultimately leads to the greater glory of God himself. The existence of evil and divine goodness is not, then, necessarily incompatible. God may simply have a very good reason for allowing evil and suffering. Preserving such greater good would then constitute rational and moral justification for God permitting malevolence and sorrow.

In addition, an omnipotent God who has created morally responsible creatures may choose to eliminate evil through a careful process that initially allows for evil and suffering. Omnipotence after all, in a biblical context, doesn't mean that God can literally do anything (e.g., God can't sin or perform the absurd). Rather, omnipotence means that God can do all things consistent with his rational and moral nature. Creating persons who are at least capable of some degree of independence may logically limit God's options. To quote Christian philosopher Alvin Plantinga, "To create creatures capable of *moral good*, therefore, He [God] must create creatures capable of moral evil."[11] It again seems reasonable to conclude that if God created human beings with free agency, then eliminating evil would likely require a process that involves evil and suffering. Eradicating evil, even for God, may not be an immediate and painless task. Evil and suffering may be necessary for the greater good of humanity and may lead to the greater glory of God.

Alvin Plantinga has suggested something like the following in response to the problem of evil:

1. God is omnibenevolent and omnipotent.
2. God created a world that now contains evil and he had a good reason for doing so (for purposes of a greater good).
3. Therefore, the world contains evil, but evil is consistent with the Christian view of God.[12]

Another approach may reflect how God will act over time concerning the problem of evil:

1. An omnibenevolent God *would want* to eliminate evil.
2. An omnipotent God *could* eliminate evil.
3. Since evil still exists, then God will eliminate it in the future.

While these responses certainly don't solve all the problems connected with God's relationship to evil,[13] the reasoning of Swinburne, Plantinga, and other Christian philosophers has been successful in showing that evil is not necessarily inconsistent with the Christian view of God. Thus the deductive argument against God from evil isn't logically compelling. Even the distinguished philosopher of religion William Rowe, a self-professed atheist, agrees: "Some philosophers have contended that the existence of evil is logically inconsistent with the existence of the theistic God. No one, I think, has succeeded in establishing such an extravagant claim."[14] Moreover, leading agnostic philosopher of religion Paul Draper concurs: "I do not see how it is possible to construct a convincing logical argument from evil against theism."[15]

Some skeptical thinkers, while admitting that the logical-deductive argument from evil fails to formally disprove God's existence, nonetheless set forth what is known as the evidential-inductive problem of evil. This position insists that the *vast amount* of evil that exists in the world makes God's existence highly improbable.

Inductive Argument from Evil

Let's consider three responses to this refined perspective problem of evil.[16]

1. *Measuring evil is extremely difficult.* Alvin Plantinga explains, "Of course, there doesn't seem to be any way to measure moral evil—that is, we don't have units like volts or pounds or kilowatts so that we could say 'this situation contains exactly thirty-five turps of moral evil.'"[17]

2. *Weighing evil is beyond humanity's capacity.* There is really no way of knowing how much evil is required in order to achieve a perceived moral good. Omniscience seems to be a requirement—ironically for the atheist that's an attribute only God possesses.

3. *Evil's weight must be properly counterbalanced.* To calculate the probability of God's existence in light of evil one must also include all the evidence that weighs in favor of God's existence. Therefore, the apologetics arguments for God's existence and the truth of Christianity need to be appropriately factored.

In light of these three points alone, the evidential or inductive problem of evil seems far from persuasive. From a Christian theistic worldview, God is in the best position to decide exactly how much evil justifies good ends.

Since some atheists, like many other people, are often outraged by evil, one may wonder what the atheist solution is to the problem of evil. Will evil be overcome in an atheist world? Or is there really any evil at all in a godless universe?

Does Naturalistic Atheism Offer a Coherent Explanation of Evil?

It seems difficult to conceive how evil could exist in a godless world. If the atheist affirms a naturalistic, materialistic worldview, then it seems that human beings are just part of the cosmic accident—mere *matter in motion*. As products of a blind and purposeless evolutionary process, there appears to be no compelling reason to believe that human beings possess true inherent dignity and objective moral worth. Yet if the worth of human beings is at best questionable, then what is one to conclude about acts of genocide, ethnic cleansing, and infanticide? From an atheist perspective, it is awfully hard to argue with the comment made by Dostoevsky's character Ivan Karamazov: "If God doesn't exist, everything is permissible."[18]

While a particular atheist may find these things personally objectionable, another atheist may readily agree with them. But one viewpoint is no better than the other because both are purely subjective and arbitrary. Things happen in a godless, merely physical world, but who's to say that any of it is actually bad?

Paul Copan explains the naturalistic, atheistic dilemma:

> If God doesn't exist, why expect nature to be configured a certain way rather than another? Why be disappointed when it's not? Isn't it just tough luck? Assuming a pattern to which things should conform suggests a design-plan, which in turn implies a Designer.[19]

For evil to exist, one must be able to make an objective moral judgment. But in a godless world it seems that morals can only be arbitrary, subjective, and relativistic in nature because there is no objective metaphysical foundation. Therefore, without God there may be obstacles, inconveniences, and unpleasantries in conjunction with one's subjective desires and needs, but this can hardly be called *evil*. Atheists may choose to act in an expedient or pragmatic way in life, but this cannot be equated with prescriptive morality (the moral *should* or *ought*). And in order to have evil, prescriptive morality is needed. As Christian philosopher Chad Meister concludes, "If evil truly exists, what we could call 'objective evil'—then there also exist objective moral values, moral values which are binding on all people, whether they acknowledge them as such or not."[20]

Summarizing the Skeptical Arguments from Evil

1. The *deductive argument from evil* reasons that the theistic God's existence is logically incompatible with evil.
2. The *inductive argument from evil* reasons that the amount of evil in the world makes the theistic God's existence highly improbable.

Yet most atheists do seem to believe that some things or actions in the world can be judged evil. There is, to their thinking, something morally amiss in the universe. This is, of course, their major objection against God. But when they object to evil, they must appeal beyond their strictly natural world to an objective standard of goodness because something can only be evil if it has transgressed the good. Evil by its very nature implies a standard of goodness. As Gerard J. Hughes notes:

> The problem of evil cannot even be stated unless it is assumed that it is proper to speak of moral truth; and it cannot be stated with much force unless it is assumed that moral does not simply depend on human conventions which could well have been quite different.[21]

Yet all of this reasoning raises serious difficulties for atheists since they must account for the apparent *problem of good*. Ironically, the problem of evil may serve as a powerful evidence for God's existence; an objective standard of goodness needs an adequate metaphysical foundation. The existence of a theistic God explains both the existence of goodness as well as its opposite: evil.

Consider, then, the following argument for God's existence from the concepts of good and evil:

1. If objective moral values exist, then God probably exists as the best explanation for such ethics (serving as a necessary metaphysical foundation).
2. Evil (the transgression of moral goodness) exists.
3. Therefore, God probably exists.[22]

Borrowed Moral Capital

Some Christian philosophers have pointed out that when atheists remain indignant about evil and God's relationship to it, they are actually borrowing from the theistic worldview[23] since their own worldview provides no adequate basis on which to make such moral claims. This assessment of the nonbeliever's moral confusion in light of his indebtedness to God's inherent moral law is clearly spoken of in Scripture (Rom. 1:18–2:16). Biblically speaking, consider the incongruent scenario that has been played out by various secular thinkers in their moral complaint against God concerning evil. The atheist, in effect, depends on the objective moral system of theism in order to raise moral objections against the theistic God. As Christian philosopher Greg L. Bahnsen succinctly puts it: "Antitheism presupposes theism to make its case."[24]

Atheism offers no adequate answers for evil and suffering. Atheists cannot even speak about evil without relying on borrowed moral capital, and they cannot explain the problem of good. Given that atheism's argument from evil fails to make its case against God, it seems logically appropriate to consider why the God of Christianity may choose to allow evil and suffering. The next chapter will explore historic Christianity's response to this enduring issue.

14

God's Good Purposes for Evil and Suffering

> As the Christian sees things, God does not stand idly by,
> coolly observing the suffering of his creatures. He enters into
> and shares our suffering. He endures the anguish of seeing
> his Son, the second Person of the Trinity, consigned to the
> bitterly cruel and shameful death of the cross.
>
> Alvin Plantinga, *Philosophers Who Believe*

Christian revelation provides a less than complete, systematic, and comprehensive explanation for the problem of evil and suffering. God, for reasons known only to him, has chosen to explain some but not all the details of his cosmic plan. As Scripture proclaims, "The secret things belong to the LORD our God" (Deut. 29:29). Undoubtedly, many mysteries will remain until the dawning of the eternal age to come, and the purposes behind evil and suffering reside at the top of that list. Yet Christianity does present unique and satisfying responses to the challenges that evil and suffering raise. What follows are some of these distinct Christian responses in summary form.

Is Evil a *Something*?

Augustine of Hippo (AD 354–430) gave considerable reflection to the problem of evil, especially because it was one of the central issues that had kept him from embracing Christianity in his early life.[1] One of his provocative

conclusions on the matter was that evil, though real, is not a thing or substance or stuff.[2] Rather, evil is a *privation* (Latin, *privatio*), that is, a lack or
absence of something.

Augustine believed evil is specifically the lack of something that should be
present in a person or thing. Evil is therefore defined in the negative (Latin,
negatio). Analogously, one may think of blindness not as a positive thing but
rather as the absence of sight. Similarly, a cavity is not so much a thing as it is a
lack (a hole), namely a lack of enamel in a tooth. Yet like evil, while blindness
and cavities are not things, they are realities of life. It must be underscored
that Augustine did not deny the reality of evil.

Augustine asserted that evil is specifically a privation of being and goodness.
To be precise, evil is the absence of the goodness (in the will of the creature)
that should be there. As he asserted, "What are called vices in the soul are
nothing but privations of natural good."[3] Augustine believed, therefore, that
evil is properly defined as an imperfection or corruption of the good. Evil may
be thought of in this way as a type of ontological parasite on goodness.[4] As
Augustine says, "For what is that which we call evil but the absence of good?"[5]

An important apologetics upshot springs from Augustine's line of reasoning on evil. If evil is not a positive substance, as he believed, then God did
not create evil as he did everything else. Therefore, God is not the creator of
evil. The source of evil is rather found in the corruption of the good that God
originally made.

Augustine's theory of defining evil as a privation of being or goodness has
not been universally accepted among Christian philosophers and theologians,
let alone by non-Christian thinkers. It could also be fairly said that Augustine's
definition of evil fails to account fully for the dynamic and fluid nature of evil
that is implied in the Bible's depiction of evil and sin. So Augustine's definition
of evil has been characterized by some as incomplete.

Nevertheless, Augustine brought forth two profound apologetic insights
regarding the nature of evil:

1. *He concluded that evil is in some sense parasitically dependent on goodness.* This serves as a powerful argument that the problem of evil presupposes
the prior existence of goodness. For as he points out, "There can be no evil
where there is no good."[6] This (as discussed in the previous chapter) is a key
response to those who seek to deny God's existence on the basis of evil. Evil,
by its very nature, is dependent on the good.

2. *He discerned that evil is not a substance or a thing.* Rather evil can, in
one sense, be thought of as a nonphysical, conceptual moral judgment (a
violation of the presumed good). Yet critical conceptual realities like moral
judgments (as well as mathematical and logical constructs) need to be accounted for in the world of human beings. These abstract realities comport
well with Augustine's Christian theistic worldview, but they seem foreign and

unaccounted for in a godless, naturalistic worldview. Augustine was clear, however, that evil, though not a substance or thing, was real and originated in the will of the creature.

Evil and the Will of the Creature

Scripture is unequivocal that the choices of God's creatures have resulted in evil. The misuse of freedom on the part of those whom God created has generated two distinct rebellions.

1. *Lucifer sought to usurp God's authority.* Although he was an angel who possessed a high position in the order of God's angelic creatures (Ezek. 28:12–19), he led a revolt in the angelic ranks (Isa. 14:12–20; Jude 1:6). Lucifer—now known as Satan or the devil—along with his demonic cohorts is a powerful agent of evil and directly opposes the moral good of God. The Bible mentions in numerous places Satan's diabolical influence in the world and among humankind (John 12:31; 2 Cor. 4:4; Eph. 2:2; 1 John 5:19).

But how could a finite being who was created good and who lacked any external evil influence possibly choose evil? Augustine again provides a provocative explanation.[7] He suggests that Lucifer's sin was actually one of idolatry. Lucifer didn't directly choose evil. Rather he chose a good thing—himself—but subsequently exalted himself above the highest good: God. Lucifer was overcome by the ultimate sin of pride (1 Tim. 3:6).

2. *A similar rebellion took place among human beings* (Gen. 3). Adam and Eve, the first humans, misused their freedom to rebel against God's sovereign rule. Tempted by Satan, they chose to go their own autonomous way. Their disobedience of God's commands resulted in immediate alienation from God, which was manifest in spiritual and physical death (review chapter 9). Yet because Adam represented all humanity before God, the sinful state and inclinations of the first humans have been passed on to all subsequent human beings (original sin; see Rom. 5:12–21). Consequently, all people are pervasively sinful (Pss. 51:5; 58:3) and capable of evil (Jer. 17:9; Matt. 15:19).

It can be reasonably argued that most of the evil and suffering present in the world stem directly from the will of the creature. This truth explains much about evil. The Scriptures teach, however, that God is in sovereign control of all things. How does God's sovereignty factor into the equation?

What about God's Sovereignty?

The Bible reveals that not only is God the transcendent Creator of all things (Gen. 1:1), but he is also the providential sustainer of all things (Acts 17:25–27;

Col. 1:17; Heb. 1:3). This means that nothing happens outside of God's sovereign control and direction, for he "works out everything in conformity with the purpose of his will" (Eph. 1:11). Even evil, calamity, and suffering are under God's unique sustaining and controlling power (Exod. 4:11; Isa. 45:7; Lam. 3:38). Yet while the Bible reveals God's sovereignty, it also declares that human beings are morally responsible for their actions before God (Matt. 16:27; Rev. 22:12).

While God's sovereignty and human responsibility are paradoxical truths,[8] they are nevertheless both taught in Scripture, sometimes in the very same verse (Luke 22:22; Acts 2:23). The Bible nowhere explains how God can be the cause of all events and actions yet also hold human beings accountable for their individual actions. God's sovereignty and human responsibility are compatible truths, but just how God works out this compatibility is known only to him. Those in the Augustinian-Reformed tradition say that the answer to this great mystery lies in God's infinite wisdom and power. As the Scripture reveals, God is capable of things far beyond the comprehension and capacity of mere mortals (Rom. 9:14–23; 11:30–36).

So while God's cosmic plan involves evil, calamity, and suffering, the Scriptures indicate that God never directly performs evil himself, nor does he coerce his creatures to engage in evil and commit sin (James 1:13).[9] And while God's sovereign governing power makes evil a sure reality, the Scriptures convey that God is not the author of evil and that in holding his creatures accountable for their sin, he is just. The clear message of Scripture is that God is directing all things toward his ultimate righteous and just ends (Dan. 4:35; Rom. 11:36). Reformed theologian Louis Berkhof remarks about God's sovereignty and the reality of sin:

> The decree of God is His eternal plan or purpose, in which He has foreordained all things that come to pass. . . . It covers all the works of God in creation and redemption, and also embraces the actions of men, not excluding their sinful deeds. But while it rendered the entrance of sin into the world certain, it does not make God responsible for our sinful deeds. His decree with respect to sin is a permissive decree. . . . It may be said, however, that the decree merely makes God the author of free moral beings, who are themselves the authors of sin. Sin is made certain by the decree, but God does not Himself produce it by His direct action. At the same time it must be admitted that the problem of God's relation to sin remains a mystery which we cannot fully solve.[10]

Because evil and suffering are under the direct control of the sovereign God, one may wonder why God permits such things to happen. What follows is an attempt to come to grips with that challenging question.

Why Does God Allow Evil and Suffering?

Christians should avoid presumption and glibness concerning the causes of evil and suffering because the question remains a mystery. Attempting to explain why there is evil in a world made by a good God is called theodicy (justifying the ways of God).

While much more could be said regarding the issue of theodicy, five broad points can be marshaled to help answer this difficult question:

1. *God has a morally sufficient though not yet fully disclosed reason for allowing evil and suffering.*[11] God assures his people that his decrees and actions are always righteous and holy. The Scriptures are replete with declarations of God's moral nature and of his dealings with humankind as just. As the patriarch Abraham declares in Genesis 18:25, "Will not the Judge of all the earth do right?" And the psalmist pronounces in Psalm 89:14, "Righteousness and justice are the foundation of your throne."

But while God has a morally justifiable reason for all he does, as the sovereign Ruler of the universe, he seldom chooses to explain himself to his creatures. Nor is he or his decisions subject to the critique of finite and imperfect human beings. And if God did explain his ultimate purposes to human beings, is there any reason to think that mere creatures could understand God's majestic ways? Even God's classic discussion with Job about the problem of evil and suffering reveals God's inscrutable wisdom and Job's limited understanding of God's purposes in creation and in redemption (Job 38:1–11; see also Isa. 55:8–9). As the apostle Paul declares:

> Oh, the depth of the riches of the wisdom and knowledge of God!
> How unsearchable his judgments,
> and his paths beyond tracing out!
> "Who has known the mind of the Lord?
> Or who has been his counselor?"
> "Who has ever given to God,
> that God should repay them?"
> For from him and through him and for him are all things.
> To him be the glory forever! Amen. (Rom. 11:33–36)

Theodicy (the Justification of Evil in Relation to God)

In an attempt to discover whether evil has a justifiable purpose on God's part, philosophers have offered two classifications:

1. Gratuitous: purposeless or unjustifiable evil
2. Inscrutable: unfathomable or indiscernible evil

---

2. *God allows evil and suffering because of the greater good that results from it.* The basic Christian answer for why God allows evil and suffering is that God plans to bring about a greater good from it. According to Scripture, the greatest good for humanity came out of the greatest act of evil. Jesus Christ, none other than God in the flesh, came to reveal God's love to humankind. But though he was perfectly holy and blameless, he was falsely accused, convicted, beaten, and then executed as a common criminal. Jesus underwent the agony of Roman capital punishment: crucifixion. But God had planned this incredible miscarriage of justice from all eternity (Acts 2:22–23). Out of this horrible incident of pain and suffering came divine redemption for sinners. God brought the greatest good out of the greatest evil. Consider Augustine's words again as he notes that God only allows evil for purposes of the greater good:

> For the Almighty God, who, as even the heathen acknowledge, has supreme power over all things, being Himself supremely good, would never permit the existence of anything evil among His works, if He were not so omnipotent and good that He can bring good even out of evil.[12]

While Christians should be cautious about claiming to readily identify God's purposes behind specific incidents of evil and suffering, there are some scriptural purposes revealed concerning how God uses evil and suffering for good in the world.

3. *God may use evil and suffering to get a nonbeliever's attention and ultimately draw that person to himself* (Zech. 13:7–9; Luke 13:1–5; John 9). If God protected people from the consequences of their sin, they would be far less likely to sense their deep estrangement from him. A life without pain and suffering would serve to reinforce the sinful illusion that people are truly independent and in control of their destiny. Without trials and difficulties, people would likely think everything is okay and fail to recognize their desperate need for God.

Christian apologist Walter R. Martin used to say that some people will not look up until they are flat on their back. Evil and suffering can shock people out of their life of diversion and indifference to spiritual things. Nothing serves to awaken a soul to its desperate plight like pain and suffering. Evil, pain, and suffering in this way may be used by God's grace to bring a person to faith. As C. S. Lewis so eloquently put it: "God whispers to us in our pleasures, speaks in our conscience, but shouts in our pains: it is His megaphone to rouse a deaf world."[13]

The New Testament story of the prodigal son illustrates how God's grace works in and through the difficult times of people's lives to get their attention and to draw them to God. Jesus's story notes both the providential benefits of adversity and the overwhelming nature of God's grace:

When he came to his senses, he said, "How many of my father's hired servants have food to spare, and here I am starving to death! I will set out and go back to my father and say to him: Father, I have sinned against heaven and against you. I am no longer worthy to be called your son; make me like one of your hired servants." So he got up and went to his father.

But while he was still a long way off, his father saw him and was filled with compassion for him; he ran to his son, threw his arms around him and kissed him.

The son said to him, "Father, I have sinned against heaven and against you. I am no longer worthy to be called your son."

But the father said to his servants, "Quick! Bring the best robe and put it on him. Put a ring on his finger and sandals on his feet. Bring the fattened calf and kill it. Let's have a feast and celebrate. For this son of mine was dead and is alive again; he was lost and is found." So they began to celebrate. (Luke 15:17–24)

4. *Natural evil or physical forces, while capable of unleashing much destruction and harm, are actually necessary for making Earth a habitable planet*. The cosmos that God made is both aesthetically beautiful and physically ominous. Humankind must therefore exercise prudence and caution when it comes to the powerful forces of nature. Much physical devastation that affects human beings can be avoided if people respect nature and share scientific advancements that help protect people from impending natural calamities. Technologically advanced societies bear responsibility for helping the less-advanced cultures to preserve life and protect property from nature's forces. Natural evil (or disaster) is too often the result of moral evil in the form of irresponsible behavior or the lack of concern for the welfare of others.

The pain and sorrow caused by natural disasters are real and heartbreaking. Christians are called by God to be at the forefront of efforts to help people who are victims of such tragedies. All people are made in the image of God and deserve relief and charitable support. Through the centuries Christian organizations have led the way in helping the less fortunate around the globe who are suffering.

But so-called natural disasters are far from being all bad. Such powerful natural forces as earthquakes, hurricanes, tornadoes, and volcanoes (all of which were part of Earth before humans arrived) also carry with them many benefits for the planet and thus for human beings.[14] Planetary scientists consistently affirm that natural events such as hurricanes and earthquakes must occur for Earth to maintain the delicate balances of atmospheric and other environmental conditions necessary for human life to exist and to thrive. Far from being just terrorizing acts of God, the powerful forces of nature illustrate God's fine-tuned care for Earth and thus his provision and preparation for human beings.

Scripture speaks of God's providential care for his creation that often comes through the amazingly powerful forces mentioned above.

> You care for the land and water it;
>   you enrich it abundantly.
> The streams of God are filled with water
>   to provide the people with grain,
>   for so you have ordained it.
> You drench its furrows and level its ridges;
>   you soften it with showers and bless its crops. (Ps. 65:9–10)

Although natural evil occurs, God's moral and spiritual purposes are enacted in and through the secondary causes of nature. In other words, God remains in complete, sovereign control of the laws of nature and their effects.

5. *God's sovereignty and glory will be displayed by his cosmic conquest over evil.* The *Westminster Shorter Catechism* (a Reformation statement of faith of 1647) begins with the reflective question: "What is the chief end of man?" The answer is, "Man's chief end is to glorify God, and to enjoy him for ever."[15] In fact, all of God's great works (creation and redemption) are intended to display his sovereignty and glory. God's cosmic prevailing over evil and sin, however, will even more surely exhibit his splendor and dominion. This triumph over evil has already begun with the life, death, and resurrection of the divine Messiah, Jesus Christ. God's power to conquer evil is anticipated in creation but executed in redemption. Satan and his forces are already defeated foes with Christ's first coming as Savior (Heb. 2:14–15), and all evil and human sin will forever be vanquished at Christ's second coming as Judge and Lord (Rev. 21).[16] After these cataclysmic eschatological events, God will bring forth the new creation. Revelation 21:1–3 speaks of God creating a new heaven and a new earth along with the Holy City—the New Jerusalem. At that glorious time all evil, suffering, and sorrow will be forever eliminated. The apostle John provides a prophetic glimpse of this glorious eternal age to come in the book of Revelation:

> They will be his people, and God himself will be with them and be their God. "He will wipe every tear from their eyes. There will be no more death" or mourning or crying or pain, for the old order of things has passed away. (Rev. 21:3–4)

God's Purposes in the Christian Life

Having briefly looked at God's general reasons for allowing evil and suffering, let's now note God's purposes in the lives of his people. It may be that God uses evil and suffering to build the moral and spiritual character of his people or to express fatherly discipline (Rom. 5:3; Heb. 10:36; 12:4–11).

Courage is forged only through facing one's fears. Steel must be refined by fire. For faith to grow, it must be tested by trial. God appears to be more concerned about his children's character than about their comfort, therefore he uses evil and suffering to facilitate the believer's moral and spiritual maturity. The apostle Paul, who endured much evil and suffering, explains the causal relationship between suffering and character: "Not only so, but we also glory in our sufferings, because we know that suffering produces perseverance; perseverance, character; and character, hope" (Rom. 5:3–4).

Noble earthly parents discipline their children. Discipline isn't pleasant at the time for children, but it is crucial for their growth as responsible persons. God may similarly use the effects of evil and suffering to bring about discipline in the life of his children. As the writer of Hebrews declares, "Endure hardship as discipline; God is treating you as his children" (Heb. 12:7). The assuring guarantee that the Christian has, however, is that God will not allow evil and suffering in a person's life without producing a greater good for him or her. The apostle Paul sets forth that divine promise in Romans 8:28: "And we know that in all things God works for the good of those who love him, who have been called according to his purpose."

Facing evil and suffering is never easy, even if one knows God is ultimately in control. What practical things can the Christian keep in mind during difficult times?

Christians' Assurance in Confronting Evil and Suffering

In closing this chapter and this book, I'd like to offer three thoughts to help those who sometimes find themselves in the throes of the struggle:

1. *Believers need to know that they never suffer alone.* God is acquainted with suffering. Jesus Christ came into the world as a man and suffered with human beings and for them. God himself entered into the painful and ugly mix. Of all the world's religions, only in Christianity does God suffer *with* humanity and *for* humanity! His suffering on Earth and especially on the cross can transform the individual suffering of his people.[17] Even now Jesus serves in his role as the great High Priest in which he intercedes for believers during their great adversities. Jesus is not aloof or indifferent to human suffering; he suffered as a real man. The author of Hebrews declares Christ's glorious role as a sympathetic High Priest:

> Therefore, since we have a great high priest who has ascended into heaven, Jesus the Son of God, let us hold firmly to the faith we profess. For we do not have a high priest who is unable to empathize with our weaknesses, but we have one who has been tempted in every way, just as we are—yet he did not sin. Let us then approach God's throne of grace with confidence, so that we may receive mercy and find grace to help us in our time of need. (Heb. 4:14–16)

2. *God calls all his children to live with faith.* He wants us to have confidence and trust in the goodness and sovereignty of God despite the presence of evil and suffering. Scripture points to the powerful examples of Abraham, Moses, Job, and Paul. To paraphrase a hymn, we don't know what tomorrow holds, but we do know who holds the future. Faith is trusting in the character of God when circumstances are painful and confusing. Christians can trust God in the midst of suffering because we are aware of his character and his promises. Many generations have known his faithfulness. The apostle Paul assures the church through asking and answering a probing question about evil and suffering: "Who shall separate us from the love of Christ? Shall trouble or hardship or persecution or famine or nakedness or danger or sword? . . . No, in all these things we are more than conquerors through him who loved us" (Rom. 8:35, 37).

3. *Evil and suffering are not merely a logical or philosophical problem; they are a deeply personal problem.* When people suffer they need comfort and reassurance. Christians can confront evil and suffering in a powerfully practical way by comforting those afflicted by evil and by easing the pain of people around them who are suffering. The Christian church, as Christ's hands and feet in a needy world, exists to extend loving care and concern for its members and others who are wounded by evil and suffering.

How Historic Christianity's Most Comforting Dangerous Idea Changed the World

Knowing that there is a moral rhyme and reason to the universe makes all the difference. Historic Christianity's message that God is both loving and just and has good reasons for allowing pain and suffering provides genuine hope for fragile human beings. God also promises to do away with evil finally and forever in Christ's eternal kingdom.

Christ's church has been commissioned to provide a livable and hopeful world- and life-view to the lost people of the earth. In addition, Christians bear a responsibility to help comfort those souls who have been the victims of pain and sorrow. But how has the church fared in discharging this difficult and sacred responsibility over the centuries?

Certainly the church has never been perfect but instead has struggled with many moral faults. But Christians throughout history have worked diligently to (among other things) abolish slavery, build orphanages for homeless children, erect hospitals for the sick, provide hospice facilities for the dying, set up soup kitchens for the hungry, and fund scholarships for the needy. In other words, despite its serious flaws, the Christian church has sought to express Christ's love to a fallen and hurting humanity.

God's Solution

The historic Christian answer to the problem of evil and suffering is found in the person of Jesus Christ. God has come in the flesh to heal his people's suffering and to destroy the power of evil. The suffering of God in Christ is the ultimate solution to the problem of evil for human beings.

Historic Christianity's seventh dangerous idea is that God has a purpose and a good for all the evil and suffering humanity experiences. Christianity is the only belief system whose central message (the gospel) focuses on God coming into the world to suffer, die, and rise again and, through that act, to conquer all evil and suffering once and forever.

Living and Thinking Dangerously

The Christian faith consists of many more dangerous ideas than the seven discussed in this book. May the transforming power of these magnificent seven spark an interest to explore all the truths of the faith such that the *danger* will spread.

To God be the glory.

Further Suggested Reading

Logical Problem of Evil and Suffering

Frame, John M. *Apologetics to the Glory of God*. Phillipsburg, NJ: Presbyterian and Reformed, 1994. Chapters 6–7.

Lewis, C. S. *The Problem of Pain*. New York: Macmillan, 1962.

Peterson, Michael. *Evil and the Christian God*. Grand Rapids: Baker, 1982.

Plantinga, Alvin C. *God, Freedom, and Evil*. Grand Rapids: Eerdmans, 1974.

Psychological Problem of Evil and Suffering

Eareckson Tada, Joni, and Steve Estes. *A Step Further*. Grand Rapids: Zondervan, 1978.

Kreeft, Peter. *Making Sense Out of Suffering*. Ann Arbor, MI: Servant, 1986.

Lewis, C. S. *A Grief Observed*. Reprint, San Francisco: HarperSanFrancisco, 2001.

Yancy, Phillip. *Where Is God When It Hurts?* Revised and expanded edition. Grand Rapids: Zondervan, 1997.

Discussion Questions

1. Why is the problem of evil the number one reason given for not believing in God?

2. Why is viewing evil as an illusion such an inadequate response?

3. If God has good reasons for allowing evil, what may some of those reasons be?

4. How does the philosophical problem of evil differ from the psychological problem of evil?

5. How is Jesus Christ the ultimate answer to the problem of evil and suffering?

Acknowledgments

Writing a book involves an enormous investment of time, energy, and focus. I am very fortunate that a number of people encouraged me in this exacting task and that others worked diligently to improve the quality of this work.

Expressing gratitude for this assistance begins with my family. My wife, Joan, patiently endured the many hours I spent researching and writing and also offered me encouragement on the project when I needed it the most. The continual respect and loving support extended to me by my three children—Sarah, Jacqueline, and Michael—remain a source of deep strength for me.

My friends and colleagues at Reasons To Believe (RTB) also served as a source of personal encouragement—a number of them even used their editorial talents. I am especially thankful to my friend Joe Aguirre, whose editorial skill and advice helped to strengthen and sharpen this book's content. Editors Sandra Dimas and Kathy Ross also offered many helpful suggestions that improved the readability and the overall quality of this book. And Marj Harman and Linda Kloth improved the accuracy of the book by carefully checking all the notes and references.

I'm also appreciative that RTB's scholar team, including Hugh Ross, Fuz Rana, Dave Rogstad, and Jeff Zweerink, along with apologist Bob Stuart, continue to challenge me to think carefully and critically about issues of truth and reality. My interaction with these men over the years has, in various ways, served to shape the apologetics reasoning evident in this book.

For the professional guidance and kind assistance of the people at Baker Books, I remain indebted. Specifically, special thanks to Baker's executive editor Robert Hosack for his support and to Wendy Wetzel for her editorial counsel.

I also appreciate the members of my weekly Sunday school class at Christ Reformed Church in Anaheim, California, who have heard me talk about the content of this book over many years.

My daughter, Sarah, helped to inspire me in the writing of this work—thus the book is dedicated to her.

Finally, glory and praise to the Triune God: Father, Son, and Holy Spirit.

Faith seeking understanding,
Kenneth Richard Samples
Advent 2011

Notes

Introduction Historic Christianity's Dangerous Ideas

1. For a historic Christian analysis of today's competing worldviews, see Kenneth Richard Samples, *A World of Difference: Putting Christian Truth-Claims to the Worldview Test* (Grand Rapids: Baker, 2007).

Chapter 1 Easter Hope

1. Lynne Ann DeSpelder and Albert Lee Strickland, *The Last Dance: Encountering Death and Dying*, 4th ed. (Mountain View, CA: Mayfield, 1996), 5–6.

2. Walter Ralston Martin (1928–89), my first teacher and mentor in the historic Christian faith, would often repeat this line in his lectures and sermons.

3. For a Christian theistic perspective on the critical issue of the origin of life, see Fazale Rana and Hugh Ross, *Origins of Life* (Colorado Springs: NavPress, 2004).

4. For a Christian theistic critique of the naturalistic worldview, particularly its view of the mind and rationality, see "Naturalism: A Secular Worldview Challenge," in Samples, *World of Difference*, chap. 12.

5. Stephen T. Davis, *Risen Indeed: Making Sense of the Resurrection* (Grand Rapids: Eerdmans, 1993), 203.

6. Ibid., 203–4.

7. The portion of this chapter that explains and defends the historic resurrection of Jesus Christ is a revision and expansion of "Did Jesus Christ Actually Rise from the Dead?" in my book *Without a Doubt: Answering the 20 Toughest Faith Questions* (Grand Rapids: Baker, 2004), chap. 10.

8. For a detailed harmonization of the material from the Gospels relating to the resurrection, see John Wenham, *Easter Enigma: Do the Resurrection Accounts Contradict One Another?* 2nd ed. (Grand Rapids: Baker, 1993).

9. For apologetic evidence of the resurrection of Jesus as well as critiques of alternative naturalistic theories, see William Lane Craig, *Reasonable Faith*, 3rd ed. (Wheaton: Crossway, 2008), 333–404; William Lane Craig, *Assessing the New Testament Evidence for the Historicity of the Resurrection of Jesus* (Lewiston, NY: Edwin Mellen, 1989); Gary R. Habermas and Michael R. Licona, *The Case for the Resurrection of Jesus* (Grand Rapids: Kregel, 2004); Gary R. Habermas, *The Risen Jesus and Future Hope* (Lanham, MD: Rowman and Littlefield, 2003); and N. T. Wright, *The Resurrection of the Son of God* (Minneapolis: Fortress, 2003).

10. See William Lane Craig, "Did Jesus Rise from the Dead?" in *Jesus Under Fire*, ed. Michael J. Wilkins and J. P. Moreland (Grand Rapids: Zondervan, 1995), 146–53.

11. John Dominic Crossan, *Jesus: A Revolutionary Biography* (San Francisco: HarperCollins, 1994), 174; also see Craig, "Did Jesus Rise?," 141–76.

12. Craig, "Did Jesus Rise?," 153.

13. Gary R. Habermas, "The Resurrection Appearances of Jesus," in *In Defense of Miracles*, ed. R. Douglas Geivett and Gary R. Habermas (Downers Grove, IL: InterVarsity, 1997), 262.

14. Gary R. Habermas, "Tracing Jesus's Resurrection to Its Earliest Eyewitness Accounts," in *God Is Great, God Is Good*, ed. William Lane Craig and Chad Meister (Downers Grove, IL: InterVarsity, 2009), 208.

15. James D. G. Dunn, *Jesus Remembered*, vol. 1 of *Christianity in the Making* (Grand Rapids: Eerdmans, 2003), 855.

16. A. J. Hoover, *The Case for Christian Theism: An Introduction to Apologetics* (Grand Rapids: Baker, 1976), 230.

17. Davis, *Risen Indeed*, 4.

18. Hoover, *Case for Christian Theism*, 234.

19. Blaise Pascal, *Pensées*, trans. A. J. Krailsheimer, rev. ed. (New York: Penguin, 1995), 249.

Chapter 2 Objections Examined

1. J. P. Moreland, *Scaling the Secular City* (Grand Rapids: Baker, 1987), 151–54.

2. Craig L. Blomberg, *The Historical Reliability of the Gospels* (Downers Grove, IL: InterVarsity, 1987), 18.

3. Richard L. Purtill, *Thinking about Religion* (Englewood Cliffs, NJ: Prentice Hall, 1978), 81–93.

4. A. N. Sherwin-White, *Roman Society and Roman Law in the New Testament* (Grand Rapids: Baker, 1978), 186–93.

5. Julius Müller, quoted in Craig, *Reasonable Faith*, 284–85.

6. Blomberg, *Historical Reliability*, 81–84.

7. Edwin M. Yamauchi, "Easter: Myth, Hallucination, or History?" Leadership University, accessed August 23, 2001, http://www.leaderu.com/everystudent/easter/articles/yama.html; and Habermas and Licona, *Case for the Resurrection*, 89–92.

8. Peter Kreeft, *Between Heaven and Hell* (Downers Grove, IL: InterVarsity, 1982), 74.

9. F. F. Bruce, *The New Testament Documents: Are They Reliable?*, 5th ed. (Downers Grove, IL: InterVaristy, 1960), 45–46.

10. Peter Kreeft and Ronald K. Tacelli, *Handbook of Christian Apologetics* (Downers Grove, IL: InterVarsity, 1994), 185.

11. For a present-day critique of the resurrection of Jesus Christ by numerous atheists or skeptics, see Jeffrey Lowder and Robert M. Price, eds., *The Empty Tomb* (Amherst, NY: Prometheus, 2005).

12. See Stephen T. Davis, "The Counterattack of the Resurrection Skeptics," *Philosophia Christi* 8 (Summer 2006): 55–56.

13. See Yamauchi, "Easter."

14. This theory was publicly debated by philosophers Greg Cavin (advocated) and William Lane Craig (critiqued). Accessed January 8, 2002, at http:www.leaderu.com/offices/billcraig.

15. Habermas, "Resurrection Appearances of Jesus," 272–74.

16. William Lane Craig, *Knowing the Truth about the Resurrection* (Ann Arbor, MI: Servant, 1988), 110.

17. Davis, *Risen Indeed*, 168.

18. Augustine, *Confessions*, trans. R. S. Pine-Coffin (New York: Penguin, 1961), 1.6.25.

19. Merrill C. Tenney, *The Reality of the Resurrection* (New York: Harper and Row, 1963), 141.

20. Hoover, *Case for Christian Theism*, 234.

Chapter 3 Religious Pluralism and God in the Flesh

1. William L. Rowe, *Philosophy of Religion*, 2nd ed. (Belmont, CA: Wadsworth, 1993), 174–75.

2. The most primitive form of Buddhism, *Theravada*, is godless in belief.

3. Purtill, *Thinking about Religion*, 105–6.

4. For a presentation and defense of the Christian doctrine of the Trinity, see Kenneth Richard Samples, "How Can God Be Three and One?" in *Without a Doubt* (Grand Rapids: Baker, 2004), 63–76.

5. Craig A. Blaising, "Hypostatic Union," in *Evangelical Dictionary of Theology*, ed. Walter A. Elwell (Grand Rapids: Baker, 1984), 540.

6. For a discussion of the principle of kenosis, see Bruce Milne, *Know the Truth*, 3rd ed. (Downers Grove, IL: InterVarsity, 2009), 200; and Wayne Grudem, *Systematic Theology* (Grand Rapids: Zondervan, 1994), 549–52.

7. Milne, *Know the Truth*, 200.

8. Ibid.

9. See the Chalcedonian formulation in Alister E. McGrath, *An Introduction to Christianity* (Cambridge, MA: Blackwell, 1997), 131–32.

10. For a discussion of how the two natures can be in union without contradiction, see Samples, *Without a Doubt*, 132–33.

11. The following material in support of the deity of Jesus Christ was partially derived from Murray J. Harris, *Jesus as God* (Grand Rapids: Baker, 1992), 315–17; and John Jefferson Davis, *Handbook of Basic Bible Texts* (Grand Rapids: Zondervan, 1984), 68–74.

12. The material in support of the humanity of Jesus Christ was partially derived from Milne, *Know the Truth*, 173–74.

13. John Hick, "A Pluralist View," in *More Than One Way? Four Views on Salvation in a Pluralistic World*, ed. Dennis L. Okholm and Timothy R. Phillips (Grand Rapids: Zondervan, 1995), 54–55.

14. John R. W. Stott, *Basic Christianity*, 2nd ed. (Downers Grove, IL: InterVarsity, 1971), 21–34. Some of Stott's descriptive statements about Jesus (e.g., p. 27) have been set forth in this section, and his scriptural analysis has been expanded.

15. D. A. Carson, *The Gospel according to John* (Grand Rapids: Eerdmans, 1991), 358.

16. Ibid., 394–95.

17. See Stott, *Basic Christianity*, 29–32.

18. See Robert L. Reymond, *Jesus, Divine Messiah* (Phillipsburg, NJ: P&R, 1990).

Chapter 4 Explanations for Christ's Life

1. Louis P. Pojman, *Philosophy*, 5th ed. (New York: Oxford University Press, 2002), 34–37.

2. Ibid., 36.

3. T. Edward Damer, *Attacking Faulty Reasoning*, 4th ed. (Belmont, CA: Wadsworth, 2001), 115.

4. See Josh McDowell, *Evidence that Demands a Verdict* (San Bernardino, CA: Here's Life, 1979), 103–9. In McDowell's defense, he addresses other possible alternatives in other parts of the book.

5. Reymond, *Jesus, Divine Messiah*.

6. See Samples, *Without a Doubt*, 96–97.

7. John Warwick Montgomery, *History and Christianity* (Minneapolis: Bethany, 1965), 66–72.

8. R. T. France, *The Evidence for Jesus* (Downers Grove, IL: InterVarsity, 1986), 19–58; and Gary R. Habermas, *The Historical Jesus* (Joplin, MO: College Press, 1996), 187–228.

9. Stott, *Basic Christianity*, 23–26.

10. C. S. Lewis, *Mere Christianity*, 3rd ed. (New York: Macmillan, 1952), 56.

11. For an assessment of Father Divine, see Walter Martin, *The Kingdom of the Cults* (Minneapolis: Bethany, 1977), 213–21. For an assessment of David Koresh, see Kenneth Samples et al., *Prophets of the Apocalypse* (Grand Rapids: Baker, 1994). For an assessment of Jim Jones, listen to Walter Martin's audio recording, "Jonestown, the Death of a Cult," available for purchase at http://www.waltermartin.com/prodserv.html.

12. Montgomery, *History and Christianity*, 62–63.

13. Ronald H. Nash, *Worldviews in Conflict* (Grand Rapids: Zondervan, 1992), 153.

14. Montgomery, *History and Christianity*, 64.

15. Huston Smith, *The World's Religions*, rev. ed. (San Francisco: HarperSanFrancisco, 1991), 143–44.

16. Ibid.

17. James T. Fisher and Lowell S. Hawley, *A Few Buttons Missing* (Philadelphia: Lippincott, 1951), 273.

18. For evangelical Christian assessments of the New Age movement, see Douglas R. Groothuis, *Unmasking the New Age* (Downers Grove, IL: InterVarsity, 1986); Elliot Miller, *A Crash Course on the New Age Movement* (Grand Rapids: Baker, 1989); and John P. Newport, *The New Age Movement and the Biblical Worldview* (Grand Rapids: Eerdmans, 1998).

19. For an evangelical Christian assessment of the "lost years of Jesus" claim, see Ron Rhodes, *The Counterfeit Christ of the New Age Movement* (Grand Rapids: Baker, 1990), 27–56; and Douglas Groothuis, *Revealing the New Age Jesus* (Downers Grove, IL: InterVarsity, 1990), 147–73.

20. Rhodes, *Counterfeit Christ*, 48.

21. Ibid., 44–46.

22. Ibid., 51.

23. Ibid., 47.

24. Hugh Ross, Kenneth Samples, and Mark Clark, *Lights in the Sky and Little Green Men* (Colorado Springs: NavPress, 2004), 147–58.

25. Ibid., 162–63.

26. Ibid., 164.

27. Ibid., 157–58.

28. Kreeft and Tacelli, *Christian Apologetics*, 151–52.

29. J. B. Phillips, "Angels' Point of View," in *New Testament Christianity* (London: Hodder and Stoughton, 1956).

30. Abraham Kuyper, "Sphere Sovereignty," in *Abraham Kuyper: A Centennial Reader*, ed. James D. Bratt (Grand Rapids: Eerdmans, 1998), 488.

Chapter 5 Cosmology and Creation Out of Nothing

1. Stephen W. Hawking and Roger Penrose, *The Nature of Space and Time* (Princeton, NJ: Princeton University Press, 1996), 20.

2. Paul Davies, *The Cosmic Blueprint* (New York: Simon and Schuster, 1988), 203.

3. The portion of this chapter that explains and defends the historic Christian doctrines of creation and providence is a revision and expansion of the chapter "God's World—Creation and Providence," in my book *World of Difference*, 153–69.

4. My discussion of the doctrine of creation in this chapter was influenced by the following sources: Davis, *Basic Bible Texts*, 45–47; C. John Collins, *Science and Faith* (Wheaton: Crossway, 2003); Milne, *Know the Truth*, 72–81; Louis Berkhof, *Summary of Christian Doctrine*, 2nd ed. (Grand Rapids: Eerdmans, 1947), 51–58; Louis Berkhof, *Systematic Theology*, new combined ed. (Grand Rapids: Eerdmans, 1996), 126–64; Grudem, *Systematic Theology*, 262–314; Robert L. Reymond, *A New Systematic Theology of the Christian Faith* (Nashville: Nelson, 1998), 383–414; Millard J. Erickson, *Christian Theology* (Grand Rapids: Baker, 1985), 365–86; Millard J. Erickson, *Introducing Christian Doctrine*, ed. L. Arnold Hustad (Grand Rapids: Baker, 1992), 120–27; and J. I. Packer, *Concise Theology* (Wheaton: Tyndale, 1993), 21–22.

5. Creation events (Gen. 1–2); creation's power and complexity (Job 9, 34–41); creation generally (Pss. 8; 19; 65; 102; 104; 139; 147–48); Israel's Creator (Isa. 40; 44; 48).

6. For a discussion of the doctrine of the Trinity, see Samples, "How Can God Be Three and One?" in *Without a Doubt*, 63–76.

7. Erickson, *Introducing Christian Doctrine*, 123.

8. Richard A. Muller, *Dictionary of Latin and Greek Theological Terms* (Grand Rapids: Baker, 1985), s.v. "*ex nihilo*."

9. Paul Copan and William Lane Craig, *Creation Out of Nothing* (Grand Rapids: Baker, 2004), 43.

10. Ibid., 78–83.

11. Ibid., 82.

12. For eight such biblical expressions, see Erickson, *Introducing Christian Doctrine*, 122.

13. Copan and Craig, *Creation Out of Nothing*, 27.

14. Cornelius Plantinga Jr., *Engaging God's World* (Grand Rapids: Eerdmans, 2002), 20, 22.

15. Samples, *Without a Doubt*, 75.

16. Copan and Craig, *Creation Out of Nothing*, 16.

17. Ibid., 25.

18. For a discussion of these three views of creation, see Norman L. Geisler, *Baker Encyclopedia of Christian Apologetics* (Grand Rapids: Baker, 1999), s.v. "creation, views of," 172–77.

19. For clear and thoughtful Christian critiques of pantheism and panentheism, see Winfried Corduan, *No Doubt about It* (Nashville: Broadman and Holman, 1997), 92–99; and Norman L. Geisler and William D. Watkins, *Worlds Apart*, 2nd ed. (Eugene, OR: Wipf and Stock, 2003), 75–146.

20. For a clear and thoughtful Christian critique of the metaphysical concept of monism (as expressed in Eastern mysticism and metaphysical naturalism), see Dean C. Halverson, ed., *The Compact Guide to World Religions* (Minneapolis: Bethany, 1996), 30–31, 160–97.

21. For clear and thoughtful Christian critiques of some of these religious philosophies, see Winfried Corduan, *Neighboring Faiths* (Downers Grove, IL: InterVarsity, 1998); and Halverson, *Compact Guide*.

22. For clear and thoughtful Christian critiques of some of these basic or folk religions, see Corduan, *Neighboring Faiths*; and Halverson, *Compact Guide*.

23. For clear and thoughtful Christian critiques of secularism, materialism, and atheism from a Christian theistic perspective, see Corduan, *No Doubt about It*, 83–88; and Halverson, *Compact Guide*, 144–59, 182–97.

24. For a summary of the problems associated with the naturalistic worldview, see Nash, *Worldviews in Conflict*, 116–29. For a Christian critique of naturalistic explanations for the emergence of the cosmos, see Copan and Craig, *Creation Out of Nothing*, 249–66.

25. For a clear and thoughtful Christian critique of nihilism, see James W. Sire, *The Universe Next Door*, 3rd ed. (Downers Grove, IL: InterVarsity, 1997), 74–93.

26. For a Christian critique of methodological naturalism, see Alvin Plantinga, "Methodological Naturalism?" *Access Research Network*, part 1, http://www.arn.org/docs/odesign/od181/methnat181.htm (accessed August 7, 2006); and part 2, http://www.arn.org/docs/odesign/od182/methnat182.htm.

27. For a clear and thoughtful Christian critique of finite godism and process theology, see Geisler and Watkins, *Worlds Apart*, chaps. 4 and 6. For the same on open theism, see John M. Frame, *No Other God* (Phillipsburg, NJ: P&R, 2001).

28. For a clear and thoughtful Christian critique of deism, see Corduan, *No Doubt about It*, 90–92; and Geisler and Watkins, *Worlds Apart*, 147–85. For the same on Islam, see Corduan, *Neighboring Faiths*, 77–112; and Halverson, *Compact Guide*, 103–20.

29. For introductory articles on the life and thought of Saint Augustine that includes his interaction with Manichaeism, see Kenneth Richard Samples, "Augustine of Hippo: From Pagan,

to Cultist, to Skeptic, to Christian Sage," *Facts for Faith* 5 (first quarter 2001): 36–41; see also http://www.reasons.org/augustine-hippo-part-1-pagan-cultist-skeptic-christian-sage; and "Augustine of Hippo: Rightly Dividing the Truth," *Facts for Faith* 6 (second quarter 2001): 34–39; see also http://www.reasons.org/augustine-hippo-pt-2-2-rightly-dividing-truth. For an evangelical assessment of Zoroastrianism, see Corduan, *Neighboring Faiths*, 113–34.

30. For a philosophical and theological critique of the Mormon view of God, see Francis J. Beckwith, Carl Mosser, and Paul Owen, eds., *The New Mormon Challenge* (Grand Rapids: Zondervan, 2002).

31. Gottfried Wilhelm Leibniz, "The Principles of Nature and of Grace, Based on Reason," in *Philosophic Classics*, *Bacon to Kant*, ed. Walter Kaufmann, vol. 2 (1714; repr., Englewood Cliffs, NJ: Prentice Hall, 1961), 256.

Chapter 6 Divine Providence and the Emergence of Science

1. USGS, "Magnitude 9.1—Off the West Coast of Northern Sumatra," U.S. Geological Survey, December 26, 2004, http://earthquake.usgs.gov/earthquakes/eqinthenews/2004/usslav/#summary.

2. Erickson, *Introducing Christian Doctrine*, 123.

3. Davis, *Basic Bible Texts*, 49. My discussion of the doctrine of providence in this chapter was influenced by the following sources: Davis, *Basic Bible Texts*, 49–52; Collins, *Science and Faith*, 161–79; Milne, *Know the Truth*, 81–89; Berkhof, *Summary of Christian Doctrine*, 59–63; Berkhof, *Systematic Theology*, 165–78; Grudem, *Systematic Theology*, 315–54; Reymond, *New Systematic Theology*, 398–414; Erickson, *Christian Theology*, 387–410; Erickson, *Introducing Christian Doctrine*, 128–37; and Packer, *Concise Theology*, 54–56.

4. Berkhof, *Summary of Christian Doctrine*, 59–63; Grudem, *Systematic Theology*, 316–36; and Erickson, *Introducing Christian Doctrine*, 128–37.

5. These points were influenced by Davis, *Basic Bible Texts*, 49–52; and Packer, *Concise Theology*, 54–55.

6. Erickson, *Introducing Christian Doctrine*, 128–29.

7. See Packer, *Concise Theology*, 56; and Grudem, *Systematic Theology*, 322–30.

8. See Kenneth Richard Samples, "Aren't Christianity and Science Enemies?" in *Without a Doubt*, 187–200.

9. Hugh Ross, *The Genesis Question*, 2nd ed. (Colorado Springs: NavPress, 2001), 195–97; and Reijer Hooykaas, *Religion and the Rise of Modern Science* (Grand Rapids: Eerdmans, 1972).

10. Michael Peterson et al., *Reason and Religious Belief* (New York: Oxford University Press, 1991), 210–14.

11. These twelve points were influenced by Delvin Lee Ratzsch, *Science and Its Limits* (Downers Grove, IL: InterVarsity, 2000), 36; and Nancy R. Pearcey and Charles B. Thaxton, *The Soul of Science* (Wheaton: Crossway, 1994). The portion of this chapter that explains how the Christian worldview influenced the character and presuppositions of science is a revision and expansion of the chapter "Aren't Christianity and Science Enemies?" in my book *Without a Doubt*, 187–200.

12. Ratzsch, *Science and Its Limits*, 138.

13. John C. Polkinghorne, *Science and Creation* (Boston: Shambhala, New Science Library, 1988), 20.

14. Rodney Stark, *For the Glory of God* (Princeton, NJ: Princeton University Press, 2003), 147.

15. McGrath, *Introduction to Christianity*, 166.

16. Ratzsch, *Science and Its Limits*, 139.

17. Stark, *Glory of God*, 147.

18. Leibniz, *Principles of Nature and of Grace*, 256.

Chapter 7 The Explanatory Power of Atheism versus Christian Theism

1. Richard Dawkins, *The God Delusion* (Boston: Houghton Mifflin, 2006), 317.

2. John Horgan, *The End of Science* (New York: Broadway, 1996).

3. Robert A. Harris, *The Integration of Faith and Learning* (Eugene, OR: Cascade, 2004), 197.

4. The portion of this chapter that explains and defends the profound realities that are accounted for by the God of the Bible is a revision and expansion of Kenneth Richard Samples, "How Can Anyone Know That God Exists?" in *Without a Doubt*, 21–33.

5. For an introductory discussion of the cosmological argument, see Edward L. Miller, *God and Reason*, 2nd ed. (Upper Saddle River, NJ: Prentice Hall, 1995), 45–67.

6. Richard Taylor, *Metaphysics*, 4th ed. (Englewood Cliffs, NJ: Prentice Hall, 1992), 100–101.

7. William Lane Craig, "God Is Not Dead Yet," *Christianity Today*, July 2008, 24. This popular article influenced my use of the traditional arguments for God's existence in this chapter.

8. Ibid.

9. This discussion of the two lines of scientific evidence is based on Miller, *God and Reason*, 52–54.

10. Hugh Ross explains big bang cosmology and how its proponents defend their theory in his book *The Creator and the Cosmos*, 3rd ed. (Colorado Springs: Navpress, 2001).

11. John Barrow and Joseph Silk, *The Left Hand of Creation* (New York: Oxford University Press, 1983), 38.

12. For a detailed scientific discussion of this topic, see John D. Barrow and Frank J. Tipler, *The Anthropic Cosmological Principle* (New York: Oxford University Press, 1986), 166–73, 401–3.

13. See Craig, *Reasonable Faith*, 116–24.

14. For a detailed discussion of the Kalam cosmological argument, see ibid., 111–56.

15. To consider the coherence of certain Eastern views of God, see Purtill, *Thinking about Religion*, 95–109; and Mortimer J. Adler, *Truth in Religion* (New York: Macmillan, 1990), 69–92.

16. See Jeffrey A. Zweerink, *Who's Afraid of the Multiverse?* (Glendora, CA: Reasons to Believe, 2008). See also Craig, *Reasonable Faith*, 134–39.

17. Ockham's razor: the simplest complete explanation is best. See Samples, *World of Difference*, 34.

18. Pascal's Wager: risk-reward analysis makes believing in the truth of historic Christianity a prudent wager. See Samples, *Without a Doubt*, 77–87.

19. See Alex Vilenkin, *Many Worlds in One* (New York: Hill and Wang, 2006), 176.

20. CNN Wire Staff, "Theology Unnecessary, Stephen Hawking Tells CNN," *CNN*, September 11, 2010, http://edition.cnn.com/2010/WORLD/europe/09/11/stephen.hawking.interview/index.html?eref=edition.

21. Stephen Hawking and Leonard Mlodinow, *The Grand Design* (New York: Bantam, 2010).

22. Michael Holden, "God Did Not Create the Universe, Says Hawking," *Reuters*, September 2, 2010, http://www.reuters.com/article/2010/09/02/us-britain-hawking-idUSTRE6811FN20100902.

23. Paul Davies, "Taking Science on Faith," *New York Times*, November 24, 2007, http://www.nytimes.com/2007/11/24/opinion/24davies.html.

24. For an introduction to the anthropic principle, see Patrick Glynn, *God: The Evidence* (Rocklin, CA: Prima, 1997), 21–55; and Ross, *Creator and the Cosmos*, 92.

25. Robin Collins, "A Scientific Argument for the Existence of God: The Fine-Tuning Design Argument," in *Reason for the Hope Within*, ed. Michael J. Murray (Grand Rapids: Eerdmans, 1998), 48.

26. Freeman J. Dyson, *Disturbing the Universe* (New York: Basic, 1979), 250.

27. For an extended essay of the fine-tuning argument, see Collins, "A Scientific Argument," 47–75.

28. Paul Davies, *The Mind of God* (New York: Simon and Schuster, 1992), 169.

29. Roger Penrose, *The Emperor's New Mind* (Oxford: Oxford University Press, 1989), 344.

30. Paul Copan, *Loving Wisdom* (St. Louis: Chalice, 2007), 85.

31. Taylor, *Metaphysics*, 110–16.

32. Gregory E. Ganssle, "Dawkins's Best Argument against God's Existence," in *Contending with Christianity's Critics*, ed. Paul Copan and William Lane Craig (Nashville: B&H Publishing Group, 2009), 80.

33. Ibid.

34. Moreland, *Scaling the Secular City*, 77–103, see especially 80–82.

35. Samples, "Augustine of Hippo: Rightly Dividing the Truth."

36. Concerning the laws of logic, see Peter A. Angeles, *The HarperCollins Dictionary of Philosophy*, 2nd ed. (New York: HarperCollins, 1992), s.v. "laws of thought, the three"; and Ronald H. Nash, *Life's Ultimate Questions* (Grand Rapids: Zondervan, 1999), 193–208.

37. See Alvin Plantinga, "Two Dozen (or so) Theistic Arguments," *Analytic Philosophy of Religion*, accessed February 23, 2011, http://philofreligion.homestead.com/files/theistic arguments.html.

38. Copan, *Loving Wisdom*, 105.

39. Ganssle, "Dawkins's Best Argument," 81.

40. Ibid., 82.

Chapter 8 More Signposts to the Almighty

1. For a defense of the Moral Argument, see Copan, *Loving Wisdom*, 89–95.

2. J. L. Mackie, *The Miracle of Theism* (Oxford: Clarendon, 1982), 115–16.

3. For a Christian assessment of existentialism, see C. Stephen Evans, *Existentialism: The Philosophy of Despair and the Quest for Hope* (Grand Rapids: Zondervan, 1984).

4. Lewis, *Mere Christianity*, 45–46.

5. Pascal, *Pensées*, S146/L114,131. For an introduction to Blaise Pascal and his thought, see Samples, "Why Should I Gamble on Faith?" in *Without a Doubt*, 77–87.

6. Samples, *Without a Doubt*, 91–103.

7. See Ron Rhodes, *Christ before the Manger* (Grand Rapids: Baker, 1992), 233–37.

8. For a defense of miracles from a Christian perspective, see Geivett and Habermas, *In Defense of Miracles*.

9. See Samples, "Testing the Christian Theistic Worldview," in *A World of Difference*, 265–76.

10. Davies, "Taking Science on Faith."

Chapter 9 Moral Goodness and the Human Condition

1. Islam has approximately 1.5 billion adherents worldwide and claims that fifty countries in the world have an Islamic majority. See http://www.islam.com/introislam.htm, accessed September 15, 2010.

2. The following works provide a helpful understanding of the religion of Islam and have influenced my thinking on the subject: Smith, *World's Religions*, 221–70; John L. Esposito, *Islam: The Straight Path*, 3rd ed. (New York: Oxford University Press, 1998); Seyyed Hossein Nasr, *The Heart of Islam* (San Francisco: HarperSanFrancisco, 2002); and Seyyed Hossein Nasr, *Islam: Religion, History, and Civilization* (San Francisco: HarperSanFrancisco, 2003).

3. The following works provide a helpful understanding of the various aspects of the religion of Islam from the standpoint of historic Christianity and have influenced my thinking on the subject: Corduan, *Neighboring Faiths*, 77–112; Dean Halverson, ed., *The Illustrated Guide to World Religions* (Bloomington, MN: Bethany, 2003), 103–24; and Norman L. Geisler and Abdul Saleeb, *Answering Islam*, 2nd ed. (Grand Rapids: Baker, 2002).

4. Islam.com, "Introduction to Islam," accessed September 15, 2010, http://www.islam.com/introislam.htm.

5. Islam.com, "Questions and Answers III," accessed September 15, 2010, http://www.islam.com/qans3.htm.

6. The portion of this chapter that explains the sinful nature of humankind and the atoning death of Christ is a revision and expansion of the chapter "Why Did Jesus Have to Die?" in Samples, *Without a Doubt*, 148–57.

7. For a thorough theological discussion of sin from a biblical perspective, see Berkhof, *Systematic Theology*, 219–61; Grudem, *Systematic Theology*, 490–514; and Erickson, *Christian Theology*, 561–658.

8. Erickson, *Christian Theology*, 564–80.

9. Charles Caldwell Ryrie, *Ryrie Study Bible*, exp. ed. (Chicago: Moody, 1994), 2004–5; and Grudem, *Systematic Theology*, 490.

10. Adapted from "Biblical Terms for Sin," *ESV Study Bible* (Wheaton: Crossway, 2008), 2530.

11. Erickson, *Christian Theology*, 781–823.

12. For a brief discussion of the view known as federalism, see Berkhof, *Summary of Christian Doctrine*, 75–76.

13. Reymond, *New Systematic Theology*, 430–36.

14. Davis, *Basic Bible Texts*, 56.

15. Stott, *Basic Christianity*, 75.

16. Reymond, *New Systematic Theology*, 450–53.

17. Davis, *Basic Bible Texts*, 57–58.

Chapter 10 God to the Rescue

1. "2010 Copiapó Mining Accident," *Wikipedia*, accessed February 15, 2011, http://en.wikipedia.org/wiki/2010_Copiap%C3%B3_mining_accident.

2. See Thomas C. Oden, *The Justification Reader* (Grand Rapids: Eerdmans, 2002). Oden's thesis is that the vast majority of Christianity's greatest teachers through the centuries (including the early church fathers) have affirmed the biblical doctrine of salvation by grace alone through faith alone in Christ alone.

3. Ibid., 82.

4. Anthony A. Hoekema, *Saved by Grace* (Grand Rapids: Eerdmans, 1989), 144–45.

5. Benjamin Breckinridge Warfield, *Biblical and Theological Studies*, ed. Samuel G. Craig (Philadelphia: P&R, 1952), 425.

6. The discussion of the atonement in this chapter was influenced by the following sources: John Murray, *Redemption Accomplished and Applied* (1955; repr., Grand Rapids: Eerdmans, 1975); Leon Morris, *The Atonement* (Downers Grove, IL: InterVarsity, 1983); Berkhof, *Summary of Christian Doctrine*, 113–17; Milne, *Know the Truth*, 150–63; and Erickson, *Christian Theology*, 761–841.

7. See discussion throughout Murray, *Redemption*; also see Morris, *Atonement*.

8. Alister E. McGrath, *Theology: The Basics* (Malden, MA: Blackwell, 2004), 71.

9. Davis, *Basic Bible Texts*, 78–79.

10. Murray, *Redemption*, 30.

11. See Oden, *Justification Reader*, 2.

12. Ibid., 37.

13. See McGrath, *Introduction to Christianity*, 134–43.

14. Berkhof, *Summary of Christian Doctrine*, 113.

15. See Louis Berkhof, *The History of Christian Doctrines* (Grand Rapids: Baker, 1937), 131–39.

16. Reymond, *New Systematic Theology*, 468.

17. Augustine, *On the Proceedings of Pelagius*, *New Advent*, accessed March 6, 2011, http://www.newadvent.org/fathers/1505.htm; and Alister E. McGrath, *Historical Theology* (Malden, MA: Blackwell, 1998), 35–37, 79–85.

18. Augustine, *On Nature and Grace*, in *Four Anti-Pelagian Writings*, trans. John A. Mourant and William J. Collinge (n.p.: Catholic University of America Press, 1992), 25; and Allan D.

Fitzgerald, ed. *Augustine through the Ages: An Encyclopedia* (Grand Rapids: Eerdmans, 1999), s.v. "predestination."

19. McGrath, *Historical Theology*, 36.

20. Ibid.

21. Ibid., 35.

22. Reymond, *New Systematic Theology*, 468.

23. For more on an evangelical assessment of Augustine's views concerning Adam's fall, see Berkhof, *History of Christian Doctrines*, 131–39; McGrath, *Historical Theology*, 79–85; and Harold O. J. Brown, *Heresies* (New York: Doubleday, 1984), 200–207.

24. See "Gratitude," part 3, Heidelberg Cathechism, in *Ecumenical Creeds and Reformed Confessions* (Grand Rapids: CRC Publications, 1988), 53–77.

Chapter 11 Secular Humanism and the *Imago Dei*

1. See Friedrich Nietzsche, *The Gay Science*, trans. Walter Kaufmann (New York: Vintage, 1974), 167, 181–82, 279–80.

2. See Friedrich Nietzsche, *The Will to Power*, trans. Walter Kaufman and R. J. Hollingdale (New York: Vintage, 1967), 3–82.

3. Dinesh D'Souza, "Staring into the Abyss: Why Peter Singer Makes the New Atheists Nervous," *Christianity Today*, March 2009, http://www.christianitytoday.com/ct/2009/march/22.60.html.

4. See Friedrich Nietzsche, *The Antichrist*, in *The Works of Friedrich Nietzsche*, vol. 11, ed. Alexander Tille, trans. Thomas Common (1896; repr., New York: Macmillan, 1908), 250–51, 347–51.

5. See Nietzsche, *Will to Power*, 261–453, especially 366–67.

6. See Nietzsche, *Gay Science*, 191–92.

7. See Peter Singer's website for numerous articles setting forth his views, accessed March 6, 2011, http://www.utilitarian.net/singer.

8. Peter Singer, *Practical Ethics*, 3rd ed. (New York: Cambridge University Press, 2011), 151.

9. Regarding *speciesism*, see ibid., 48–70.

10. Peter Singer, *Ethics* (Oxford: Oxford University Press, 1994), 6.

11. Peter Singer, quoted in Michael Specter, "The Dangerous Philosopher," *The New Yorker*, September 6, 1999, 46.

12. D'Souza, "Staring into the Abyss."

13. The portion of this chapter that explains the meaning of the *imago Dei* is a revision and expansion of Samples, "The Historic Christian View of Man," in *World of Difference*, 171–88.

14. Grudem, *Systematic Theology*, 442–50. Grudem's discussion of the *imago Dei* is clear and helpful.

15. Geoffrey W. Bromiley, ed., *The International Standard Bible Encyclopedia* (Grand Rapids: Eerdmans, 1982), s.v. "image of God," 2:803.

16. Grudem, *Systematic Theology*, 443.

17. Muller, *Latin and Greek Theological Terms*, s.v. "*imago Dei*."

18. Erickson, *Christian Theology*, 513.

19. Berkhof, *Summary of Christian Doctrine*, 69–70.

20. Grudem, *Systematic Theology*, 445–48; and Berkhof, *Summary of Christian Doctrine*, 69–70.

21. Cornelius Plantinga, *Engaging God's World*, x.

22. It appears that there are two types of *immortality* implied in Scripture. First, through being made in the image of God, human beings have a derived or created immortality, which means the soul will survive the death of the body. This *consciousness* in the intermediate state following death is true for believers (Luke 23:43; 2 Cor. 5:6–8; Phil. 1:21, 23–24; Heb. 12:23; Rev. 6:9–10; 14:13) and nonbelievers (Eccles. 12:7; Luke 16:22–23; 2 Peter 2:9). Second, immortality is

spoken of as being the gift of God through redemption in Jesus Christ (Rom. 2:7; 2 Tim. 1:10). Of course only God alone has an inherent immortality (1 Tim. 1:17; 6:16).

23. Charles Hodge, *Systematic Theology* (1872; repr., Grand Rapids: Eerdmans, 1986), 2:97.

24. Herman Bavinck, *In the Beginning*, ed. John Bolt, trans. John Vriend (Grand Rapids: Baker, 1999), 187.

25. Ibid., 159–60.

26. Anthony A. Hoekema, *Created in God's Image* (Grand Rapids: Eerdmans, 1986), 5–10.

27. Davis, *Basic Bible Texts*, 53.

28. Hoekema, *Created in God's Image*, 21–22.

29. Ibid., 22.

30. Davis, *Basic Bible Texts*, 54.

31. Grudem, *Systematic Theology*, 449–50; and Erickson, *Christian Theology*, 516.

32. Davis, *Basic Bible Texts*, 54.

33. Hoekema, *Created in God's Image*, 16.

34. See the chapter on capital punishment in J. P. Moreland and Norman L. Geisler, *The Life and Death Debate* (Westport, CT: Praeger, 1990), 103–21. Also see the chapter on capital punishment in John Jefferson Davis, *Evangelical Ethics*, 3rd ed. (Phillipsburg, NJ: P&R, 2004), 203–18. The penalty of life imprisonment for murderers is not justice because the punishment (life in confinement) does not match the crime (the taking of an innocent life).

35. Davis, *Evangelical Ethics*, see especially chaps. 1 and 6.

36. These points concerning the Bible's perspective on the unborn were derived from ibid., 134–39. For a summary of the scientific evidence for the full humanity of the unborn, see Moreland and Geisler, *Life and Death Debate*, 34–36.

37. See Francis J. Beckwith and Norman L. Geisler, *Matters of Life and Death* (Grand Rapids: Baker, 1991).

38. Moreland and Geisler, *Life and Death Debate*, 63–82.

39. Davis, *Evangelical Ethics*, 200.

Chapter 12 How Human Beings Differ

1. See chap. 11, p. 164.

2. John Calvin, *Calvin: Institutes of the Christian Religion*, 1.1.1, ed. John T. McNeill, trans. Ford Lewis Battles, vol. 20 of Library of Christian Classics (Philadelphia: Westminster Press, 1960), 35.

3. *Westminster Shorter Catechism*, Q. 1, in *Reformed Confessions Harmonized*, ed. Joel R. Beeke and Sinclair B. Ferguson (Grand Rapids: Baker, 1999), 3.

4. Augustine, *Confessions*, bk. 1, 1.

5. Ibid., bk. 1, 20.

6. For a provocative and clear discussion of humankind's fallen condition and how that often leads to the state of the *divided self*, see Nash, *Worldviews in Conflict*, 46–53.

7. Cornelius Plantinga, *Engaging God's World*, 6–7.

8. Pascal, *Pensées*, S181/L148.

9. Ibid., S36/L417.

10. Augustine, *Confessions*, bk. 1, 5.

11. Kenneth L. Barker, gen. ed., *The NIV Study Bible*, 10th anniversary ed. (Grand Rapids: Zondervan, 1995), 8.

12. Fazale Rana with Hugh Ross, *Who Was Adam?* (Colorado Springs: NavPress, 2005), 48–49, 199–225.

13. See Harold H. Titus, Marilyn S. Smith, and Richard T. Nolan, *Living Issues in Philosophy*, 9th ed. (Belmont, CA: Wadsworth, 1995), 28–29. This philosophy text lists eight ways in which humans differ from the rest of nature. This chapter utilizes some of that material but also reorganizes and adds to it.

14. Paul Tillich, *The Courage to Be*, 2nd ed. (New Haven: Yale University Press, 2000), 47.

15. Titus, Smith, and Nolan, *Living Issues*, 29.

16. Socrates, *Apology*, 38e.

17. For a refutation of moral relativism and a defense of moral absolutism, see Samples, *Without a Doubt*, 229–38.

18. Alvin Plantinga, quoted in "Right and Wrong," in *Great Thinkers on Great Questions*, ed. Roy Abraham Varghese (Oxford: Oneworld, 1998), 102.

19. J. P. Moreland, *Christianity and the Nature of Science* (Grand Rapids: Baker, 1989), 11.

20. Stephen W. Hawking, *A Brief History of Time* (New York: Bantam, 1988), 171, 175.

21. Pascal, *Pensées*, S146/L114; S164/L131. For a discussion of Pascal's view of man and the explanatory power of Christianity, see Samples, *Without a Doubt*, 77–87.

22. Thomas V. Morris, *Making Sense of It All* (Grand Rapids: Eerdmans, 1992), 129.

23. The discussion of sin in this chapter was modified from Samples, *Without a Doubt*, 150.

24. For a discussion of salvation in and through faith in Jesus Christ, see Samples, *Without a Doubt*, 48–57.

25. See Mark Roseman, *The Wannsee Conference and the Final Solution* (New York: Henry Holt, 2002).

26. Hugh Ross conveyed this to me in a private conversation, Glendora, CA, 2001.

27. This argument was influenced by philosopher J. P. Moreland's argument in "The Image of God and the Failure of Scientific Atheism," in *God Is Great*, ed. Craig and Meister, 33.

28. See Alvin J. Schmidt, *How Christianity Changed the World* (Grand Rapids: Zondervan, 2004).

29. George Grant, *The Last Crusader* (Wheaton: Crossway, 1992), 127.

Chapter 13 Squaring Evil with God's Goodness

1. The portion of this chapter that explores the problem of evil and suffering is a revision and expansion of Samples, "How Can a Good and All-Powerful God Allow Evil?" in *Without a Doubt*, 239–54.

2. For a Christian assessment of Hinduism, see Corduan, *Neighboring Faiths*, 189–219. For a Christian assessment of the pantheistic-monistic worldview, see Samples, *World of Difference*, 233–45.

3. See Karl Menninger, *Whatever Became of Sin* (New York: E. P. Dutton, 1973).

4. Purtill, *Thinking about Religion*, 95–109.

5. Historian Stephen Ambrose calls World War II the greatest catastrophe in history in his introduction to C. L. Sulzberger, *The American Heritage New History of World War II* (New York: Viking, 1997).

6. David Hume, *Dialogues Concerning Natural Religion*, ed. Henry D. Aiken (New York: Hackett, 1998), 63. To see the full context of Hume's statement through his created philosophical dialogue (Philo), see pp. 62–67.

7. Rabbi Harold Kushner, *When Bad Things Happen to Good People* (New York: Anchor Books, 2004).

8. For further analysis of the view known as *finite godism*, see Geisler, *Baker Encyclopedia of Christian Apologetics*, s.v. "finite godism."

9. Richard Swinburne, quoted in "The Problem of Evil," in *Great Thinkers*, ed. Varghese, 191.

10. Copan, *Loving Wisdom*, 128.

11. Alvin C. Plantinga, *God, Freedom, and Evil* (Grand Rapids: Eerdmans, 1974), 30.

12. Ibid., 12–29.

13. For various Christian responses to the problem of evil, see Norman L. Geisler, *The Roots of Evil* (Grand Rapids: Zondervan, 1978); Michael Peterson, *Evil and the Christian God* (Grand Rapids: Baker, 1982); Ronald H. Nash, *Faith and Reason* (Grand Rapids: Zondervan,

1988), 177–222; and John M. Frame, *Apologetics to the Glory of God* (Phillipsburg, NJ: P&R, 1994), 149–90.

14. William L. Rowe, "IX. The Problem of Evil and Some Varieties of Atheism," *American Philosophical Quarterly* 16 (October 1979): 335, n. 1.

15. Paul Draper, "The Argument from Evil," in *Philosophy of Religion*, ed. Paul Copan and Chad Meister (Malden, MA: Blackwell, 2008), 146.

16. See Doug Powell, *Holman QuickSource Guide to Christian Apologetics* (Nashville: Holman Reference, 2006), 341–45.

17. Alvin Plantinga, *God, Freedom, and Evil*, 55.

18. This is the form of the quotation that is most frequently used. Though not in exactly this form, the idea is found throughout the book. See Fyodor Dostoevsky, *The Brothers Karamazov*, trans. Richard Pevear and Larissa Volokhonsky (New York: Farrar, Straus and Giroux, 1990), especially pp. 263, 593, 696–97.

19. Copan, *Loving Wisdom*, 128.

20. Chad Meister, "God, Evil and Morality," in *God Is Great*, ed. Craig and Meister, 109.

21. Gerard J. Hughes, quoted in "The Problem of Evil," in *Great Thinkers*, ed. Varghese, 194.

22. Adapted from Copan, *Loving Wisdom*, 127.

23. See Greg L. Bahnsen, *Always Ready*, ed. Robert R. Booth (Texarkana, AR: Covenant Media Foundation, 1996), 170.

24. Ibid.

Chapter 14 God's Good Purposes for Evil and Suffering

1. Augustine, *Confessions*, bk. 7, sec. 5, 138–39. For introductory articles on the life and thought of Saint Augustine, see Samples, "Augustine of Hippo: From Pagan, to Cultist, to Skeptic, to Christian Sage"; and Samples, "Augustine of Hippo: Rightly Dividing the Truth."

2. For a helpful discussion of Augustine's view of evil, see Edward Miller, *God and Reason*, 163–70.

3. Augustine, "The Enchiridion on Faith, Hope, and Love," chap. 11 in *Basic Writings of Saint Augustine*, ed. Whitney J. Oates (1976; repr., Grand Rapids: Baker, 1992), 1:662.

4. John M. Frame, *Apologetics to the Glory of God* (Phillipsburg, NJ: P&R, 1994), 155–56.

5. Augustine, "Enchiridion," chap. 11, 1:662.

6. Ibid., chap. 13, 1:663.

7. See Fitzgerald, *Augustine through the Ages*, s.v. "evil."

8. For a discussion of the paradoxical nature of God's sovereignty and human responsibility, see Hoekema, *Saved by Grace*, 5–10.

9. For a helpful discussion of how evil relates to God's providence, see Grudem, *Systematic Theology*, 322–30.

10. Berkhof, *Summary of Christian Doctrine*, 46–47.

11. Bahnsen, *Always Ready*, 172.

12. Augustine, "Enchiridion," chap. 11, 1:662.

13. C. S. Lewis, *The Problem of Pain* (New York: HarperCollins, 2001), 91.

14. See Krista Kay Bontrager's articles on natural evil, "Grappling with Natural Evil," *Reasons to Believe*, March 1, 2010, http://www.reasons.org/grappling-natural-evil; and "Good God, Cruel World," *Reasons to Believe*, January 1, 1999, http://www.reasons.org/good-god-cruel-world.

15. Beeke and Ferguson, *Westminster Shorter Catechism*, Q. 1 and A. 1, 3.

16. Premillennialists believe that evil will finally be removed only after the literal earthly millennium of Christ. For an amillennial interpretation of eschatological events, see Anthony A. Hoekema, *The Bible and the Future* (Grand Rapids: Eerdmans, 1979).

17. Alister E. McGrath, *Intellectuals Don't Need God and Other Modern Myths* (Grand Rapids: Zondervan, 1993), 104–5.

Scripture Index

Subject Index

Kenneth Richard Samples serves as senior research scholar with a focus on theological and philosophical apologetics at Reasons To Believe (RTB). A nonprofit and interdenominational organization, RTB provides research and teaching on the harmony of God's revelation in the words of the Bible and the facts of nature.

An avid speaker and debater, Kenneth has appeared on numerous radio programs such as *The Frank Pastore Show*, *VoiceAmerica*, *Newsmakers*, *Stand to Reason*, *The White Horse Inn*, *Talk New York*, *The Bob Grant Show*, *The Janet Mefferd Show*, *Issues Etc.*, and *Apologetics.com*.

Prior to joining RTB in 1997, Kenneth worked as senior research consultant and correspondence editor at the Christian Research Institute (CRI) for seven years. During that time he regularly cohosted the popular call-in radio program *The Bible Answer Man*.

Kenneth is the author of *A World of Difference: Putting Christian Truth-Claims to the Worldview Test* and *Without a Doubt: Answering the 20 Toughest Faith Questions*. He has also contributed to *Lights in the Sky* and *Little Green Men: A Rational Christian Look at UFOs and Extraterrestrials*, as well as several other books. In addition, his articles have been have been published in *Christianity Today*, *Christian Research Journal*, and *Facts for Faith*.

Kenneth participates in RTB's apologetics podcasts, including *Straight Thinking* and *I Didn't Know That*. He also writes Reflections, a weekly blog dedicated to helping believers think through their worldview (http://reflections byken.wordpress.com).

An experienced educator, Kenneth has taught courses in philosophy and religion at several colleges and is an adjunct instructor of apologetics at Biola University. He also teaches adult classes at Christ Reformed Church in Southern California. Kenneth holds undergraduate degrees in philosophy and social science and a master's degree in theological studies. Over the years he has held memberships in the American Philosophical Association, the Evangelical Philosophical Society, the Evangelical Theological Society, and the Evangelical Press Association.

Kenneth lives in Southern California with his wife, Joan, and their three children. He is an enthusiastic student of the American Civil War and World War II and is also an avid Los Angeles Lakers fan.

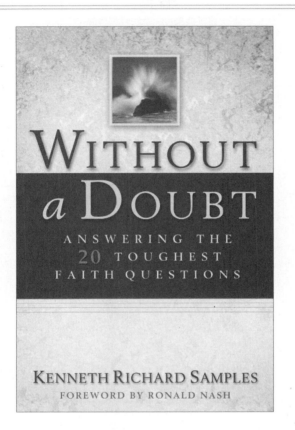

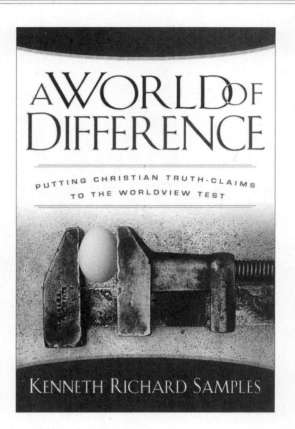